Making Peace
with God

BOOKS AUTHORED AND COAUTHORED BY PHILIP GOLDBERG, PH.D.

The 6 Secrets of a Lasting Relationship

Making Peace with Your Past

The Best That I Can Be

Pain Remedies

Passion Play

Get Out of Your Own Way

A Different Kind of Healing

This Is Next Year (a novel)

The Babinski Reflex

The Intuitive Edge

How to Manage Your Boss

Executive Health

Natural Sleep

The TM Program

Making Peace with God

A PRACTICAL GUIDE

Harold Bloomfield, M.D.

&

Philip Goldberg, Ph.D.

JEREMY P. TARCHER/PUTNAM
A MEMBER OF PENGUIN PUTNAM INC.
NEW YORK

Except for the personal experiences of the authors, all cases and characters in this book are composites from acquaintances and clinical work. Names and details have been changed to protect privacy and confidentiality. This book is not intended as a substitute for advice from a trained counselor, therapist, or other mental health professional. If you are currently in counseling or therapy, check with your mental health provider before altering or discontinuing your therapeutic regimen.

Every effort has been made to ensure that the information contained in this book is complete and accurate. However, neither the publisher nor the authors are engaged in rendering professional advice or services to the individual reader. The ideas, procedures, and suggestions contained in this book are not intended as a substitute for consulting with a licensed therapist. All matters regarding your health require medical supervision. Neither the authors nor the publisher shall be liable or responsible for any loss or damage allegedly arising from any information or suggestion in this book.

Most Tarcher/Putnam books are available at special quantity discounts for bulk purchase for sales promotions, premiums, fund-raising, and educational needs. Special books or book excerpts also can be created to fit specific needs. For details, write Putnam Special Markets, 375 Hudson Street, New York, NY 10014.

Jeremy P. Tarcher/Putnam
a member of
Penguin Putnam Inc.
375 Hudson Street
New York, NY 10014
www.penguinputnam.com

Library of Congress Cataloging-in-Publication Data

Bloomfield, Harold H., date.
Making peace with God : a practical guide / Harold Bloomfield and Philip Goldberg.
p.   cm.
ISBN 1-58542-159-6
1. Religion. I. Goldberg, Philip, date. II. Title.
BL27 .B57   2002   2001052729
291.4—dc21

Printed in the United States of America
1   3   5   7   9   10   8   6   4   2

This book is printed on acid-free paper. ∞

Book design by Meighan Cavanaugh

To all who yearn
for the peace of God

Contents

Making Peace with God

1.

WHY GOD?

A Piece of God Yearning for the Peace of God

You, O God, have made us for yourself,
and our heart is restless until it rests in you.

St. Augustine

What is normally a barren plain of sandy soil has become, overnight, a sprawling sea of people and tents. Against the dusty backdrop, the reds, greens and golds of women's saris and the orange robes of monks stand out like brush strokes on parchment, and the vibrant colors are highlighted by white splashes of smiles—more smiles than one expects to see from huddled masses in extreme discomfort. Many had traveled hundreds of kilometers to get there, stuffed like sardines into stifling railroad cars, rickety buses and groaning pickup trucks that tilted with every curve and jolted the passengers' spines with every bump. Many are sleeping on the cold, lumpy ground, wrapped in tattered shawls, trying to cook and stay warm with makeshift fires, drinking and eating what they managed to carry with them or can be purchased for a few rupees on site, unashamedly depositing human waste wherever they can. Even the fortunate ones quartered in dormitory-style tents, and the more affluent in air-conditioned hotels, have to put up with conditions that, in normal circumstances, would be considered unbearable. Here, they seem no more annoying than a long traffic light.

It is the largest spiritual gathering ever assembled. By some estimates 70 million pilgrims would pass through Allahabad, a mid-sized city in northern India, during the course of the month-long spiritual festival—mostly Hindus from everywhere on the vast subcontinent, but also Christians, Jews, Muslims, Buddhists, Jains and others, from more than fifty countries. Monumental crowds congregate in Allahabad every twelve years for the Kumbha Mela, and this one, in January, 2001, is extra special, for a *Maha* (great) Kumbha Mela comes around only once every 144 years. On the most auspicious days, as many as 20 million amass at the site, forty times the number at Woodstock.

With the exception of journalists, organizers and curiosity seekers, the multitude has congregated for one purpose only: to purify their souls and connect with the Divine. They chant, pray, meditate, make offerings and bask in the presence of swamis, yogis and holy men, many of whom leave their caves and monasteries only on such rare occasions. For most, the centerpiece of the pilgrimage is to bathe in the prescribed manner at the confluence of three holy rivers: mother Ganges, brown and slow at this point in its meandering; the swift, green Yamuna; and the unseen Saraswati, said to be flowing underground. Only the sacred intention and devotional activity of the participants can explain one of the most remarkable features of this most remarkable assembly: the serenity that permeates the chaos.

The mela is far from quiet; there is no escape from the barrage of ear-splitting announcements, fervent discourses and passionate chants that blare from the tinny loudspeakers. Nor is it bucolic; it is a ceaseless hubbub of motion, and the dust kicked up by millions of feet and the smoke from fires built for warmth, food preparation and rituals sting the eyes and choke the lungs. As for solitude, one can hardly find refuge from the human crush. At peak bathing times, as the faithful undress, enter the sacred water, clamber back to shore and change clothes, you are elbow to elbow with a human herd, with no easy way to break for empty space should you need a toilet or feel claustrophobic. When crossing the Ganges on a footbridge, you have to walk with mini steps because if you take a normal stride you will step on someone's heels, and you hold your arms close to your sides because even the smallest of natural swings will propel your hand into a stranger's hip.

And yet, it is peaceful. You do not feel threatened, you do not feel apprehensive, you do not worry that someone's frustration will boil over or some drunk or druggie will freak out. No one is rude, no one elbows for advantage, no one snaps or curses or complains. Even the beggars and the hawkers of goods are polite. The faces register neither annoyance nor impatience, but rather calmness and ease and, in many cases, joy. Holiness is a subtle but palpable presence; at times it penetrates so deeply you feel blessed by an ineffable grace. In his or her own way, every soul in this colossal crowd is *making peace with God.*

The Yearning Burning in Our Souls

Yearning for God in every thought, directing every breath
toward the One, intending no harm, that is prayer.

BAWA MUHAIYADDEEN

That is what we are all doing, knowingly or not, each in his or her own way. We are *all* pieces of God yearning for the peace of God. It is not just momentary serenity we're after, or fleeting ecstasy, or the absence of tension and anxiety. We don't just want to make things OK with the Almighty and carry on in a state of peaceful coexistence. That might do for a start, but what we truly ache for is to know God intimately, feel God vividly, and beyond even that, to dissolve the illusion of separation from the Divine and experience what the Bible calls the peace which passeth understanding.

Like raindrops longing to return to the sea, like bewildered infants crying out for the original bliss we left behind in the womb, we long to unite with the Source from which we spring and become one with all that is. That is the ultimate aim of every human desire and the engine that drives the spiritual quest. It is a yearning that cuts across time and tradition. "From bliss we have come, in bliss we live and have our being, and in that sacred bliss we will one day melt again," declare the Upanishads of ancient India. "To know the sweetness of the Infinite within us," wrote the fifteenth-century Christian mystic Nicholas of Cusa, "that is the cause, the reason, the purpose, the *only* purpose of our being." Writes contemporary rabbi Michael Lerner, "At heart, our deepest desire is to realize our oneness with that power, that transcendent reality that is both within us, at the core of our being, and all around us, saturating every part of this sacred universe."

The longing for union is the soul's equivalent of the genetic drive to procreate, an essential component of our human blueprint. The instinct might be expressed consciously or unconsciously, explicitly or implicitly, with feverish passion or subdued caution; it may lead to pleasure and virtue or get misdirected in ways that cause pain and injury. But it is always present, always driving us onward, to experience more, know more, feel more, love more, be more.

That goes not only for reverent Hindus at the Kumbha Mela or the sacred temples of Varanasi, and not just the millions of Muslims who make the pilgrimage to Mecca for the annual hajj, or the Catholics who gather in St. Peter's Square on Easter Sunday or the devout Jews who journey to Jerusalem to pray at the Western Wall. Not just their brethren who stay home and fill the churches and temples and mosques at prescribed times. Not just the everyday faithful—the Muslims who stop what they're doing five times a day to prostrate themselves on prayer rugs; or the Christians who begin and end their days with a prayer and say grace before meals; or the Jews who light candles to welcome the sabbath or kiss the mezuzah as they enter and leave their homes; or the Hindus who offer fruit and flowers to idols on homemade altars; or the Buddhists who meditate in silence and intone blessings to relieve all beings of suffering. And not just the Native Americans who dance and sing in praise of Mother Earth or Father Sky or the Great Spirit; or the tribal peoples of Africa who drum and chant and call out fervently to Amma or Chukwu or deities of other names; or the Pentecostalists who speak in tongues; or the Hasidim who dance in celebration of the Almighty; or the Sufis who whirl ecstatically and recite the ninety-nine names of God. Not just New Agers repeating affirmations or visualizing their Higher Selves, and not just 12-Steppers vowing to turn themselves over to a higher power.

And, for that matter, not just the overtly religious and spiritual, but also the ardently secular and the skeptical agnostics and, yes, even the determined atheists, for they too have a relationship with whatever they conceive of as the universal Whole. Some may cringe at the word God. They may prefer terms like nature or evolution. They might think of themselves as biological entities in a vast ecological web of life, or build their philosophies around the most current scientific knowledge, but still their inner peace depends in large part on coming to terms with whatever they view the universe to be, whether friendly or unfriendly, purposeful or meaningless, random or designed. They still wrestle with what it's all about, what their place in the larger landscape might be and how they relate to the power or force—or seeming lack thereof—that shapes the cosmos of which they are part.

You may love the word God or prefer another term; you may think of God as nameless or assign a name such as Allah or Hashem; you may conceive of God as formless or embodied in a figure such as Jesus or Mary or Krishna or Avalokiteshvara; you may draw inspiration from the Torah or the New Testament, the Koran or the Tao Te Ching, the Vedas or the Diamond Sutra; you may understand God to be masculine or feminine or neither or both; you may think of God as Father or Mother or Friend or Ruler, or as a force or an energy field; you may see God as immanent or transcendent, as within you or outside of you or both within and without, as an active player in human life or as a creator who has left us to our own devices. All such differences merely give shape to our individual tasks, but the goal in every case is the same: to make peace with the Ultimate.

Seeds of God

Our real Self is not different from the ultimate Reality called God.

UPANISHADS

We yearn for the Divine because we *are* divine. It is our essential nature, the part of our identity that is created "in the image and likeness of God"— and we are drawn to realize it the way rivers are obliged to run toward the sea and plants bend toward the sun. "The seed of God is in us," said the fourteenth-century Christian mystic Meister Eckhart. "Given an intelligent and hard-working farmer, it will thrive and grow up to God, whose seed it is; and accordingly its fruits will be God-nature. Pear seeds grow into pear trees, nut seeds into nut trees, and God seed into God." The memory of oceanic One-ness is part of our soul's code. It is buried deep in our awareness; our very brains are programmed to reclaim it, as research in the new field of neurotheology has revealed. And when we homesick creatures manage to wend our way home to our Source, we attain the ultimate peace that has been called by various names: God-consciousness, Self-realization, salvation, moksha, satori, nirvana, enlightenment.

Some of us are conscious of being "God seed." They are the spiritual seek-ers and devoutly religious who derive much of life's meaning and purpose from their relationship with the Sacred. Many sense a divine presence early in life, and the fortunate ones hold fast to that sublime connection despite the pressures of maturation and materialism. Like kids who know before they start school that they are destined to make music or fly airplanes, some feel called to the ministry, or head for a monastery or ashram at the earliest date. Others simply know in their hearts that as they build a family and a career they will be in the world but not of it, one eye always on God. Dennis Carpenter*, a sem-inary student in Chicago, is one of the early bloomers. "I can remember at a very young age feeling that I was bathed in a loving presence," he says. Physi-cally abused as a young boy, he would rush to his room after a beating from his father, into the comforting arms of that sacred protection. "Sometimes it wouldn't be there, and I would wonder why," he says. "But at one point I just knew that my purpose in life was to learn how to have it with me all the time." Most abused children blame themselves for their beatings, and many believe that God is punishing them. Not so Dennis. "It was my sanctuary," he says of that Presence. "When I was about five, I started calling it God. We'd go to church every Sunday, and the God they'd talk about couldn't wait to banish everyone to hell. I just knew they had it all wrong."

---

*Names with * after them have been changed to honor the individual's request for anonymity.

For most of us, the innate drive to transcend finite existence and bask in the Eternal takes a more circuitous route. Driven by what Freud called the pleasure principle, we rush toward pleasure and run from pain. We don't just *want* to be happy, we are driven instinctively toward happiness like bees are driven to make honey. That natural urge propels us toward more and better sources of delight, thrills of greater intensity and ever-new sources of ego gratification. We turn to the usual suspects, to sex and money, career and family, achievement and excitement, houses, cars and other goodies, and when each of these runs its course, we renew the search in the same old places, like kids who want to see the same magic trick over and over again. But, like those kids, we eventually get bored, or we wise up to the fact that it's all an illusion. We question our choices and priorities. We suspect that no amount of temporary pleasure or attainment will ever satisfy the deepest aspirations of the soul, and we start to probe deeper within ourselves to find out what we're really looking for.

Spiritual Crises

Where do we come from? Where are we going? What is the meaning of this life? That is what every heart is shouting, what every head is asking as it beats on chaos.

NIKOS KAZANTZAKIS

Stirrings of spiritual yearning are felt most often at times of personal upheaval: divorce, parenthood, the loss of a job or a financial setback, the death of a loved one, a serious illness or injury. For reflective individuals, such events almost guarantee a reappraisal of who we are and what really matters. The period most likely to stir things up is midlife, when we realize that the number of years we have left may be fewer than the years we have already lived. Typically, it's a time of looking back to see what our lives have stood for. We ponder our mistakes, question our values and search for lost dreams. We accuse ourselves of lacking authenticity, of selling out and abandoning our ideals. For the lucky ones, the crisis leads not to a binge or a red sports car or a series of young sex partners, but to a conscious commitment to the spiritual quest.

If it doesn't happen in midlife or another time of crisis, the breakthrough might wait until we hit retirement age, when the nest is empty and the work that defined us no longer structures our days. When cocktails and golf and early bird specials lose their pizzazz, when friends start to talk about nothing but ailments and grandchildren—or, worse, start to die like flies in autumn— and our joints creak and our own impending demise has us wondering what awaits us beyond the grave—well, if we don't start thinking about our souls then, we never will.

In his pioneering work on self-actualization, psychologist Abraham Maslow demonstrated that once our most basic needs have been met, we are driven, "in the same naturalistic scientific sense that an acorn may be said to be pressing toward an oak tree," to the unfoldment of our fullest and highest potential. Because it is our nature to constantly seek more and more fulfillment, we climb the ladder of human needs rung by rung, and sooner or later we discover a yearning for the Infinite, where all desires and needs come to rest. It is the ultimate extension of our craving for connection—at first to our parents, then to our peer groups, our lovers, our spouses, our children—which we experience as a desire to love and be loved. "The basis of our need to love lies in the experience of separateness and the resulting need to overcome the anxiety of separateness by the experience of union," wrote Erich Fromm in *The Art of Loving*. "The religious form of love, that which is called the love of God, is, psychologically speaking, not different. It springs from the need to overcome separateness and to achieve union." There may be countless reasons why you are not at peace with God, but they all boil down to one thing: separation.

All of our heated striving, whether for power or sex or pleasure or truth or human betterment, is, at bottom, an attempt to transcend the limits of our separate personas and unite with something bigger and greater than ourselves— and the biggest of the big and the greatest of the great, beyond which the mind cannot conceive, is the nameless mystery that humans have given a thousand names, the formless essence to which we have attributed a thousand forms. "God is that which concerns us ultimately," said theologian Paul Tillich. The idea is echoed by all traditions. Said the twentieth-century Hindu master Paramahansa Yogananda, "No matter what the world gives you, your heart will still wish for God." Your desire to make peace with God, therefore, is an expression of an even deeper, more primal instinct: to tear down the stubborn wall between you and the holy of holies and become, at long last, whole.

The Dark Nights of Your Soul's Yearning

Nothing whatsoever is achieved in spiritual life without yearning.

RAMAKRISHNA

You may have been drawn to this book, knowingly or not, because of a spiritual crisis in your life—a crisis of faith, perhaps, in which you wonder if God actually exists, or if this universe, fashioned by either chance or design, is really worthy of your trust. You may feel angry with God because your prayers have not been answered and your deepest desires have not been fulfilled. You may be enraged by the continuing presence of evil in the world and the ubiquity of human suffering—the random or meaningless kind in particular, and your own and that of your loved ones especially. You may find yourself screaming at God, "I have been good, I have followed the rules, I have done all the right things, and still you deny me success and happiness and fill my days with sorrow!"—only to cringe with guilt or tremble in fear because you had the temerity to lash out at the Almighty.

Your need to make peace may stem from a belief that you don't measure up in God's eyes. In your heart of hearts you may think that God disapproves of you. You may crave forgiveness for your sins, whether those sins are real or imagined, whether you have actually committed them or merely contemplated them. You may feel unworthy of God's love and cry out for help to become more deserving. Perhaps a marriage that was made in heaven has plummeted to hell, leaving you to ponder how two soul mates, two pieces of

God, could tear themselves apart. Or you have tumbled into an abyss of grief over the death of a loved one and you wonder if you're a fool to believe that you will one day be reunited in another realm. Or you are staring into the pitiless face of death yourself—because you are aging or suffering from a serious illness or approaching a landmark birthday—and you are trying desperately to come to terms with the meaning of it all before it's too late.

Perhaps you feel spiritually homeless because the tradition you were raised in has failed to live up to your standards, frustrated because it fails to inspire you or give you the spiritual guidance you crave. You may be disillusioned because those who are supposed to represent God on earth have let you down. Perhaps you seethe with resentment because a member of the clergy has defiled the sanctity of your faith with hypocrisy, exploitation or abuse. You may feel like a leaf in a storm, twisted this way and that by winds of dogma blowing from different directions.

Your spirit may be crying out for answers to the Big Questions: Who am I? *Why* am I? Where did I come from? Where am I going? You may have started a conversation with God only to find that it's one-sided. You may be aching to know what God has in mind for your passage on earth—what you were meant to do or learn, what service you can render, what gifts you were meant to leave behind—and you're trying to shake the universe out of its silence. You may be a veteran of the spiritual path or a long-time follower of a religious tradition who has run into a maddening detour or an apparent dead end. You may be frustrated by your unfulfilled desire to feel God's presence. Or, you may have no specific reason at all, just that the yearning has now made itself known.

Whatever your immediate concerns, it is important to remember that the dark, icy patches we stumble through can be a prelude to peace and grace. The challenge is to recognize a spiritual crisis for what it is: a phase of growth, an opportunity to accelerate your spiritual development, a time for discipline, reflection and emotional honesty. Historically, saints and sages have struggled through God-crises as much as ordinary seekers have and, in most cases, far more intensely. Often their greatest challenges arose after years of diligent spiritual practice had carried them to magnificent heights of transformation, triggering what John of the Cross called a dark night of the soul and the Vedas called "long exiles from the light." For them, having tasted the ecstasy of divine illumination, to suffer an apparent setback was more than a disappointment; it was a devastating loss. Something sublime had been taken from them. "I tasted," cried St. Augustine, "and now I hunger and thirst. You touched me, and now I burn with longing for your peace."

For Wendy, a nurse in Southern California, the dark night started in the middle of a discount drugstore. She had been immersed in what she calls a profound, intimate union with God for several months. "I never felt such total acceptance, such absolute love and bliss," she says. "So much so that the entire world ceased to exist. It disappeared into an insignificant dream. It was only God and me and eternity. And yet it was more alive, more real, than this world is to me now." And then, as "Oh Come, All Ye Faithful" played on the intercom and shoppers pondered which roll of gift-wrap to buy, the connection was severed as suddenly as it had come. "I continued to have a relationship with God for a few years," recalls Wendy. "But it was compromised. I wasn't always aware of his absolute presence, as I had been before. I would have a taste of it, and it would go away. It was painful."

Emptiness had replaced the ecstatic fullness she had known before. "I was not receiving that magnificent love, and I had to get it back," says Wendy. When she couldn't, she felt helpless and undeserving. "I wanted to know what I had to do to be worthy of getting that close to God again. So I prayed a lot, and I tried to be as pure as possible." After a number of years, some of which were spent in on-the-edge rebellion, "running as hard as I could to get away from God," she reached a point where she couldn't stand it anymore. "So one day," she says, "I yelled at God: 'You've got to do something! You've got to bring me closer or let me forget, so the pain will stop." Not long after that, she met her first spiritual teacher. Since then, her path has been to learn how to integrate the divine presence into everyday life. "It's more grounded this time," she says. "Before, I didn't really want to be in this world. I just wanted the bliss."

Still, the memory of her exquisite union with God haunts her. "I really yearn to have it again," she says, "but I'm learning to accept the yearning and see the beauty in it, to see it as a blessing, because if it wasn't for that yearning, I wouldn't be able to go forward."

Whenever and however it arises, the yearning for God is bittersweet. Sweet like the skin's craving for the touch of an absent lover and the flutter of the heart when the phone rings. Bitter like the lonely nights with the empty pillow and the vacant chair. The yearning can be a thrill and a comfort, or it can ache and gnaw and hurt, especially if you're not sure that you'll ever achieve the intimacy for which you long. Through it all, it is vital to understand that your separation from God is, in itself, a form of connection. "Two prisoners whose cells adjoin communicate with each other by knocking on the wall," wrote the French philosopher Simone Weil. "The wall is the thing which separates them but is also their means of communication. It is the same with us and God. Every separation is a link."

The Love—and Fear—of God

Nearness to Thee is my hope, and love for Thee is my companion.

BAHÁ'U'LLÁH

The hunger to close the gap between your individual self and the Self of all selves can be regarded as a form of connecting. In his poem, "Love Dogs," the Sufi mystic Rumi depicts a despondent man who gives up praying because God has never answered his prayers. Khidr, the guide of souls, says to the man, "This longing you express *is* the return message. Listen to the moan of a dog for its master. That whining is the connection." In other words, the longing you feel to "dwell in the house of the Lord forever" is, in itself, a form of grace. That you want to end the separation and become ever more intimate with the Beloved is a sign of love—yours for God and God's for you.

The soul's longing for the Divine has been compared to a man who hears the roar of the ocean from a distance. The sound is first of all evidence, or at least a strong hint, that the ocean exists. It is also a clarion call to begin the journey. And once the quest has begun, the song of the sea becomes a navigational system, a homing beacon that keeps you moving in the right direction as you grope your way to its source. With this in mind, you can use the pain of separation from God as an impetus to continue the sacred quest. "The grief you cry out from," sings Rumi, "draws you toward union."

Along the way, your relationship with God may run into the same kind of problems as your human relationships, largely because you, like everyone else, project onto God your feelings about yourself and other people. The conflict might stem from misunderstanding or disappointment or a reluctance to commit because you're afraid of plunging into the fathomless abyss and losing your individuality. And heavy on your shoulders falls the weight of ambivalence: you love God and you fear God; you sense God's presence and you doubt God's existence; you thank God and you resent God; you try to please God and you challenge God to please you; you think you understand God and you are totally baffled by God; you humbly bow to God and you shake your fists at God; you stand proud before God and you cower before God; you feel close to God and you feel galaxies apart from God. Those conflicts might make you feel guilty or ashamed. But why should they, when God's own design leaves room for such upheavals? How can you not be ambivalent about the Creator when Creation itself is awash in contradictions, paradoxes and enigmas?

Wrestling with God-related doubt, anger and confusion is not a sign of spiritual inadequacy. It does not make you a sinner or a fool or a flawed human being. Your tension with the Divine shows that you're alive, that you dare to ponder the imponderable and question both the handed-down assertions of tradition and your own cherished assumptions. It shows that you are brave enough to feel powerful emotions, even if they frighten you or cause you anguish, rather than suppress or deny them. Above all, it shows that you are fortunate to *have* a relationship with God, and that the relationship is dynamic, passionate and engaged—just what any relationship should be if it is to grow in intimacy, strength and peace.

The Fruits of Peace

May his peace abide with you. May his presence
illuminate your heart now and evermore.

Sufi blessing

Making peace with God is its own reward. It bestows upon the sincere seeker a degree of wholeness, joy and serenity that can be found no other way. But there are specific rewards as well. If you bring to the work ahead your highest intention and your full attention, you will, on your own terms, be able to:

- Live the bliss of deep peace
- Become partners with God in cocreating your reality
- Clarify your understanding of God
- Resolve your doubts and restore your faith
- Look God in the eye without guilt or shame
- Resolve your anger, even your rage, toward God
- Forgive God (and yourself for breaking with God)
- Create a mature relationship with God, based on dignity, integrity and truth
- Come to terms with your mortality
- Resolve your feelings toward spiritual institutions and authority figures
- Transform your fear of God into awe and wonder
- Renew your sense of meaning and purpose
- Strengthen your commitment to your spiritual path
- Live your spirituality and keep your promises to God and yourself
- Discover your fundamental covenant with God

This grand spiritual journey brings with it concrete benefits for mental and physical well-being. Until recently, modern health professionals have been indifferent to religion and spirituality, often downright antagonistic. At best, a patient's religious beliefs and practices were considered a source of solace or hope; at worst, they were considered an obstacle to health in that "superstition" or "blind faith" might deter needy patients from taking advantage of proven scientific remedies. In psychiatric settings, spirituality was widely considered a detriment because it fostered what was held to be an illusory view of reality. The father of modern psychology, Sigmund Freud, wrote that religion "imposes equally on everyone its own path to the acquisition of happiness and protection from suffering. Its technique consists in depressing the value of life and distorting the picture of the real world in a delusional manner—which presupposes an intimidation of the intelligence. At this price, by forcibly fixing them in a state of psychical infantilism and by drawing them into a mass delusion, religion succeeds in sparing many people an individual neurosis. But hardly anything more."

If "sparing many people an individual neurosis" was all religion had to offer, it would have been enough, as Jews say of God's miracles at Passover, and in fact it would have been more than many schools of psychotherapy can boast. Nevertheless, therapists often joke about how grateful they are that religious institutions have driven millions of suffering clients to their doors with a fear of divine wrath and guilt about their sins. But, while there have always been psychologists who took spirituality seriously—from William James in the early twentieth century, to Carl Jung, to Abraham Maslow and other apostles of humanistic psychology, to today's transpersonal psychologists—the idea that faith and spiritual practice might actually be beneficial has only recently taken root in the mainstream. Two decades of scientific data have forced health professionals to take notice.

A survey conducted by the National Opinion Research Center, for instance, found that "symbolic relations with a divine other are a significant correlate of well-being." Another group of researchers found that such a relationship is "a stronger predictor for well-being than race, sex, income, age, marital status, or church attendance." A number of psychological studies have found that those who are spiritually active are less likely to suffer from anxiety or depression. Among those who *are* depressed, the actively religious—as measured by factors such as attendance at services and the use of private prayer—get over their conditions faster than their nonreligious counterparts. Spirituality is also associated with a lowered risk of substance abuse and suicide attempts. And psychological tests of coping styles indicate that spirituality helps people deal with challenge and adversity in a healthier manner.

Religious participation and spiritual practice have been correlated with a variety of measures associated with quality of life. In reviewing the psychiatric literature on the subject in the journal *Psychiatric Annals* (August 2000), Dr. Edward P. Shafranske concludes that, "Meta-analyses have found religious commitment to be associated with reduced risk in factors important to mental health, such as suicide, drug use, alcohol abuse, delinquency, marital satisfaction, and depression." Such findings have overcome the historical skepticism of the psychiatric community. The most recent (fourth) edition of the *Diagnostic and Statistical Manual of Mental Disorders* (DSM-IV), the virtual Bible of the profession, includes for the first time the category "Religious or Spiritual Problem." In addition, all psychiatric residency programs are now required to include in their curricula courses on religious and spiritual issues. This is a major development; in the past, people who went to therapists with a spiritual crisis were frequently misdiagnosed or had their principal concerns ignored entirely. Indeed, religious involvement itself was often considered evidence of psychopathology. Now it is far more likely that someone torn by spiritual or religious conflict will be seen by a therapist who knows how to deal with it or will make an appropriate referral.

A similar evolution has taken place in medicine. Because of the solid data linking spirituality and health, the most scientifically demanding institutions in the world now take religious involvement seriously. In 1993, only 3 of the 125 medical schools in the United States offered courses that examined the health implications of spirituality and religion. By 2001, the number was approaching eighty, and other schools had declared their intention to add such courses.

Hundreds of studies have found that religious commitment and spiritual practices are helpful in lowering blood pressure, enhancing immune function and improving the chances of survival following heart surgery, among other indices of improved health. Researchers at the Duke University Medical Center, for instance, studied 4,000 men and woman over sixty-five and found that those who prayed, read scriptures and attended services regularly were 40 percent less likely to have a stroke or heart attack than subjects who were not religious. Another Duke study found that seniors who attended services at least once a week were half as likely as their non-religious counterparts to have elevated levels of interleukin-6, a protein that impairs the function of the immune system. It seems that religious practice can even help you live longer: a massive study of more than 5,000 people over a period of twenty-eight years found that those who attended religious services at least once a week were 23 percent less likely to die during the time of the study. Another study of 21,000 people over an eight-year period found that those who attended services more than once a week lived an average of seven years longer than those who were no-shows.

Researchers explain the evidence of improved mental and physical health by postulating that religious participation fosters optimism, encourages good health habits, facilitates coping, reduces stress, provides a sense of meaning and coherence and, for many, offers vital social support. Some findings, however, can't be explained, most notably the extraordinary effect of intercessory prayer on medical conditions. It seems that sick people not only do better when they pray, they also do better when other people pray *for* them — even when they don't *know* someone is praying for them.

Interestingly, studies suggest that simply being religious or professing a belief in God is not quite enough; the *quality* of one's relationship with the Divine is also important. In one experiment, for example, researchers found that "people who experienced disappointment, frustration or unforgiveness in their relationships with God reported more emotional distress than other people." A survey of elderly patients in a hospital found that those with religious anxiety — as indicated by statements such as "wondered whether God had abandoned me," "questioned God's love for me," and "decided the devil made this happen" — are likely to die sooner than their more sanguine counterparts. While the conclusions of the study must be considered tentative, Dr. Kenneth I. Pargament, the lead researcher, speculates that the inability to resolve anger, guilt and anxiety toward God might contribute to poor health. In other words, it's good for your health to have a relationship with God, and it's even healthier when that relationship is at peace.

Overall, the body of research on spirituality and healing is remarkable in its range and consistency. According to Dr. Jeff Levin's review of the literature, the effects are significant "regardless of the age, sex, race, ethnicity, nationality, or religious denomination of the people studied, and independent of the design used and of when or where these studies took place." It should be emphasized that it does not seem to matter which faith tradition a person follows. It can also be inferred that *no* institutional involvement is necessary, since significant results have been derived from nonsectarian spiritual practices such as yoga and meditation. Thirty years of research on the benefits of Transcendental Meditation alone—on blood pressure, heart rate, health-care utilization and a host of other medical indices—would support that conclusion. Whatever the context, it is clear that enhancing inner peace, faith and hope, and reducing stress, fear and worry are crucial factors in the fight against mental and physical distress—precisely what would be expected when someone is making peace with God.

That's just the hard data. The more profound truth, beyond anything that can be quantified, is that when you make peace with God you feel more whole. As a result of this greater integration, you acquire more ease in the ebb and flow of life. Good things tend to happen, and the bad stuff does not seem to have as lasting an impact. Because your cup runneth over, you find yourself acting with a generosity of spirit that naturally adds more compassion, empathy and love to your relationships. Your appreciation for life as it is, here and now, is heightened, and gratitude comes to replace resentment and self-pity. And because the present moment is richer and fuller, you can look back at your past without regret and move into your future with greater optimism and confidence, knowing that you can handle whatever comes your way and cocreate with the Creator all of the blessings you desire for yourself, your loved ones and the rest of humanity.

God Is Within;
We Are Never Without

I have sought your nearness. With all my heart I called to you,
and going out to meet you I found you coming to meet me.

JUDAH HALEVI

Making peace implies that a relationship exists between two separate entities and that the relationship is in a state of conflict or tension. Where God is
concerned, that perception, in and of itself, can disturb the peace. "That was
my problem," says Evelyn Barr*, a forty-six-year-old English professor who was
raised by a Catholic mother and a Jewish father and now calls herself a "non-
denominational mystic." "I don't see God as something out there, separate
from me. All there *is* is God and God is all there is. Nothing is not God. So
how can I have a personal relationship with something that has no boundaries, that's in fact not a *something* at all, and not a *someone* either?" That was
Evelyn's understanding about God and it made perfect sense. But it was not
satisfying, because she *felt* as though God were apart from her. Separation was
her reality, as it is for most of us as we look through the glass darkly and try to
glimpse the light of unity through the grime. She wanted to communicate
with God in hopes of closing the gap, but she didn't know how to communicate with the formless. "I solved the problem by reasoning that if God is everything, then she can be a she as well as a he, and she can have whatever
qualities I need her to have. So now I talk to God as if to a girlfriend."

Evelyn's dilemma is as old as the human imagination—and so is her solution. Sages and seers, mystics and ministers, scholars and parishioners, have all
wrestled for millennia with the paradoxes of God. "God is, but at the same time
God also is not," wrote Aldous Huxley in *The Perennial Philosophy*. "The Universe is governed by blind chance and at the same time by a providence with
ethical preoccupations. Suffering is gratuitous and pointless, but also valuable
and necessary. The universe is an imbecile sadist, but also, simultaneously, the
most benevolent of parents. Everything is rigidly predetermined, but the will is

perfectly free. This list of contradictions could be lengthened so as to include all problems that have ever vexed the philosopher and the theologian."

God is transcendent and also immanent, formless and form, beyond time and space and within time and space, perfect unity and infinite diversity, one and many, motionless and perpetual motion. "God in his eternal stillness is hidden from every mortal eye. God in her eternal dancing is manifested everywhere," writes James Finley in *The Contemplative Heart*. The paradoxes of God have been resolved by the great ones who have left their marks on spiritual history in precisely the way Evelyn resolved it: by humbly yielding to the illogical logic of a higher intelligence. If God is both everything and no thing, then why can't God have two seemingly contradictory aspects: on the one hand, boundless, absolute and impersonal; on the other hand, circumscribed and personal? It's hard to relate to the aspect of God that is entirely transcendent. It's hard to praise that God or venerate that God or talk to that God or even curse that God, because there is nothing and no one to focus your attention on. And so we turn to the personal aspect of God.

Some would say that we merely fabricate a personal God for the sake of convenience, assigning finite attributes to the Infinite to compensate for our inability to perceive the everlasting oneness of the universe. But is there anything wrong with that? Like suspending disbelief in a theater to participate more intimately with the drama, it has long and honorable history. And it reflects rather accurately the paradoxical nature of existence. Even the enlightened ones, who were fully awake to their unity with God and lived and breathed that truth, allowed themselves the luxury of a certain degree of separation. Otherwise, what would they have done with their overflowing love, their gratitude and their urge to fall on their knees to worship or burst into songs of praise? For example, Shankara, the founder of Advaita Vedanta, taught that the only reality is the Absolute (Brahman), the nondual One without a second. In that view, everything we perceive as separate and distinct, including ourselves, is like waves on an ocean—perturbations and fluctuations that seem to have a form all their own but are actually pure ocean and nothing but pure ocean. And yet Shankara could write a hymn of praise to God: "Oh, Lord, even after realizing that there is no difference between the individual soul and Brahman, I beg to state that I am yours and not that you are mine. The wave belongs to the ocean, not the ocean to the wave."

Even knowing that there is, in truth, no separation between us and the Divine, we allow ourselves to have a relationship with a personal God because doing so has value and utility—and because in our ordinary level of consciousness the separation is real. As is the inkling of the ultimate union and the yearning to capture its bliss. And so, like Shankara, like Jesus, who could say both "I and the Father are one" and "hallowed be Thy name," we submit to the illusion of separation. To facilitate communication with the Divine, we fix on what in Hinduism is called the *ishta*, one's ideal form of God. Some even attribute unique personas and assign names of their own to God—or Gods. A rabbi we spoke to, for instance, has a holy trinity of her own: three different personalities, with corresponding names, for the aspects of God that she needs to connect with at different times. There's Sissy, the sibling she can tell anything to; Sol, the learned elder who gives her practical advice; and Rose, the wise old crone who knows all. "If this keeps up," she jokes, "I'll have to become a Muslim. They have ninety-nine names for God, each one representing a different quality." Then there's the pop culture imagery in the novel *Dream A Little Dream,* by Susan Elizabeth Phillips, in which a character has a Counselor God, Oprah Winfrey; a Mom God, Mrs. Cunningham (Richie's mom) in *Happy Days;* and an Enforcer God, Clint Eastwood. Eventually, the trio dissolves into the unity of one God: Mr. Rogers.

Whatever works. What matters is finding a way to relate to God that feels authentic and meets your needs. "I consider my personal God to be my companion," explains a dentist from Boston, who has purposely attached no particular name or image to God and hops back and forth between the masculine and feminine pronouns. "He's a being with whom I can be totally myself. She asks of me only to be true to who I am and what I'm becoming. God doesn't want me to be better or worse. When I turn to him, I feel like I was in a psychic prison and had suddenly been declared innocent. I don't have to be on my guard; I can say whatever I think as long as it's the true voice of my soul. She understands the contradictions in my nature because she put them there in the first place. I never feel misjudged by God. I can tell her my envies, re-

grets, hates, vanities and meanness, and when I share these feelings, it is healing. I can be completely silent with God, I can cry with God, I can laugh with
God, and, yes, I can even sin with God. He understands that at times I'm going to neglect him, and I might get enraged with him, but through it all, God
knows me and loves me."

As for the absence of peace in the relationship, unlike lovers and friends,
God does not share our imperfections and does not contribute to the tension.
It may sound unfair, but the truth is, the problems are all of your own making,
and the responsibility for solving them is yours, not God's. It's up to you to resolve the conflict. After all, the indwelling essence of all that is, the universal
intelligence whose nature is love, is not an adversary who has to be coaxed to
the bargaining table. God does not need to make peace; God *is* peace. It's you
who needs to make peace. And to achieve it you have to eliminate the black
holes in your consciousness that suck away the light. Your doubts about God;
your illusions and delusions about God; your magical expectations of
God; your anger, disappointment and fear toward God; your secret pockets of
guilt, shame and sinfulness that make you feel unworthy of the blessings that
are your birthright—all these are veils that come between you and God, and
they have to be dealt with. "God is always ready, but we are very unready,"
wrote Meister Eckhart. "God is near us, but we are far from Him. God is
within, and we are without. God is friendly—we are estranged."

In short, making peace with God requires making peace with yourself,
your life and all that is. It means taking steps to close the gap between you and
the Divine—a gap that does not really exist but only seems to.

Your Quintessential Self

Man is his own star.

JOHN FLETCHER

In the forthcoming chapters we will be taking an integrative approach to
making peace with God, working with all five aspects of what we call the

Quintessential Self: mental, physical, emotional, relational and spiritual. Yes, the road ahead can be understood as a purely spiritual journey, but we are spiritual beings having a human experience, and our humanness includes our minds, our bodies, our feelings and our relationships. We relate to God through each of those avenues, and for peace to be secure and lasting, they all must be involved in the process. Think of them as the five points of a star whose center is your higher self, or soul, pure consciousness.

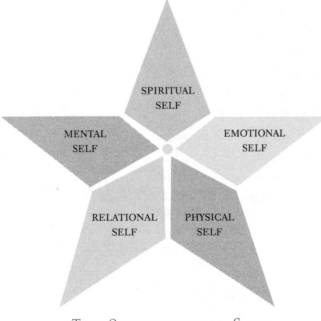

THE QUINTESSENTIAL SELF

The Mental Self: Rethinking possible misbeliefs and false assumptions about who or what God is; understanding the roots of your attitudes toward God; opening your mind to new ways to conceptualize your relationship to God.

The Emotional Self: Recognizing, resolving and releasing all the "bugaboo emotions" (anger, hurt, shame, guilt, sadness, etc.) you feel in relation to God;

shining a light on the shadow, where you've hidden disowned feelings and tendencies; loosening the constrictions that prevent you from fully expressing the most godlike qualities of the heart—love, compassion, forgiveness, reverence and gratitude.

The Physical Self: Gaining the physical strength to support your spiritual quest and avoiding the dis-ease that distracts the attention; healing your body of the physical residue of past traumas and psychospiritual crises; refining the machinery of perception so it can rise to a level of sensory awareness that apprehends the presence of God in all things.

The Relational Self: Resolving any human relationships (with parents, friends, religious authorities, etc.) that may have created tension between you and God; ending the habit of projecting onto God your feelings about yourself and other people; lifting your personal relationship with God to the highest possible level.

The Spiritual Self: Finding—or creating—the spiritual path that is most appropriate for who you are at this stage of your journey; elevating the other four aspects of the Quintessential Self to the highest level of integration; awakening to your true nature as a spiritual being in human form; taking all necessary steps to achieve union with the Divine, so you may shine brightly as a star of God.

Your Relationship with God

When you first begin, you find only darkness and as it were
a cloud of unknowing. You don't know what this means
except that in your will you feel a simple, steadfast
intention reaching out toward God.

FROM *The Cloud of Unknowing*

To begin the process of making peace, take some time to reflect upon your relationship with God. The following exercises will help you clarify your thoughts and feelings.

1. Write down in one or two sentences your own definition, feeling and experience of God.

2. Circle which of the following words fit your conception, feeling and/or experience of God.

Father	Mother	Friend
Protector	Beloved	Ruler
Judge	Spirit	Intelligence
Energy	Creator	Forgiveness
Love	Merciful	Punishment
Helper	Provider	Transcendent
Within	Above	Presence
Kind	Fierce	All-knowing
Participant	Uninvolved	Almighty

3. What role does God play (or not play) in your life?

4. If you could ask only three questions of God, what would they be?

5. If you could have God fulfill three specific wishes or requests, what would they be?

6. To identify the ways in which you most need to make peace with God, answer yes or no to the following questions:

   • Do you feel you have turned away from God—or that God has turned away from you?
   • Do you ever feel unworthy of receiving God's love?
   • Do you sometimes get angry at God?
   • Do you ever doubt God's existence?
   • Do you ever feel afraid of God's wrath?
   • Do you ever wonder why God allows evil and suffering to exist?
   • Are your spiritual beliefs in conflict with those of your family or your religious heritage?
   • Do you yearn to experience—or reexperience—God's presence?

7. Examine Your Spiritual History.

   • How would you characterize the way your parents or step-parents felt about God?
   • What did they teach you, explicitly and implicitly, about spirituality?
   • In what ways, if any, was your spirituality affected by other family members, e.g., uncles, aunts, siblings, grandparents?
   • Was God a source of love and joy?

- Was God used to intimidate or shame you, or make you feel sinful and unworthy?
- What influence, if any, did specific clergy have on your developing attitudes toward God and religion?
- Were religious occasions a pleasant, rich experience, or did you resent having to take part?
- How has your attitude toward God changed in adulthood?
- Have you come to question any of your early beliefs? Reject them? Disdain them?
- What were the turning points in your religious or spiritual development?

8. Finally, what drew you to this book at this time? What are your goals in relation to God? Be as specific and open as possible.

Experiencing the Peace of God

Everyone holds a precious jewel, all embrace a special gem;
if you do not turn your attention around and look within,
you will wander from home with a hidden treasure.

DOGEN

As you proceed through this book, it will be extremely helpful to keep in mind the distinction between peace *with* God and the peace *of* God. Making peace with God is a process, something to be achieved through evolving and becoming; the peace *of* God is a birthright, something that is eternal and unconditional, but has to be recaptured. Making peace with God is an act of do-ing; the peace of God is a state of being. Making peace with God is an activity of the mind, heart, body, senses and spirit; the peace of God is a non-activity that transcends mind, heart, body, senses and spirit. The peace of God is al-ways available. There is no place or time where it cannot be accessed, even—miraculously, amazingly—while you are struggling to make peace *with* God. That is because the very nature of the divine essence we call God is peace, and its Presence is within and around you, in the repose of the present. At any mo-ment, you can, in the famous phrase from Psalm 46, "be still and know that I am God."

You might be used to calling it by a spiritual term—grace, satori, Christ-consciousness, Buddha-mind, samadhi—or something more ordinary—serenity, tranquility, inner silence, the deep hush—but by any name, it is, in its deepest form, the peace of God. And, said the nineteenth-century Hindu sage Ramakrishna, "The nearer you come to God, the more you feel peace."

The process of making peace with God deepens and makes more durable the peace of God. At the same time, experiencing the peace of God enhances, supports and clarifies your peacemaking efforts. Think of it in metaphoric terms: You may have to repair a leaky roof, but in the meantime your house still gives you shelter; that shelter makes it easier to fix the roof, and fixing the roof enhances your shelter. You may have to resolve some differences with your business partner, but meanwhile you are bound by contract; your agree-ment offers protection and guidelines for settling the dispute, and the process of resolution reinforces the spirit of the contract. You may be upset with your children for getting into trouble, but your love for them remains unshaken; that love guides your response to the kids and, in turn, is strengthened by their need for your guidance. Similarly, you can be mad at God, doubt God, resent God, mistrust God, feel rejected by God, and while you're wrestling with and metabolizing those disturbing feelings, you can still, beyond the illusory melo-drama, be still and know the peace of God.

Therefore, to the degree that you can access it—whether through formal spiritual activities such as prayer, meditation or worship services, or by walking in nature, listening to music or playing with a child—the peace *of* God will serve you well as you work toward making peace *with* God. (Chapter 6 contains many suggestions and practices for experiencing the peace of God; feel free to have a sneak preview.)

We encourage you to approach the work ahead as a sacred spiritual quest. Making peace with God is seldom a straightforward, linear journey with a neat beginning, middle and end. It meanders, it winds, it moves in fits and starts, with bursts of speedy progress mixed with apparent setbacks and roadblocks. It can be a joyful, exhilarating ride, but at others times it can be challenging. Along the way you may have to give up a lot. You may have to give up your resentments, your anger, your fears, your arrogance, your grandiosity and perhaps the feeling of being victimized by the Almighty. You may have to forgive yourself for not being "perfect" or for feeling unworthy. You may have to learn to accept God as he or she is rather than the way you think God should be. You may even have to give up the faulty way you see yourself in relation to God. Is it worth it? There can be no greater goal than to reach what every people, every culture and every religion has had at its overarching goal: the peace of God.

From Judaism: "Help us, O God, to lie down in peace, and awaken us to life on the morrow. May we always be guided by Your good counsel, and thus find shelter in Your tent of peace . . ."

From Christianity (St. Francis of Assisi): "Lord, make me an instrument of Your peace. Where there is hatred, let me sow love; where there is injury, let me sow pardon; where there is doubt, faith; where there is despair, hope; where there is darkness, light; and where there is sadness, joy."

From Islam: "Guide us, O God, on the path of perfect harmony, the path of those whom You have blessed with the gifts of peace, joy, serenity and delight . . ."

From Buddhism: "May all beings be free of suffering. May all have happiness and contentment. May all be peaceful and at ease. . . . May all be free. May all beings abide in the great innate peace."

From Hinduism: "May there be peace in the higher regions; may there be peace in the firmament; may there be peace on earth. . . . The Supreme Lord is peace. May we all be in peace, peace, peace, peace; and may that peace come into each of us."

2.

WHAT ROAD
MUST I TRAVEL, GOD?

The 9 Paths to Quintessential Peace

Our idea of God tells us more
about ourselves than about Him.

THOMAS MERTON

In a sense, there are an infinite number of paths to God, one for each of us. In Hindu mythology, the young Lord Krishna is depicted as a cowherd whom the local *gopis* (milkmaids) find irresistible. When Krishna plays his celestial flute, the gopis drop everything and flock to him, wanting nothing more than to be with their beloved. So Krishna multiplies himself, taking on a singular form—young, old, tall, short, etc.—to match each milkmaid's desire. This ancient allegory illustrates that a multitude of qualities can be attributed to God; worshippers tend to fix upon the ones that suit their personalities, tally with their beliefs and serve their psychospiritual needs. The tale also teaches that the yearning for divine union can be expressed in many ways, and the route to God is highly individual.

The tasks that lie before us as we make peace with God, the methods we use and the pitfalls and challenges we face, are as unique as our profiles. Nevertheless, each of us is primarily disposed to one of nine distinct pathways, based on the archetypes described in this chapter.[1] These archetypes can be

---

[1] Those who are familiar with the Enneagram will find that these nine archetypes correspond loosely to the personality drives in that system, specifically applied to making peace with God.

seen as dominant personality drives, each with specific tendencies and strengths, as well as a dark side that creates obstacles to peace that must be consciously examined and overcome.

As you read about the archetypes, you will find in each one something to identify with and insights to help you on your spiritual journey. That is because we all have traits in common with every personality drive. Two or three of the archetypes will probably remind you strongly of yourself. One might stand out above all. You will say, "That's me!" Well, it's *not* you. Like all systems of personality classification, this one is as useful—and as limited—as a good map or metaphor. The archetypes define a collection of qualities that describe how some individuals think, feel and act most of the time. They draw a rough sketch of the ego, that aspect of consciousness that gives us our sense of individuality. The ego is the voice of I, me and mine. Like the chalk outlines that police draw to indicate the position a body was in when it was found, the ego defines the boundaries of an illusion. It convinces us that the small self we identify with—consisting of our bodies, our values and attitudes, the roles we play, etc.—is the true center of our being. It tries to sell that lie like a consummate con artist who knows that the minute we catch on to what we really are, the jig is up. The central task of all spiritual seekers is to break through the illusion that we are what our ego defines as "self," and courageously embrace the true Self that we share with all that is.

One of the myriad paradoxes of the spiritual path is that, while it feels as though we're trying to get to a specific destination, we're in fact already there. We don't have to find the Self, we *are* the Self. We don't have to achieve union with God, we are already one with God. At the same time, we may as well *not* be, because we don't *know* that we are. It's the same as saying, "The sun's not shining," when the sun is actually shining as it always does, it's just obscured by clouds. Our identification with the ego is a self-imposed cloud. It's a time-bound, space-bound mirage that blocks our awareness of the eternal Self. But another paradox is this: the ego may be an illusion, but it's also real. As real as a cloud. It is just as foolish to pretend that our individual personalities don't exist as it is to pretend that they're all we are. Our small self is the vehicle we're riding in (some would say we selected it, or even designed it) on the pathless path to the Infinite. While we must always remember that we are not what we drive, we need to take our vehicle seriously, care for it without obsessing over it and use it to full advantage until we no longer need it.

With that in mind, reading about the nine archetypes will give you a greater understanding of your own spiritual needs and challenges, as well as insight into other people in your life—your love partner, the parents who raised you, the clergy and congregants in your spiritual affiliation or house of worship, your friends and coworkers—whose primary orientation may be different from your own. It will also give you a fresh vantage point on your past and help you define what you need to do now in order to make peace with God. If you discover that one archetype describes your personality better than any of the others, consider it your primary orientation, the one to pay the closest attention to as you proceed through the book. But hold it lightly. Don't get lost in analysis or allow it to define you, any more than you would allow your astrological sign to define you. The archetypes are simply summaries of some of the roles we play on the stage of life, where, as Shakespeare reminds us, we are all players.

Bear in mind that no archetype is better than any of the others. They are just different postures we adopt toward God, peculiar expressions of the eternal yearning for union. As we mature spiritually, the distinct personality traits that once defined who we are become less significant. Like trendy clothes, or former lovers we thought we couldn't live without, or youthful convictions we once thought we'd defend to the death, they are attachments to which we cling less and less.

It is also vital to remember that each archetype encompasses a broad range of qualities. Within each are individuals who are totally secular and divorced from spirituality, as well as those who are devoted one hundred percent to union with God—and everyone in between. More important, the traits within each archetype exist on a continuum from integration to disintegration. Depending on the individual's level of awareness, spiritual development and emotional maturity, he or she will exhibit qualities that are stronger or weaker, more evolved or lesser evolved, noble or crude, constructive or destructive, catalysts to peace with God or obstacles to peace. As we move toward the peace which surpasses understanding, we naturally evolve toward the best qualities of our principle archetype and away from its weaknesses. But all growth occurs through the interaction of seemingly opposite values. By becoming conscious of traits that hold us back, we can more easily overcome them and harness our strengths for spiritual growth. To make the discussion most useful, therefore, we have devoted more space to the qualities that get in the way of peace with God, emphasizing what can be done to rise above them.

What follows are descriptions of the nine archetypal paths to God, in this order: the Reformer, the Lover, the Achiever, the Creator, the Thinker, the Security-Seeker, the Adventurer, the Boss and the Peacemaker.

The Reformer

If thou shouldst say, "It is enough,
I have reached perfection," all is lost.

ST. AUGUSTINE

Reformers tend to see God as the Great Rule-Maker, the giver of commandments that, if followed, make all things good, pure and holy. Idealistic, compassionate and highly moral, Reformers at their best make terrific preachers, crusaders and healers. Their commitment to doing what is right makes them loyal followers and devoted disciples, but when they believe that the prevailing structure is not consistent with the highest and best ideals, they lead the movement to change the rules. They hold themselves and others to elevated standards, and when people or institutions do not measure up, they turn their productive energies toward reformation and transformation. Like water assumes different forms—rivers, rain, ice, etc.—and reshapes the earth, Reformers adapt to the needs of their surroundings in order to purify and restructure them. When they rise to the level of a Jesus, Buddha or Mohammed, or a Gandhi, Mandela or Martin Luther King, Jr., Reformers change the course of history. If they had their highest aspirations fulfilled, everyone would

celebrate their differences while holding to the great truth of our divine Oneness, and heaven would descend on earth.

Restless in their quest for self-improvement, uncompromising in their self-
assessment, Reformers want to be the best that they can be and help others do
the same. They look at themselves with brutal honesty, see what needs to be
done and take on with fixity of purpose the task of removing obstacles and
cleansing impurities. Problem-solvers by nature, their orientation is to figure
out the rules of the road and follow them to the letter. If they can do that, they
feel they will surely (depending on their religious orientation) earn the grace
of God, pile up points for the afterlife or rise quickly to spiritual enlightenment.

THE REFORMER'S SPIRITUAL CHALLENGE

The yearning of Reformers for perfection makes it hard for them to tolerate a world that is, on the surface at least, imperfect. They can be hypersensi-
tive, judgmental, critical faultfinders, always on the lookout for something
that needs correcting. When caught up in their egos, they are driven to fix
everyone or convert them to their belief system. When they don't succeed,
they get angry—at God for creating an imperfect world, at human beings for
messing up God's perfect world or at themselves for not doing enough to make
things right. Their perfectionism can also make them fickle; when people or
environments are beyond their capacity to reform, they're likely to switch alle-
giances to something that appears to be perfect, or at least perfectible. They
often turn each new teaching, guru, church, book or insight into The Answer—
until they discover that it too is imperfect.

The ranks of fundamentalists in every religion are filled with Reformers.
They think that theirs is the only true way to goodness and God, and they want
everyone else to wake up and get with the program. While their missionary
zeal is born of the best intentions, they will, at their most extreme, stop at nothing to win converts. As history has sorrowfully witnessed with the Crusades,
the Inquisition and various jihads, desperate Reformers can destroy the very

souls whom they set out to save. In positions of authority, they can be obsessive rule-makers and rule-enforcers. Dogmatic, unbending, intolerant and self-righteous, they feel that they must convert the infidels and unbelievers—or eliminate them—so God's perfection can be realized on earth. Their fervor can destroy a corrupt institution only to install in its place a brand-new style of oppression.

Most Reformers, of course, do not go to such extremes. But they always work hard for what they believe in, and sometimes their noble sense of purpose and high standards of responsibility turn them into overburdened work-horses for a cause. In moments of weakness, they might turn toward God and yell, "Why did you give me this heavy cross to bear?"—when they unwittingly piled the wood onto their own shoulders. Or, finding themselves still suffering despite having worked hard to perfect themselves, they might rise up in frustration and shout, "I followed all the rules, God! Why am I being punished?"

On the other hand, when they shine their perfectionist gaze on themselves, Reformers can be ruthlessly self-critical. They are highly prone to guilt and shame. "I'm not compassionate enough." "I have not lived up to God's standards." "I can't rise above my sexual drives or my material ambitions." They work relentlessly at being perfect, and when they invariably fall short of their expectations, they can sink into self-loathing and despair. Overly serious, they can become Goody Two-shoes, suppressing their human instincts and denying themselves pleasure and joy. They often end up burned out or sick from a stress-induced illness. Or, the negative emotions they've buried burst into extreme forms of acting out; they break all the rules they tried to live by and indulge in behavior they later feel guilty about.

Not being at peace with God feels tragic to Reformers. It reinforces their conviction that they are inherently flawed or tainted. In order to make peace, they need to reform themselves—only not in the way they think they do. Their adopted credo should be Lighten Up! They need to realize that on the spiritual level the imperfections of the world are all part of God's creation, perfect in their imperfection. By getting in touch with the natural compassion that lies at the positive end of the Reformer spectrum, they can learn to accept reality for what it is, other people for what they are and God for what God is.

Even more important is *self*-acceptance; Reformers need to go easy on themselves for being human. When they do, they just might give themselves permission to enjoy the pleasures of life on earth.

Perhaps most of all, Reformers need to take a break from evaluating everything around them and look clearly and deeply within. Their persistent efforts to make themselves better people are usually restricted to the level of outer behavior. They need to understand that the real problem is not what's going on "out there," but their own tendency to criticize, find fault and become easily aggravated. Because they tend to neglect what is nurturing and healing to the soul on the grounds that it's self-indulgent, it is extremely important for Reformers to find refuge on a regular basis from the irritating imperfections of the world. It is only at the core of the Self, where the infinite peace of the Divine awaits, that perfectionists can find true perfection and a perfect shield.

The Lover

Love walks the golden trail that leads to God.

PARAMAHANSA YOGANANDA

Lovers are devoted to God as the ultimate Beloved and feel very deeply God's infinite love. They want to drink the nectar of divine love, and their way of getting to it is through worship, devotion and surrender. In India, the way of the Lover is called bhakti yoga, the path of the heart, in which the aspirant's single-minded adoration of his guru or God diminishes the grip of ego as it melts into union with the Divine.

Spiritual romantics, Lovers are in love with love. At their best, they find it easy to subordinate their own desires in favor of generosity, heart-felt empathy and profound compassion. Some become ecstatic, God-intoxicated devotees, who sing and dance and weep with praise, so single-minded in their passion that they lose concern for anything but God the Beloved. Others tilt their swelling hearts toward their fellow creatures, finding genuine joy and deep satisfaction in giving. They know that the giver always gets more than the re-

ceiver. Humble and self-effacing, they are natural caregivers. Think of Mother
Teresa and others whose path to God is selfless service to the needy, or the
bodhisattvas of Buddhist lore who forego their own final liberation and remain
in human form to help relieve the suffering of all beings. For spiritual Lovers
who choose family life, the ego sacrifice of parenting, the mutual give and take
of marriage and the ecstasy of sexual union can serve as sacred vehicles for experiencing God's love.

Because the epitome of both lover and beloved is the Divine Mother,
Lovers often worship the sacred feminine, perhaps in the form of Mary, perhaps as a goddess figure. In their highest expression, they also *take on* the qualities of the Divine Mother. This applies to male Lovers as much as to females,
for the qualities of the Mother are shared by both sexes (as are the "male" qualities of Protector and Provider). This gives Lovers the ability to take on different
roles—nurturer, nutritionist, psychologist, educator, healer, etc.—depending
on the needs of those they love. Like the divine parent, spiritually mature
Lovers are capable of seemingly endless unconditional giving, hardly ever de-
pleting their reservoir of love. As love is the delicate magnetic force that uni-
fies diversity and brings wholeness to variety, they readily embrace the spiritual
vision of union with God and go about the task with utmost humility.

The Lover's Spiritual Challenge

For Lovers in their least evolved state, the act of loving is not so generous,
not so sacred. The yearning stems from emptiness rather than fullness. Its aim
is to satisfy the cravings of the small self, not to transcend them. And their love
comes with strings attached. Often possessive and needy, they want something
in return, usually the kind of love that they themselves are not yet capable of
giving. They need to feel special in the eyes of the beloved. Where God is concerned, this can translate not only to a strong desire for divine bliss, but sometimes even more—a sign that they have been anointed as one of the chosen.

Often, what appear to be acts of service and pure generosity might really be
calculated attempts to get something back—at the very least, appreciation and

praise. In the context of a spiritual or religious group, they are the obsequious ones who are always casting about for ways to claim the attention of the guru or to be singled out for a round of applause by the minister for their sacrificial service to the congregation. Lovers, in their quest for more and more love, can become overly accommodating.

They are also prone to "mood-making"—pretending to themselves and others that they are holier, humbler and more compassionate than thou. Their false humility actually stems from a quality they profess to loathe: pride. "Look at me!" they silently declare. "See how selflessly I love? How devoted I am? How perfectly free of ego I've become?" This charade is seldom a conscious one, for they are as determined to hide their dark side from themselves as they are from others. To compensate, many Lovers project their shadow onto others and blame them when things go wrong. Easily hurt, vulnerable to rejection and humiliation when they don't get the love they crave, they will quickly find fault with the object of their affections.

But Lovers can't very well blame God if they don't get the divine love they crave. So they blame the Devil instead, or a non-believing spouse, or a corrupt institution, or perhaps a pastor or guru whose human flaws have become apparent. Then they're off to find a replacement who will see them for the special souls they are. In the meantime, they might garner an exquisite sense of emotional satisfaction from the longing for love itself, for many Lovers love the longing as much as the loving.

Some Lovers *do* blame themselves when the blessings they want from God or another human being are not forthcoming: "I must not deserve it. I must not have loved purely enough." At which point, they might go to desperate extremes to prove themselves deserving—all the while feeling terrified that they are, in truth, not worthy at all. That's when Lovers' egos become vulnerable to their chief pitfall: martyrdom. Like Ado Annie, the character in the musical *Oklahoma*, they "cain't say no." And, like Annie, they often end up in a "turrible fix." They'll give and sacrifice, then give and sacrifice some more, always looking for ways to help, protect, nurture and otherwise prove their worth as Lovers.

Lovers must learn how to shower others with care and concern and still take care of themselves. Their credo might very well be "God loves those who love themselves." You can't flower fully as a Lover unless you can love yourself. They also have to distinguish between acts that are rooted in a sincere impulse to serve others and those that spring from neediness or dependency. Perhaps most of all, they have to stop looking for God's love in all the wrong places and get in touch with it directly, where it always abides, in the perfect stillness of the Self.

The Achiever

The end of life is not to achieve pleasure and avoid pain.
The end of life is to do the will of God, come what may.

MARTIN LUTHER KING, JR.

Achievers are in awe of God as Master Builder, the Supreme Architect of Creation and Chief Executive Officer of the Cosmos, who achieves magnificent order amidst infinite complexity. Spiritually driven Achievers gravitate toward good works, tirelessly serving God or their idea of a larger good. In Eastern terms, their path is that of karma yoga. They can be dreamers in the mode of Robert Browning's decree, "A man's reach should exceed his grasp, or what's a heaven for?" But they know that dreams must be acted upon if they are to become concrete realities. Achievers are the ones who might interrupt an endless stream of planning sessions to say, "Enough talking. Let's roll up our sleeves and get to work!" Do we need to raise more money? Get the mailing out? Build a new wing? On with it! As worker bees or team captains, they're out in front, making sure God's work is getting done, whether it's serving the needy directly or creating a charitable foundation.

Achievers, progressive by nature, are always looking to move forward in their spiritual growth, becoming veritable knights in quest of the Holy Grail. Making peace with God becomes a noble task to be accomplished. Magnanimous by nature, mature Achievers will lead the way for others, and, like spiritual warriors, slay any dragons that get in the way. At their very best, they become saints whose selfless efforts to make the world a better place inspire awe. Their deepest spiritual yearning is to turn the earth into a heavenly queendom.

The Achiever's Spiritual Challenge

The Achiever's primary pitfall is equating spiritual value with outer performance and accomplishment. Achievers are likely to treat the path to the Ineffable as if it were a contest. They want to know exactly what God expects of them, and what steps they have to take to earn the keys to heaven ASAP. Often, when they seem to be working for a higher good, they are actually serving their lower self in a calculated attempt to be spiritually rewarded. At every step, Achievers who lack integration are calling out, "How am I doing, God?" They measure their spiritual progress by whatever currency their tradition or teaching provides, and compare their score to their fellow travelers, just as in business they would compare their market share to that of the competition. Always looking ahead to higher attainment, they can't be in the Now, where the goal they seek can be gained only through nonattachment. They can become so fixed on the destination that they can't enjoy the surprise and mystery of the path.

When they acquire positions of religious authority, Achievers are highly skilled in spreading the word and attracting followers. With their natural charisma and their ability to project a persona that matches the group's expectations, they quickly gather a flock. Some leave a positive mark on spiritual history, but some join the ranks of fallen gurus, scandalized clerics and discredited institutions.

Achievers need to accept themselves as human beings, not just humans doing. Their mantra should be: God loves me for who and what I am, not just for what I accomplish. By halting their incessant activity once in a while to turn within, they might do something they find difficult: distinguish their true values from those they have absorbed from their families and religions. Achievers have trouble with stillness because it feels like doing nothing— which is precisely the point, for it is in that nothing that spirit comes alive. "Silence is the language of God," said Father Thomas Keating, "and everything else is a bad translation." Achievers need to realize through direct experience that the silence at the core of their being is not a void to be avoided, not an abyss of nothingness or a pit of darkness, but a well of blissful fullness and a fountain of light.

They also have to learn that nurturing the soul is not incompatible with achievement. The French novelist Marcel Proust once said, "Books are the work of solitude, and the children of silence." The same can be said of any worthwhile endeavor. The most creative achievements spring from the primal source of energy and intelligence within us. Achievers should bear in mind the ideals that all spiritual traditions advocate—to work for the joy of it, not just for recognition and reward; to serve the highest good; to do their duty well, and, having done it, remain unattached to the fruits of their actions. "Even an ordinary person can accomplish extraordinary things when he or she steps aside and lets God in," says Rabbi Shoni Labowitz. For Achievers, it also has to be OK *not* to accomplish extraordinary things; God may not require it of them.

The Creator

From the individual to the universal, all that we see
is the play and display of Creative Intelligence.

MAHARISHI MAHESH YOGI

The aspect of God that most appeals to Creators, of course, is that of Creator Supreme, the Master Painter, the Sacred Sculptor, the Divine Musician and the Cosmic Storyteller. Creators approach God through awe and wonder, through aesthetic appreciation and ecstatic sensory experience. They are drawn to elaborate rituals, colorful ceremonies and soul-stirring choirs. In their own artistic expression, they use creativity as a kind of sacrament. Gospel hymns, the pure baritone of a cantor, the sacred works of Bach and Beethoven; the Sphinx, Angkor Wat and the Taj Mahal; Tibetan tankas, Islamic miniatures and the Sistine Chapel; the poetry of Rumi and Rilke and "The Song of Songs"—these are immortal expressions of the adoration of God and the longing to connect to the Divine through creative expression. If Creators could invent a world, it would be a thing of beauty and a joy forever, free of vulgarity and ugliness, where everyone lived in perpetual delight.

Dramatic and passionate by nature, Creators are incurable romantics. They abhor conventionality and revere true originality. In their most integrated state, Creators are compassionate, supportive and gentle, able to form strong interpersonal connections. They feel deeply, and in their integrated state, they allow themselves to experience the complete range of emotions, from bliss to blisters, exaltation to despair, enjoying the comedy and pathos of human life. In their spiritual quest, Creators desire not only to surround themselves with beauty but to *be* spiritually beautiful themselves. Many will direct their passionate, compassionate energy into helping others lead inwardly richer lives.

Creators intuitively understand the joy of being open to the Presence of the moment, ecstatically dancing with the divine rhythms of life and rejoicing in the grandeur of Creation. Their natural sense of proportion and symmetry leads them from the chaos and disorder on the surface of life to the unity at the depths. Seeking out that which is exceptional as well as beautiful, they are dedicated to embellishing God's jewel-like handiwork. And along with their passion for pleasure and beauty comes an ardent search for meaning and purpose—"What's it all about?" They seek to develop a refinement of perception that can fully appreciate the grandeur of the Creator and the Creation. They can be great visionaries, although the details of manifesting their visions often bore them. At rock bottom, they seek to make things whole, and wholeness, in its highest form, is union with God.

The Creator's Spiritual Challenge

Lurking in the shadows of the exuberant Creator is a propensity for tragedy. One of their chief pitfalls is that they can't handle ordinary reality. It all seems too mundane, too common, too bland for them. Only the ecstatic will do. Combined with their fear of being seen as ordinary themselves, this pushes them toward new and exciting experiences, the more mind-blowing and extraordinary the better. This can lead to self-destructive behavior. Until they recognize that there are better and safer ways to satisfy their yearning for transcendence, they try to escape the confines of dreary reality through the extremes of sensory experience, often ending up addicted to some form of getting high. It is as though they took literally William Blake's statement that "the road to excess leads to wisdom," not realizing it's from "Proverbs of Hell."

The dark side of Creators is a potential black hole of madness. Prone to depression, they wear their doom and gloom like a badge of honor. Classic images of the tortured soul, the tormented genius and the doomed romantic are tailor-made for this moody archetype. They often seem to be lost souls, lurking on the fringes of society on the brink of despair. In many cases, their cavernous lows alternate with skyscraping highs in classic bipolar fashion, making them as hard to be *with* as it is to be them. Because they crave emotional intensity, they are constantly creating dramas in their lives. Their particular burden is to feel alone and abandoned. They always seem to be grieving for something lost or pining for something not yet found, sometimes behaving in such a way as to ensure that they *do* grieve and pine. In fact, many Creators are addicted to longing, unconsciously preferring it to actually having what they long for.

Creators can be overly sensitive and thin-skinned. Easily wounded, they beat themselves up constantly. While we all have an inner critic inside our heads, the Creator's is especially cruel, reviewing every performance with an acid tongue. This self-flagellation is rooted in a core of shame, the Creator's true Achilles' heel. Deep down, religious Creators often feel useless and worthless in the eyes of God.

Creators often feel that something is missing spiritually. "Why does God reward *her* and not me?" "Why is God punishing me with visions so magnificent I can't make them materialize?" "Will I *ever* break through to grace?" They can often be found rending their garments over something they lost: the once-in-a-lifetime soul mate who got away, the parent who loved them unconditionally and died too young, the ecstatic vision they had on LSD but have never duplicated, the Oneness they felt while watching the sun go down over Machu Picchu and never again recaptured. Spiritually, this translates into feeling forsaken by God. Creators tend to feel exiled from all that is holy, like an Old Testament character who is banished from the tribe by divine decree.

Their relationship with God is often contradictory. On the one hand, they have a sense of entitlement; they expect their prayers to be magically answered and their desires to be readily fulfilled. On the other hand, they feel so fundamentally rotten that they don't deserve happiness or peace. The term existential despair was made for them: "Is there really any meaning to this life? Does God really exist, and if He does, why can't I catch a break?"

Creators need to know that when Jesus said, "Blessed are they that mourn," he was not advising us to *kvetch*. They need to take pride in their talents and achievements, not despair because they haven't won an Academy Award or a Grammy or a Nobel Prize. They also have to realize that the grass is plenty green enough on their side of the fence. Thicker skin would help, too; they don't have to take personally everything they think God is doing to them. They have to accept that the divine purpose is not to punish them, but rather to embrace them and wash away their shame.

The primary inner work of Creators is to make room for balance and equanimity. They need to appreciate that life can be thrilling and peaceful at the same time. Those who are severely depressed need to have their condition properly treated. They also need to get in touch with the roots of their shame, which usually stems from early childhood, and silence the aggressive inner voices that constantly reinforce it. Gratitude is the virtue they most need to cultivate. They would do well to remember the Muslim proverb, "Write the wrongs that are done to you in sand, but write the good things that happen to you on a piece of marble."

By learning how to extract joy from the ordinary, Creators just might stumble upon the transcendent Presence they hunger for. If God is sending them a message, it is not "You don't deserve what you desire," it's, "Stop looking for me in a burning bush, a vision, a thunderclap or a flash of divine light. Excitement is as ephemeral as the wind, as impermanent as snow. You can find ecstasy just as readily, and perhaps more lastingly, in the tinkle of wind chimes, not just Beethoven's Ninth; in a potted plant, not just majestic mountains; in a storefront chapel, not just Chartes Cathedral; in reading Dr. Seuss to a child, not just in Dante or Donne; in the Sunday comics, not just Van Gogh; in the touch of a hand, not just an orgasm."

As Henry Miller observed, "we live at the edge of the miraculous." The peace of God is here for the taking, if Creators can only seize it the way they now seize thrills.

The Thinker

I hear and behold God in every object, yet I
understand God not in the least.

WALT WHITMAN

To Thinkers, God is Pure Intelligence, the Great Cosmic Mind, the Supreme Genius, the Ultimate Wise One. Studious, dogged in their quest for intellectual certainty, when Thinkers are drawn to contemplating God they often become religious scholars and theologians. When they leave their ivory towers to engage the life of the spirit, they might feel drawn to the monastery. Even if they have jobs and families, you will find them as often as circumstances allow meditating behind closed doors, pacing contemplatively in some cloistered setting or going off on a solitary retreat. Theirs is the path of knowledge, what in India would be called *gyana* (or *jnana*) yoga. Their preferred method is persistent inquiry into the nature of things, and their favored tool is the discerning intellect.

Naturally detached, Thinkers find it easy—in fact preferable—to be alone.

They are capable of forming solid, enduring relationships, as long as they are allowed to retain a certain amount of solitude. They find it easier than most to renounce material possessions and worldly affairs, or to live in voluntary simplicity for the sake of their spiritual values. Knowing is far more important to them than having or doing. They ache to know how God operates, whether they express that yearning in scientific or religious terms. Their determined independence allows them to think for themselves, questioning repeatedly and debating relentlessly until their intellectual inquiries are satisfied—if they can *ever* be satisfied, for some of the questions Thinkers are drawn to are as enigmatic as "What is the sound of one hand clapping?" To Thinkers, peace with God would be achieving the ultimate Aha! experience.

Thinkers ache for revelation, and they bring to the quest a fierce dedication to truth. They refuse to settle for dogma, conventional answers or easy explanations. Knowing how easy it is to be misled by the limitations of the senses, they press for clarity and precision, putting every hunch and inference to the test. At their most integrated, Thinkers "get" that the mind can take them only to the door of the Transcendent, so they direct their powerful intellects to figuring out how to subdue their own ongoing mental chatter and transcend thought itself.

THE THINKER'S SPIRITUAL CHALLENGE

For Thinkers the chief obstacles to making peace are literally in their minds. They outsmart themselves by thinking too much. They fail to see the limits of their intellects. They get stuck in their heads, ruminate obsessively and think their way into their own private hell. Debating themselves endlessly, they chase their own intellectual tails as they try in vain to reason their way to the Unknowable. God is not some object that can be observed and examined from afar like astronomers analyze stars. God can't be gathered and placed under a microscope like botanists study plants. God can be known only by absorption in a place beyond thought.

Some Thinkers are so uncomfortable with uncertainty, unpredictability and ambiguity that they get stuck in their own convenient conclusions. When they become know-it-alls, as many do, they can be arrogant toward those with competing views. They can close their minds, depriving themselves of new ideas and different perspectives. When logic and reason run into a dead end— as they usually do when pursuing spiritual truth—Thinkers can either become cynics or compulsive believers.

Thinkers don't like obligations and demands, preferring solitary exploration. Out of resentment, they often quietly rebel against the expectations of others, whether a parent, a spouse or a religious institution. But what they deem healthy opposition to convention is, in some cases, merely petty defiance. On a spiritual level, rebellion can isolate Thinkers, keeping them from taking advantage of valuable teachings and depriving them of the support and nourishment of spiritual companions. Solitude is of immense value on the path to God, but so is community. Hence sangha—the fellowship of seekers— is one of the Three Jewels of Buddhism. Jews require a body of ten to properly pray. And Jesus told his disciples, "Wherever two or three are gathered together in my name, there am I in the midst of them."

Teachings that call for the renunciation of desire come easily to Thinkers because they tend to be detached in the first place, and they don't put much stock in material acquisitions. However, it is one thing to be fully engaged in life yet detached from expectations and outcomes. It is quite another to be indifferent. The former is a coveted spiritual position; the latter can be just another form of self-absorption. True spiritual detachment springs from inner fullness and absolute contentment, not from emotional disengagement. If you're aloof, as Thinkers tend to be, you miss out on the spiritual benefits of interpersonal intimacy and service to others—or to God—a difficult concept for Thinkers to embrace. Their natural propensity to disconnect from life makes them emotionally distant. This causes them to miss out on chances to open their hearts. And to make peace with God you must involve the heart, not just the brain. Thinkers need to get out of their heads from time to time and engage life viscerally and emotionally. By emerging from their secluded inner sanctums to spend time with other people, they stand to learn a great deal.

Thinkers have to realize that they can't reason their way to God and that rational thought can only go so far in answering their questions *about* God. God's ways have eluded the most prodigious intellects in history, so what chance do the rest of us have? The Thinker's challenge is to accept that some things are simply unfathomable to the human mind. But Thinkers have trouble not thinking; even the most dedicated spiritual seekers among them will resist the instinct to merge with the Infinite. They're afraid they might get swallowed up and lose their autonomous minds.

Thinkers are naturally drawn to meditative practices that can be done on their own, in private. This is a huge advantage on the path to peace with God. But, while such practices are powerful and vital, they can also be overdone and used as an excuse for disengaging from the world. Thinkers are well advised to add to their repertoire disciplines performed in groups, such as chanting and worship services, as well as non-mental practices such as yoga, breath work and martial arts. To do that successfully, they may also have to overcome their tendency to resist discipline and obligations.

Perhaps most important, Thinkers have to be willing to make a commitment to work on their spiritual development. They have a tendency to step away from challenges and watch from a distance, hoping things will to come to them. Well, God won't be going to them because God is already there. The next move is theirs.

The Security-Seeker

Be strong and of a good courage, fear not, nor be afraid.
DEUTERONOMY 31:6

Because what drives them most is the need for safety, Security-Seekers tend to see God as the Great Protector or the Ultimate Provider. When life is going well, they also see God as a bestower of blessings, a benevolent parent who takes care of her child's needs and dispenses frequent treats with supreme generosity. God takes care of me, they believe, as long as I remain loyal and steadfast and follow the law. Security-Seekers feel like favored ones, graced by a bountiful universe, although deep down they often fear that the rug will be pulled out from under them and everything will be taken away.

Naturally self-sacrificing, Security-Seekers will work hard for what they perceive as God's work in the world. If they feel called to a worthy cause, they make sturdy soldiers, devoted partners, excellent team players and humble subordinates. If they had their way, they would create an ideal world in which everyone is under divine protection, where there are no threats to anyone's safety and bad things never happen to good people.

In their personal quest for peace with God, Security-Seekers are anchored, vigilant and resourceful. Rock-solid, they are not fooled by extremism and are more likely to be sensible than fanatical. Their natural curiosity and sense of balance enables them to see all sides of an issue. Their spiritual home is in the middle, where it appears safest and most secure.

THE SECURITY-SEEKER'S SPIRITUAL CHALLENGE

Security-Seekers want God to be the perfect parent who eases their fears and shields them from the danger they perceive all around them. But life doesn't always turn out to be quite that safe, and when it's not, they fear that God is another kind of parent, the Punisher. Then they feel even more anxious than they normally are, which only serves to reinforce another natural tendency of the Security-Seeker: doubt. They are the proverbial doubting Thomases. Present them with a reasonable explanation or opinion and their minds automatically shift to the Devil's advocate position. Their ability to see both sides of an issue has its advantages, but it also makes them indecisive. They can get paralyzed by ambivalence, making them excellent agnostics who can argue just as persuasively for or against the existence of God.

At their weakest, Security-Seekers become hypervigilant. Defensive in posture, they scour the environment with psychic radar in search of incoming missiles. When planning, they project worst-case scenarios instead of best-case outcomes that are equally likely to occur. They can even become paranoid, certain that a particular individual—or a mob—is out to take advantage of them.

The more typical Security-Seeker, the phobic type, is attracted to the security of religious organizations. Nothing wrong with that unless the affiliation does not serve their true spiritual needs and the Security-Seeker remains stuck within its sheltering embrace, afraid to explore alternatives. They are also drawn to strong, charismatic leaders. Many get caught up in cults, especially insulated groups with messianic missions and a belief that they must band together to protect themselves from outsiders. But Security-Seekers have mixed feelings about authorities. Their *anti*-authority tendencies can be activated at the first sign that a revered leader has clay feet. They might then join the opposition in attempting to shatter the pedestal on which the master rests.

Since God is the ultimate authority figure, they can struggle fiercely with the Almighty. "Show me an unequivocal sign! Prove that you will hold up your end of the bargain and make my world safe!" They want to be dutiful servants of a benign Lord, and they often try their damnedest. But sometimes they just can't pull it off because they're plagued by doubt: "Lord, help my unbelief!" Then they see themselves as delinquent and deficient, unable to do God's bidding and therefore unworthy of God's grace—a very unsafe, insecure place to be.

The challenge for Security-Seekers is to conquer their doubt and learn to trust themselves and God. But their faith can't be a blind one; it can't be imposed by force of will or wiggled into place by a statement of affirmation. Rather, they need to use the strength of their own Devil's advocacy and look at the reality of existence. Am I really under threat? Is the universe really malevolent? Is the worst-case projection really more likely to occur than the best? Is God really out to get me?

Even more important, they need to derive their faith from convincing experience. Like the Cowardly Lion, they need courage to counter their innate fear, and courage arises from strength—and from the *belief* in one's strength. Security-Seekers have to realize that the root of their fear is not God or a dangerous universe, but their own sense of weakness. God strengthens those who strengthen themselves. When they can face down their demons and come away unscathed, they usually realize that they are stronger and more re-sourceful than they imagined. Simple confidence that they can plunge ahead when safety is *not* assured is a tonic for the Security-Seeker's faith in God and themselves.

Most important, they need to get strong spiritually. One of their challenges is to realize that there is no true security in any worldly attachment—not a job, not a marriage, not stock options, not a home, not even a church or temple—because everything is subject to change and decay. Only by connecting to the part of them that is indestructible and eternal can the spiritually aware security-seeker find lasting security. The more they tap into the source of di-vine power within, the more they can walk through the valley of the shadow of death and fear no evil, for the rod and staff of infinite strength will be within them. Then they can finally drop their guard.

The Adventurer

He who binds to himself a joy
Doth the winged life destroy.
But he who kisses the joy as it flies
Lives in Eternity's sunrise.

WILLIAM BLAKE

To Adventurers, God is not a solemn Deity, not a fuddy-duddy or a stern taskmaster, but rather a wild, exciting Force, a Glorious Trickster, a Master Magician who wants us to embrace life with passion and enthusiasm. They relish not just God the Creator, but also God the Destroyer, as they are most willing to explore the dark side. Adventurers are just as likely to have an epiphany watching a storm at sea or a lion pouncing on its prey as viewing a glorious sunset or a butterfly. To them, the spiritual path is a thrilling saga, a grand poem, an epic quest. Once they're on it, they will try anything and ex-plore anywhere to experience God. Where do I go? The mountaintop? Fine. The cave? OK. The soup kitchen? Show me the way. Just don't let it get boring.

On the surface, Adventurers seldom seem to be the godly type. Perpetual nonconformists, they disdain formality and they love to break the mold of spiritual correctness. Proper members of the congregation may look upon them as outrageous, and even shun them as heathens and freaks, but Adventurers couldn't care less about what others may think. They're sure that God loves them because they reflect God's free spirit.

You won't see a whole lot of penitence from Adventurers. No hair shirts, no bowing and scraping to God's representatives. If they feel the need to set things straight with the cosmos, they'll go directly to the top. And they will approach the task without great ceremony, just a candid conversation with God—the equivalent of hashing things out with the boss on the golf course rather than requesting a formal hearing.

Adventurers are idealists and determined optimists. Unsinkably buoyant, they see the universe as God's funhouse and life as a series of exciting escapades. When they awaken to the value of spirituality, they go after enlightenment with gusto. They're wide open to new knowledge and new practices—anything to explore or experiment with as long as it's part of the grand adventure. They are boundary breakers—a huge advantage on the spiritual path because it's all about breaking boundaries and getting to the boundless. If an internal block is in the way, they will immediately try to find a way around it.

One obstacle they hate to deal with is spiritual boredom and stagnation. They abhor complacency. It's ever onward for Adventurers. No waiting for messiahs or saviors or heavenly afterlives. They're drawn to teachings that promise happiness in *this* life and a happening heaven on earth.

THE ADVENTURER'S SPIRITUAL CHALLENGES

The chief spiritual obstacle for Adventurers is to value the life of the spirit in the first place. For many, the inner dimension seems like a barren flatland. Why go there? As for religion, deliver me from boredom. Give us this day our daily buzz. Adventurers are usually directed outward, to the edges of life where the kicks are most intense. Always on the lookout for peak experiences, they are in danger of being exactly what they think they're not: superficial.

In many cases, they live for those highs, and the down times can be maddening. Manic and impulsive in their search for the next breathtaking escapade or awesome spectacle, they are prone to self-destructive behavior. Those who fail to take proper care of themselves can become dissipated or ill at an early age. Some hit bottom due to addiction, whether to drugs or sex or gambling or high-risk sports and business ventures — which is unfortunate because Adventurers hate pain as much as boredom. On the other hand, it is at the low point that many of them turn to God. It typically happens in their middle years, when they take stock and realize that life did not turn out to be quite as grand as they dreamed it would. Now the body can no longer stand up to the pursuit of pleasure. Now the marriage is on the rocks and the kids despise them because they weren't there for them — or they have no family, no intimacy at all in fact, because they were too busy partying. Now the thought gnaws at them, "Has all my adventuring been in vain? Am I missing something?"

For wise Adventurers, the next great adventure is the God quest, and for many it comes to be appreciated as the most amazing and exciting adventure of all. The danger, however, is that they will look at religion or spirituality as just another way of getting high, and they'll expect to stay "up" all the time. This leads to a number of potential pitfalls.

Not moving ahead according to their spiritual timetable makes them impatient and easily disappointed — with themselves and God. If their expectations are dashed or they encounter tragedy or strife, Adventurers can become disillusioned. It can be a major struggle to reconcile their image of God with the existence of suffering and pain. They feel abandoned, not quite the darlings of the Lord they thought they were. Their maturity and sense of integration depends on being able to see that the disagreeable aspects of life are as much a part of God's grandeur as the pleasures.

Another pitfall for Adventurers is their addiction to excitement. They don't just want to enjoy life; they want to be blown away. They want to be elevated, transported, lifted out of their skins to a transcendent realm of experience. For that reason, they are drawn to the spectacular aspects of spirituality, to angels and revelations, to grand epiphanies and astral projections, to mind-boggling miracles and body-shattering ecstasies—all of which are as transient as a joy-ride and as elusive as the perfect date. And the fall from spiritual intoxication to ordinary existence can be a bummer.

Their restlessness can also turn Adventurers into spiritual dilettantes. They love variety and need to keep their options open, but they lose patience quickly, especially when things get tedious or demanding. "Okay, what's next?" They can flit from one seminar, workshop or guru to the next, barely sticking around long enough to know what they're leaving behind.

Perhaps the chief obstacle for Adventurers is admitting that they're *not* at peace with God in the first place. Their compulsive positivity can be taken so far as to land them in a place of denial. In their headlong pursuit of the light, they'll not only do their best to avoid pain, conflict and anxiety, they'll disavow them altogether. "What, me worry? No problem, everything's cool, couldn't be better." As the original spin doctors, they mentally reframe whatever un-pleasantness crops up to make it palatable and unthreatening. Add to that a kind of grandiosity that many Adventurers possess, and you get a personal-ity that believes he or she has been singled out by God and is entitled to a pleasure-packed, bump-free ride to material fulfillment and spiritual salva-tion. Quickly! The problem is, while positivity is a virtue, when it's compulsive it can blind you to issues that have to be addressed. Another problem is, the truth can come on suddenly and bring the Adventurer to his or her knees: "I've been a selfish bastard. I don't give a damn about anyone else, including God. I'm arrogant. I'm lazy. I have no discipline." If they're lucky, they'll come through the ego shattering with genuine humility and improve their chances of making peace with God immeasurably.

Adventurers need to direct their spirit of adventure to the quest for peace. Truth should be their highest goal, not stimulation. Transformation takes pa-tience and perseverance, virtues that many Adventurers find in short supply.

They also need to accept that darkness is as much a part of creation as the light they so desperately seek. They have to peer into their shadows and confront their demons, and, if necessary, go through some pain for the sake of growth. They have to be willing to work at making peace with God, not back off as soon as the going gets tough. Their penchant for flattery and charm may smooth over tensions with other human beings, but God won't fall for any of that.

Adventurers need to integrate their spiritual highs with the mundane reality of everyday existence. Peak experiences are all well and good; and they can be windows to the Divine. But they are not, in themselves, the Essence. They are God's playthings, not God. It may sound boring, but there are good reasons that every spiritual tradition counsels moderation in all pursuits, including the yearning for the Divine.

The Boss

We attain God when we love, and only that victory
endures in consequence of which no one is defeated.

FROM A SIKH PRAYER

Bosses are attracted to the omnipotent, omniscient aspect of God. They sit in awe of the Almighty Ruler of the universe, the King of Kings, and bow before that immense power. Steadfast in their faith, happy to let God be the real boss even if they can't comprehend how God administers his creation and metes out justice, well-integrated Bosses make outstanding leaders of religious institutions. They are strong, confident and authoritative, fully committed to their responsibilities — including their responsibility to wield their power with integrity. They understand that to whom much is given much is expected.

Seemingly blessed with boundless energy and self-discipline, Bosses know what they want and how to get it. For the spiritually aware, that goes as much for heavenly bounty as it does for mammon. They don't expect peace with God to come easily. They're willing to do whatever it takes and meet every challenge, and when the going gets tough they really get going. They are straight shooters who tell the truth as they see it, often with blunt honesty. What you see is what you get. At their best, the Boss's vigor and indomitable will is balanced with sensitivity and compassion, enabling them to use their skills for the benefit of others, not just themselves. They're likely to take the side of the underdog, try to lift up the weak and downtrodden and lead the fight against injustice. And while they're doing it, they'll often make those they lead feel as if *they* deserve all the credit. In the Boss's best of all possible worlds, God is in charge and everyone pitches in to fulfill the Divine Plan.

THE BOSS'S SPIRITUAL CHALLENGE

In their disintegrated state, Bosses lust for control and power above all else. They are obsessed with making themselves stronger and asserting their will over others. Their fear of being dominated won't let them accept any authority other than themselves, not even God. As underlings, they will bend the rules and push the limits in order to gain some degree of power—not just because they crave it, but because they're convinced they can do a better job. As congregants they want to be minister. As priests, they think they should be Pope. At their most arrogant, they even think they can do a better job than God.

When they do arrive at the top of the heap, Bosses can be tyrannical bullies. They have a Darwinian view of the world: it's survival of the fittest all the way and only the strong survive. They can have such contempt for "weak" emotions like sadness, remorse and especially fear that they will do everything in their power to deny them a place in their hearts. If a glimmer of tenderness rises up in them for anyone other than their immediate families, they see it as an Achilles' heel. Along those lines, they won't let themselves need anyone or be beholden to anyone—not even God. When things go wrong, their first impulse is to blame someone else—again, even God—and, if possible, exact revenge. But they can't always blame others, in which case they have no choice but to turn their rage inward. They can be as tough on themselves as they are on anyone else, berating themselves for not being strong enough, crafty enough, aggressive enough. "I let my guard down. Gotta toughen up."

While many Bosses are religious by virtue of their upbringing, they tend to be nominally observant at best, participating in church, mosque or temple for the sake of their families or to advance their ambitions through social contacts. Many have a Nietzschean view of world: God is dead, individual power is what makes the world go round. Rational and pragmatic, they are not open to any reality beyond what the senses can perceive or logic can infer. "I have no use for crutches like God or religion. That's for weaklings. I believe only what I see." In some cases, they concede that God might possibly exist, but if he does, they add, he's a not a God of love and mercy but rather a despot who can't be trusted—just like they are, of course. Bosses believe you have to be fully defended at all times. Tell them the meek shall inherit the earth and they'll laugh in your face—or will take out their financial statements and show you exactly who's inheriting what.

Proudly agnostic Bosses will wear their skepticism like a badge of honor. They will challenge God, blatantly defying what are purported to be God's rules, as if daring the Almighty to strike them down. "Go on, show me what you've got!" It is a way of testing their own doubt. If there *is* a God, they argue, then I could never get away with this.

And so it goes, unless they are lucky enough to experience some form of spontaneous grace or be struck by a lightning bolt of epiphany. Or hit rock bottom. Many Bosses undergo their first spiritual breakthrough when they suffer a particularly crushing failure. So great is their reverence for power that it takes a plunge into utter defeat to get them to realize that there is a power greater than themselves, and no amount of earthly supremacy can possibly give them total control of their lives. After the knockout heart attack, business setback, divorce or alcoholic breakdown, they get up off the canvas like a defeated boxer who has grudgingly come to respect his opponent and congratulate the victor. For many, it's time for step one of the 12-Step Program: admitting that they are powerless.

Once they do connect with God in some way, Bosses often suffer a period of agonizing self-contempt. They heap scorn upon themselves for their moral weaknesses—for not resisting temptation, for giving in to sin or yielding to their baser instincts. And since Bosses tend to have oversized appetites for lust and gluttony in every form, they usually have a lot to feel guilty about. Their selfishness, their greed, their disregard for the feelings of others, their arrogance—all their old sins haunt them now because they have signed on to a higher morality. They might then define winning in a brand-new way. Now they will stop at nothing to win God's favor.

In some cases, ironically, they resort to standard Boss form in the name of holiness. I'll be the best damn servant of God in town, and don't anybody get in my way. "You want me to tithe? Here's *twenty* percent! You want humility? Watch this!"—and they'll hit the floor, face down. Some Bosses become fanatics, suppressing their doubt because doubt is just another weakness to be defeated. They are often drawn to evangelism and holy wars because being a soldier for God suits their orientation toward power and domination. Their way is not only the right way for them, it's the *only* right way, and they are among the anointed who are charged with promoting God's will on earth. Autocratic and paternalistic, they often become ayatollahs in their own domains, whether they are heading a moral crusade or organizing a bake sale to raise money for the ladies auxiliary. Comedy writer Charles Zucker expressed the motto of true-believer Bosses: "Anyone who believes less than me is a heathen, and anyone who believes more than me is a nut." Only Bosses really mean it.

Of all the pathways to peace with God, that of the Boss is the most difficult in this respect: they find it extremely hard to "let go and let God." To them, power is not something you give away voluntarily; it has to be taken from you. Surrender is a dirty word. It means capitulation to them, and nothing is more humiliating to a Boss. Thy will be done? Not on my watch! Yield to a Higher Power? What's in it for me? Bosses have to be convinced that the rewards of making peace with God outweigh the risks. Their challenge is to look upon union with God not as annihilation but as the ultimate enlargement, a merger in which they relinquish control of their operation to a larger entity in return for a fortune in spiritual stock options.

Hard as it might be, Bosses have to stop blaming other people, or God, when they don't get what they want. In a similar vein, they have to acquire a virtue that does not come easily to them: forgiveness. They are grudge-holders and revenge-seekers, and those tendencies are not exactly conducive to making peace with God. Two other Boss traits need to be turned on their heads. One is the tendency to heed only their own counsel and shut out other voices, especially contrary ones. They have to learn to listen to the wise ones, and to the subtle signs and muted whispers of the Divine. The other trait Bosses have to overcome is their disdain for "weak" emotions. They have to realize that stifling the feelings that make them vulnerable also destroys their capacity for love, joy and other treasures that moth and rust do not corrupt.

Fortunately, Bosses have other natural tendencies that don't require U-turns but merely a change of direction. Their passion for truth-telling can be redirected away from hostile confrontation and toward an honest appraisal of reality. They might discover that the universe is not really a jungle, red with tooth and claw, but a garden, green with peace. And why not turn their enormous lust for consumption toward God? What better to try to consume than the love that is inexhaustible? Bosses also have an innate regard for the power of commitment; they can use that to sign a personal covenant with God. Their "winning is everything" attitude can be channeled into winning the peace of God. And their insatiable desire for strength and power can finally be satisfied when they understand that true strength lies in being spiritually indestructible and the ultimate power trip is to surrender and align with the highest power.

The Peacemaker

Blessed are the peacemakers: for they shall
be called the children of God.

MATTHEW 5:9

For Peacemakers, God is the Great Harmonizer, the Supreme Unifier, the Prince of Peace and the Goddess of Compassion. They marvel at creation as a flawless weave of unity underlying diversity. Their dream would be to see balance restored to human affairs and the promise of a brotherhood of man fulfilled—no war, no violence, no strife. In their most evolved state, Peacemakers are devoted to becoming perfect instruments of God's healing peace, and a significant portion of their spiritual path consists of *seva*, the Sanksrit term for rendering service according to one's understanding of God's will, without regard to compensation or reward.

Because they do best where procedures are clearly laid out for them, Peacemakers are drawn to the formal aspects of religion. They love ritual and tradition, treating the requirements of their affiliation with honor and respect. As they develop spiritually, they find making peace with God as natural as loving a child. Their regard for others evolves into an unconditional love for God and ultimately to the ability to receive the same in return and yield to God's will. Their natural inclination to merge with others can help them merge with the Divine.

As seekers, Peacemakers are patient and receptive, able to take in wisdom with an open embrace and accept the counsel of experts, as long as it is presented in a soothing, supportive style. They have no trouble seeing wholeness amidst the parts and unity amidst diversity, in the spirit of William Wordsworth's vision of "a motion and a spirit that impels all thinking things, all objects of all thought, and rolls through all things." As members of a spiritual group, they are nonjudgmental and accepting, able to go with the flow and willing to do their share—qualities that the most evolved Peacemakers extend to all people and to the planet as a whole.

THE PEACEMAKER'S SPIRITUAL CHALLENGE

Peacemakers' attraction to ritual and tradition can turn them into robotic, unthinking slaves to habit. They can go through the motions, losing sight of the deeper meaning of scripture, the richness of symbols and the transformative energy of religious customs. Rites and rituals become empty, arid routines. By fastening their identity to a religious institution or an influential person, they can embrace a received package of beliefs and practices uncritically. This cuts them off from a wealth of growth possibilities. Less integrated Peacemakers also tend to lose sight of their own inner spiritual needs; their attention is almost always directed outward, ever on the alert for ways to satisfy the needs of others.

Since tension with God plays out in the deepest corners of the mind and heart, the absence of inner peace might be off the radar screen for the outer-directed Peacemaker. They're more likely to recognize when someone else is not at peace with God and to put their efforts into helping that person. Once they do see the lack of peace in themselves, however, Peacemakers have to overcome their natural inclination to wait for things to come to them. Instead of taking the initiative and working on themselves, they'll hope for spontaneous grace. This is related to another challenge: since their inclination is to locate everything of value outside themselves, they tend to place God out there as well, separate and apart, and that misdirection can be a major obstacle.

The first step is to take the first step. Peacemakers have to get off their spiritual duffs and agitate for peace in the inner realm. They need to turn their attention around and direct some of their natural empathy toward themselves for a change. Once they get in touch with what they really want and need spiritually, they have to accept the legitimacy of their noblest desires and insist on getting them fulfilled. If they run into doubt or confusion, they need to get over their reluctance to ask for things and take their concerns to a pastor or another expert—or directly to God. They can't make peace with God if they insist on pretending they have no needs of their own.

Peacemakers also have to stop trying to please everyone. They must separate their own deepest impulses from the values they've internalized from outside sources. They also have to accept that it's OK to take a stand when their motives are pure and their aims are just, even if it means rocking the boat. If they doubt that boat rocking is compatible with godliness, they should contemplate recent historical examples such as Gandhi, Martin Luther King, Jr. and Archbishop Desmond Tutu of South Africa.

Once they embark on the road to peace with God, Peacemakers can't allow themselves to get overwhelmed by what seems like a daunting task. For them, making peace with God is less a matter of hard work than it is ceasing to do what they've been doing all along. Peacemakers have to go against their natural grain. No one who is afraid of change can hope for the inner transformation that's needed to forge a lasting peace with God. And no one who doesn't look within can discover what their real needs and priorities are. They also have to guard against inertia. They have to resist distractions and make sure their coveted habits and routines truly serve their spiritual aspirations. Perhaps most of all, Peacemakers have to heed the old adage, "Physician, heal thyself." They have to ease off their mission to bring peace to others and humbly, graciously turn to God for the infinite peace that they have, without realizing it, always longed for. Then they can do a better job of healing everyone else.

"Just a Human Being"

In an interview in India, we asked the Dalai Lama what it means to him to be the Dalai Lama. His Holiness replied that the title means different things to different people: "To some it means that I am a living Buddha, the earthly manifestation of the Bodhisattva of Compassion. To others it means I am a God-King. To some, Dalai Lama is a title that signifies the office I hold. I myself am just a human being, and incidentally a Tibetan who chooses to be a Buddhist monk."

In addition to the humility in those words, what is notable is the degree to which the Dalai Lama does not identify with his title, his status or his role as spiritual leader and political head of an exiled people. It is in that spirit that we remind you to hold lightly your personal identification with any of the archetypes we just described. Remember, we all own traits attributed to the other personality types. Like Lovers, for example, Thinkers can be devoted. Like Thinkers, Lovers can be passionate about ideas.

Awareness of how the archetypes apply to you can provide a framework for the task ahead by illuminating your personal tendencies, alerting you to potential pitfalls and highlighting your strengths and challenges. But it can serve another purpose as well. Taken as a whole, the archetypes demonstrate how opposite values come together to create growth—in this case, the amazing diversity of human life unfolding within its essential unity. This is a magnificent reflection of Creation itself, a cosmic choreography of infinite variety and absolute Oneness.

We are all the children of one God, separated by illusion and ignorance from our Source and sent on our merry ways to learn and grow. To do that, we individuate. We make ourselves unique. We anoint ourselves the Dalai Lamas of our own domains. But it is useful to remember that each of us is also "just a human being" who incidentally chooses to make peace with God.

3.

WHAT GOD?

Wrestling with Doubt

You call for faith:
I show you doubt, to prove
that faith exists.

ROBERT BROWNING

man falls from a cliff. As he plummets toward his certain doom, he reaches out in desperation and grabs hold of a branch. "Is anyone out there?" he screams as he clings to the swaying limb. "God, if you exist, please save me!"

As his grip falters, he calls out again, with still greater urgency. And a voice resounds from the heavens: "I am here."

"Oh, Lord, thank you. I'm sorry I ever doubted you. I promise I'll be better. I'll do whatever you command, only please, please, spare me."

"Do you have faith?" asks the voice.

"Yes, yes, I have faith."

"Then let go of the branch."

The man thinks a moment, ponders his options and screams out, "Is anyone else out there?"

Compare that man to the monk in the famous Zen story, who finds himself in a similar predicament. Dangling precariously from a vine, the monk looks up and sees a tiger growling at him from the precipice above. He slowly lowers himself toward the ground only to see another hungry tiger looking up at him, eagerly awaiting his lunch. To make matters worse, two mice begin to gnaw at the vine. Suspended in midair with no apparent way to avoid his death, the monk notices a bright red object on the hillside. Releasing one hand from the vine, he reaches out and grabs it: a wild strawberry. He puts it in his mouth, and oh, how sweet it tastes.

One man with strenuous doubts, attaching conditions to his faith and terrified in the face of his helplessness; the other with such deep, abiding certitude about the ultimate safety of the universe and the deathless nature of existence that he can, with his life literally hanging from a thread, pluck a mouthful of sweetness from the moment.

Such is the power of faith. Without it we could not move forward into the uncertainty that lies before us at each confusing fork in the road. Our intellects and our range of perception are simply too limited to resolve every puzzle. Faith keeps us going. This holds not just for the spiritual life but for any endeavor in this unpredictable, constantly changing world. Partners take a leap of faith when they make marriage vows. Inventors need faith; explorers need faith; artists, business executives and innovators in every field need to have faith as they press ahead with their visions. Even science, that most rational of pursuits, requires faith; without faith in the orderliness of the universe and the veracity of their own observations, scientists would not go through the trouble of performing experiments.

Because faith is so essential on the spiritual path, doubt has been viewed as a major obstacle. Some religious teachings treat doubt as a curse, the work of the Devil, an affliction to be resisted at all costs and conquered by all available means. In some cases, having doubt is viewed as a sign of weakness or spiritual sloth, and the doubter is made to feel like an infidel or someone in need of an exorcist.

But doubt is not the opposite of faith; that role would be filled by nihilism or indifference. Nor is doubt the *enemy* of faith. On the contrary, doubt is faith's necessary companion. Like the impulsive cop in the movies who drives his sensible partner crazy, doubt may seem like a nuisance. But that nuisance usually turns out to be indispensable in solving the mystery and setting things right in the end. Just as the sensible cop comes to accept his partner's irksome ways and learns to work with him, so we can learn to use doubt as a catalyst to a higher, more mature faith. In a Henry James short story, a character says about his fellow artists, "Our doubt is our passion and our passion is our task." That is excellent advice for seekers of peace with God.

Faith Goes Beyond Belief

Faith is the substance of things hoped for,
the evidence of things not seen.

HEBREWS 11:1

It must be emphasized that the kind of faith that sustains the spiritual quest is not the same as belief. Belief is often portrayed as the be-all and end-all of religious life. In America, where belief in belief is strong, when people ask, "What do you believe in?" they seldom mean "What do you have faith in?" or "What vision of life propels and sustains you?" Instead, they mean, "What philosophy do you assent to?" or "Which concepts and premises do you hold to be true?" In some religious traditions, publicly stating that you accept a specific doctrine is considered the key to salvation. But merely affirming a particular belief is, at best, a starting point for authentic spiritual development. At worst it is a hindrance; it can lock you into a rigid set of ideas and trick you into thinking that it's dangerous to entertain doubt.

Genuine faith, the kind that the leading lights of spiritual history have tried to inspire in us, is something more than belief. Faith, says Reverend Scotty McLennan in *Finding Your Religion*, is "an orientation of the whole personality, a total response. It's not just belief—the holding of certain ideas—which is a function of the mind alone. . . . [I]t is much larger; it is the ability to experience the universe as meaningful." James Fowler, in his classic research on the stages of faith, called it "an alignment of the heart or will." While it might express itself in the form of a belief system, faith as such, says Fowler, is "the relation of trust in and loyalty to the transcendent about which concepts or propositions—beliefs—are fashioned."

Accepting a set of beliefs may awaken faith, and disbelief may trigger a loss of faith—and vice versa. But, whereas belief might be considered a commitment of the mind, faith is a commitment of the heart. The scholar of religion Wilfred Cantwell Smith points out that the original Latin usage of the word *credo*, from which we get creed, "came close to its root meaning of 'I set my heart on,' 'I give my heart to.'" This is similar to the Sanskrit term *sraddha*, which is normally translated as "faith" and connotes something more like "to set one's heart on." Faith, says Smith, is not just "part of the furniture" of the mind but "an orientation of the personality, to oneself, to one's neighbor, to the universe; a total response; a way of seeing whatever one sees and of handling whatever one handles; a capacity to live at more than a mundane level; to see, to feel, to act in terms of, a transcendent dimension."

That kind of deep, abiding faith can't be imposed or coerced from the outside. Nor can it be contrived. In *The Art of Loving*, Erich Fromm distinguishes between rational and irrational faith. Irrational faith is a form of submission; it entails accepting something as true only because a source of authority says it is true. Rational faith, on the other hand, is rooted in "productive intellectual and emotional activity" and "confidence in one's power of thought, observation and judgment." In other words, genuine faith does not derive from unexamined dogma or blind trust in a person or an institution. It flows from an intuitive sense of rightness, an inner conviction that has withstood analysis and argument. It is not, says Rabbi Abraham Joshua Heschel, "the clinging to a shrine but an endless pilgrimage of the heart."

But faith is seldom a fixed entity. "Faith rises and falls like the tides of an invisible sea," wrote novelist Flannery O'Connor. We waver, we tilt, we hesitate and we tremble from the agitation of doubt: doubt about the existence of God; doubt that God can be trusted; doubt about religious dogma; doubt about our chosen path and whether we will ever find the grace we are promised by sages and seers. Any number of keys can spring doubt from its cage. It is very common, for instance, for people to wake up one day with serious doubts about a fundamental precept of their religion—the virgin birth or the resurrection; the miracles in Exodus; Muhammad receiving the word of God from the angel Gabriel—and from that initial skepticism lose faith in the entire religious enterprise. But that moment of doubt is often preceded by a crisis in some aspect of the Quintessential Self. A grave physical illness, especially at an early age, can raise doubt about God's fairness. An emotional upheaval can raise doubts about God's love or traditional notions of how to get your prayers answered. In the relational area, the trigger can be a broken marital vow or a betrayal of trust by a religious figure. And, of course, any crisis of the spirit will immediately bring up doubts. This remark from a teenager in Los Angeles, for instance, speaks to a source of doubt in our pluralistic world that is increasingly common in every religion: "I just can't accept a God that plays favorites. I mean, if God is supposed to be loving and merciful and all that, how come only people who accept Jesus as their savior can get into Heaven? Like, most of my friends are going to hell and some preacher who cheats on his wife is getting in? No way."

Whatever causes doubt to erupt, it is crucial to look upon it not as a tragic breakdown of faith but as a potential breakthrough. Too often doubt is greeted as if it were a disruption, an intrusion, a threat, a spoiler of the peace. In fact, dealing with doubt on the spiritual journey can be more like stopping for gas on a long car trip: not only inescapable, but absolutely indispensable.

Don't Doubt Your Doubt

Faith which does not doubt is dead faith.

MIGUEL DE UNAMUNO

You're coasting along, secure in your faith, firm in your cherished beliefs. Then, out of the blue, doubt creeps up on you like the monster in a horror movie. Suddenly, the structure on which you've based much of your life is crumbling beneath your feet and you're afraid you'll be left with nothing to stand on. You reach for a vital idea or concept to hold on to, but they're all slipping away and there is nothing at hand to replace them. You sink into an abyss of despair, anguish and confusion. Maybe you worry that your doubt might signal a betrayal of your religion. Maybe you're afraid that if your doubt becomes known you'll be ostracized. Maybe you think you've already been abandoned by God just for having doubtful thoughts.

What do you do? Take shelter in the sanctuary of scripture? Pretend the doubt isn't really there? The natural tendency is to do everything in your power to avoid the doubt, hide it, deny it, suppress it or drive it away—anything but what we should do: invite the intruder in for a cup of tea and a nice chat. Denying doubt is not only dangerous, it's a waste of a golden opportunity to strengthen your faith.

The well-known principle "what you resist persists" applies as much to spiritual doubt as to any unpleasant emotion we might try to suppress. Doubt denied only postpones the day of reckoning. Sooner or later, in one form or another, it's going to surface, and while it's stewing in some corner of your brain under lock and key, it can leak out in disguised form—as cynicism, for example, or depression, or an inability to trust.

"I was brought up to accept everything we were taught in church and every word spoken by our minister," says Diana Russell*, a thirty-two-year-old dental assistant, of her Baptist upbringing in Kansas. "I was an inquisitive child, but I learned not to ask anything about religion because when I did, my mother got upset. She wouldn't lose her temper or anything, she'd just sort of look around to see if anyone was listening and shoot me a look, with her finger on her lips, like, 'Don't say such things.' Sometimes she'd tell me to ask my Sunday school teacher, but the teacher would frown and recite some Bible phrase to shut me up. I got the impression that asking questions meant I was a heathen and I wouldn't get to heaven. So I learned to stifle every doubt—'Get thee from me, Satan!'"

As a young adult on her own, she kept up that pattern. "I wasn't sure I could really trust the church, or God for that matter," says Diana, "but thoughts like that were so scary I stuffed them away." But the doubt she suppressed found other outlets. "I found that I was suspicious of other people," she says. "I became a pessimist. I had this sunny demeanor around church people—'God is good,' and all that—but I had all these negative thoughts about my love life, my career, the state of the world, everything but religion."

Diana developed chronic depression, persistent fatigue and a sense of emotional and spiritual emptiness. Years of straining to suppress her "sinful thoughts" had consumed so much psychic energy that she had become depleted. And each time one of those impertinent feelings had cropped up, before she could banish it, the thought arose, "You're a horrible person." Over time, her self-worth was encased in shame. Diana felt so undeserving that she assumed she was doomed to a life of misery. Ultimately, her means of escape was to break completely with her church. "I was tired of seeing myself as a sinner," she says.

She moved to Chicago, where she could explore a variety of spiritual offerings. For a while, she felt liberated. But old habits die hard. Eventually, she adopted a New Age belief system that said, essentially, if you connect to God, or your Higher Self, and think life-affirming thoughts, the universe will give you everything you want—love, happiness, material success, spiritual fulfillment, the whole enchilada. For Diana, this positive vision was the opposite of what she had grown up with. Except that everything still had to have an upbeat spin. Doubt wouldn't send her to hell, but it could block the flow of God's positive energy. If she were to acknowledge setbacks or injustices, if she were to admit that she was afraid or angry about something, she would only make things worse.

"I took it to such an extreme that I couldn't deal with reality," she says. When difficulties cropped up in her life, Diana would find a way to rationalize them as "for the best." The cost of keeping her new faith intact was being unable to solve pressing problems or to keep others from taking advantage of her. Her magical thinking could not accept challenges for what they were.

Diana stopped short of becoming a zealot and worked out a way to have faith in the basic goodness of God and the universe while allowing herself to doubt specific teachings. Others are not able to find that middle ground.

Serving God by Seeking Truth

One of the greatest dangers of suppressing doubt is going to the other extreme and becoming a fanatic. "Frantic orthodoxy is never rooted in faith but in doubt," wrote theologian Reinhold Niebuhr. "It is when we are not sure that we are doubly sure." Fanatics force themselves to be doubly certain so they don't have to confront the doubt that threatens to rock their boats.

Now an accountant in New Jersey, Al was raised in Brooklyn by atheist parents who had turned away from their Jewish heritage entirely. In his household, religion was not just ignored, it was denigrated. "My parents subscribed to Karl Marx's adage, 'Religion is the opium of the people,'" says Al. "The pious were considered superstitious hypocrites." In his twenties, he drifted from one philosophy to another. When, at long last, he found a spiritual home, he rejected not only his parents' ideas about religion but their whole "question authority" attitude toward life. He became ultra-orthodox, moving with his wife and children to a community where everything revolved around religious observance and less orthodox Jews were regarded as "not really Jewish." In his new world, debating the meaning of specific scriptural passages was encouraged, but no one questioned the fundamental tenets of orthodoxy. Al refused to set foot in his parents' home because their ideas might contaminate his children. "I was self-righteous and intolerant," he later came to realize. "I was afraid to expose myself to contrary thoughts because it would trigger my own doubts, and I couldn't handle that."

For people like Al, the insecurity of doubt is like losing an anchor on a rollicking sea of confusion. They latch on to a lifesaver that satisfies their desperate need for certainty. Their extremism not only makes them susceptible to cults, charlatans, unworthy gurus and self-damaging beliefs, but it cuts them off from "outsiders" and can even keep them from getting the most out of their chosen affiliations. "Once I allowed myself to raise fundamental questions," says Al, "I became a much more responsible parent and a better Jew. There's an ancient rabbinical saying that goes, 'You do not serve God if you do not seek truth.'"

THROWING OUT THE BABY WITH THE BATHWATER

Another danger of denial is that when doubts that had been buried in the unconscious finally erupt, you might reverse direction like a bowstring pulled to the extreme, and lash out against what you had forced yourself to believe in. "How could I have been so stupid? I can't believe I let myself buy into all that crap. I've wasted precious years of my life." And so, some people throw out the baby with the bathwater. They not only turn their backs on the religions of their birth, the philosophies they adopted as adults, the groups with whom they affiliated or the teachers they venerated, but also renounce *all* religious forms, *all* spiritual institutions, *all* teachers and, in some cases, anything and everything of a spiritual nature. "I won't let anything pull the wool over my eyes again!" they declare, and they turn the yearning for God into the pursuit of sensory pleasure and material success. Cynicism becomes their protection against being bamboozled one more time.

In a strange way, suppressing doubt is, in itself, a stronger assertion of doubt than doubt itself. It is saying, in essence, "God can't handle my uncertainty." It is saying, "God is so petty and vindictive that I'll be punished for questioning him." It is saying, "God is so fickle that she doesn't want me use the rational mind I was created with." It is saying, "God doesn't trust me to find the right answers."

Is that really how you see God? Or are you possibly projecting your worst feelings about yourself and others onto God?

Honest Doubt Is a Blessing

There lives more faith in honest doubt,
Believe me, than in half the creeds.

ALFRED, LORD TENNYSON

If you're having doubts about God, relax; you're in good company. Think of Moses on Mount Sinai, asking God, "Who am I that I should go unto

Pharaoh?" and predicting, "They will not believe me, nor hearken to my voice." Think of him later, after Pharaoh cracks down on the Israelites, asking God, "Why is it that thou has sent me?" Think of Jesus being tempted in the wilderness; if he had been totally free of doubt, the story would not have to be told, for there would have been nothing to overcome. Think of him at Gethsemane, knowing his fate, and praying, "O my Father, if it be possible, let this cup pass from me." Think of Gautama Buddha sitting under the Bodhi Tree on the eve of his enlightenment, as Mara, the Tempter, unleashed a squadron of demons to break his will. One of the demons that Buddha had to overcome was the treacherous Visikitcha, the embodiment of doubt.

It is true that some forms of doubt can be a detriment. What might be called neurotic doubt—obsessive, repetitive, unyielding—can bury you deep in a dark hole from which you can't dig out. That kind of doubt is unhealthy, for it keeps you stuck in one place. But healthy doubt that leads to honest reflection about your assumptions, motives and values is a necessary component of everyone's spiritual story, even the holiest among us. The early Christians known as the Desert Fathers, for example, spoke of the "midday devil"—the crisis of faith that invariably erupted when years of spiritual work seemed to have been for naught and they despaired of ever attaining union with God. But the saints and sages of every tradition persevered through their doubts, wandering like Moses in the wilderness of uncertainty, fortified by the kind of faith that Rabbi Heschel called "not the assent to an idea, but the consent to God." With them as an example, you can just as easily see your doubt as an indication of spiritual maturity, not a sign of weakness or unworthiness.

If not for crises of faith, there would have been no revolutions in religious thought, no new attitudes and interpretations, no bold new translations of scripture, no debates over the proper understanding of traditional doctrine. Doubt gave rise to the magnificent diversity of religious expression. Doubt led Shankara and Buddha to turn from interpretations of Vedic tradition that they felt had become distorted and carve their own enduring paths. Lack of faith in the religious values of their time fueled the rebellions of Jesus and Muhammad. Doubt fueled the scholarship of the Jesuits and made the Talmudic tradition an intellectual battleground where dissent and argument are not only encouraged but obligatory. Indeed, one of the great ironies of religious life is that some of the sects that demand conformity of belief derive from the rebellion of a great doubter. Martin Luther suffered long bouts of despair in which he felt cut off from God and alienated from the Catholic Church before he launched the reform movement that gave rise to Protestantism.

Healthy doubt is an opportunity, not an emergency. The honest process of confronting it and overcoming it can be a stepping stone to spiritual growth. As you expand in awareness, knowledge and maturity, fresh new insights invariably arise. Your sense of who or what God is and how the universe operates undergoes a shift. Some of your assumptions stop making sense. New observations and insights conflict with your previous understanding. If you suppress the confusion or find ways to dismiss the anomalies with easy answers, you can end up stuck in complacent conformity. If, on the other hand, you endure the discomfort, seize your doubt and work with it, you can expand your spiritual horizons and rise to a higher level of awareness. The phoenix that arises from the ashes of doubt can be a grander, more inclusive faith.

The willingness to treat doubt with honest respect, therefore, can be a sign of courage, not weakness; of openness, not cynicism; of curiosity, not negativism. It is, in fact, an assertion of faith. Perhaps that is why Buddha advised his followers to be lamps unto themselves. "Do not believe a thing because many repeat it," he said. "Do not accept a thing on the authority of one or another of the Sages of old, nor on the ground that a statement is found in the books. . . . Believe nothing merely on the authority of your teachers or of the priests. After examination, believe that which you have tested for yourselves and found reasonable, which is in conformity with your well-being and that of others." He's saying what all the great teachers have said: As you make your way through the mists of uncertainty, trust that the combined wisdom of your heart and mind will lead you to the truth.

Faith in Science
and the Science of Faith

Doubt, it seems to me, is the central condition
of a human being in the twentieth century.

Salman Rushdie

From the time of the so-called enlightenment of eighteenth-century Europe, faith in God and established religious authority has been steadily eroded by another kind of faith: faith in reason and science as the ultimate paths to truth, and in technology as the means to end suffering. In the 1920s, skepticism took off like the stock market only to keep on soaring instead of crashing. "God is the immemorial refuge of the incompetent, the helpless, the miserable," wrote the acerbic jazz-age journalist H. L. Mencken. At the time, the horrors of World War I were fresh in people's minds, and inventions like refrigeration and the automobile promised to deliver us from toil. Educated parlor talk revolved around the revelations of psychoanalysis and the startling discoveries of quantum mechanics and relativity theory. All of which seemed to take the wind out of the sails of faith. "In the long run nothing can withstand reason and experience, and the contradiction religion offers to both is only too palpable," wrote Sigmund Freud.

The scientific method—basically, the systematic analysis of repeated observation in accord with the rules of logic and experimentation—was so successful in solving ancient puzzles and everyday mysteries that it was easy to believe it could be applied to all areas of human inquiry. It was expected that science would march like a conquering army through the tattered forces of ignorance and attain its ultimate triumph: a complete system of deductions, derived from unimpeachable laws, which would explain every phenomenon in the universe. Many a gleeful scientist and philosopher predicted that the irrational claims of religion would end up encased in museums like the bones of extinct animals. We would have no more need for faith, revelation and superstitious rituals than we do for painting on the walls of caves.

Not long after the time of Mencken and Freud, the juggernaut of doubt picked up speed. We saw the worst mass atrocities human beings have ever perpetrated, prompting millions to cry out in their hearts the words scratched on the wall of a concentration camp by an anonymous prisoner: "Where is God?" Material progress, psychological insight and scientific discovery accelerated at an ever-quickening pace, presumably shrinking what skeptics have always regarded as the reasons people need the "crutch" of God—scarcity, misery, emotional turmoil and an inability to understand and control the natural world. Add to that the spread of literacy and secular education, the expansion of the middle class and easy access to new ideas and beliefs, and you have a seemingly surefire formula for doubt. No wonder that less than a century after Nietzsche first raised the possibility, *Time* magazine asked on its cover, "Is God dead?"

As with Mark Twain's death, the rumor was highly exaggerated. The heart's yearning for supreme peace and love, and of the mind for ultimate truth, is much too primal.

But the soil for disbelief has never been more fertile. For a population trained to think logically, to venerate objectivity and accept only that which conforms to reason or is witnessed by the senses, how can doubts about God *not* crop up? Much of what we are told about the subject is cloaked in contradiction: God is all-knowing, but we have to let him know what we want; God is unknowable, but some people know what God's will is; God will punish us if we misbehave, but we are loved and forgiven. A God of mercy, love and justice? What about Hitler and Stalin? What about all the atrocities, wars and mass murders? What about all the liars and crooks who go unpunished? What about oppression, starvation and the deaths of innocent children? As for miracles, please! We can explain most of them scientifically, and the rest are fairy tales from a primitive past. And what about God's emissaries? Look at all the bigotry and hate, the extremism, the domination, the terrorism, all in the name of God. No loving deity would permit such misdeeds in his or her name.

Contemporary life provides more openings for the thieves of faith than a hotel without doors. But what seems to be a collective crisis is more profitably seen as a collective opportunity. The doubt raised by modern sensibilities can set the stage for a strengthening of faith. Not the old-fashioned kind, perhaps, which was based on acquiescence to dogma and obedience to authority, but rather an enlightened faith built on the unshakable conviction that comes when belief survives the crucible of doubt. The *way* we acquire faith may have to be questioned, and our concepts about God may have to be upgraded, but genuine faith has never had a better environment in which to flourish—precisely *because* there are so many reasons to doubt.

It All Depends

I believe in the sun even when it is not shining.
I believe in love even when feeling it not.
I believe in God even when he is silent.

JEWISH PRAYER

In one language or another, human beings have cried out for thousands of years, "Show me your face. Prove that you exist. Reveal yourself in a way I can recognize. Stop hiding!"

Studies indicate that the primary reason people give for not believing in God is "lack of proof." Are you looking for proof? Are you waiting for a sign? What proof would satisfy you? What sign would suffice? Some people are easy to please. For them, the evidence before them is beyond a reasonable doubt. "In the faces of men and women I see God," sang Walt Whitman, "and in my own face in the glass. I find letters from God dropt in the street, and every one is sign'd by God's name." Others have more stringent standards. "If only God would give me some clear sign!" lamented Woody Allen. "Like making a large deposit in my name at a Swiss bank."

Is it right to place the burden of proof on God? Maybe the problem is on our side. Maybe we don't really know what we're looking for. Maybe we're looking in all the wrong places.

Consider this conversation, overheard at a Beverly Hills restaurant:

"I'd like to believe in God," he says as he scans the room from behind sunglasses. "I really would. I'd like to believe there's a larger intelligence and a moral force in the universe. But I need to see evidence."

"What are you looking for?" asks the woman in black. "A burning bush with a voice? Tongues of flame in the sky?"

"I don't know, maybe some genuine prophecies, predictions about large-scale events that could not be made scientifically."

She smiles and quotes Jesus from memory: "'This is an evil generation: they seek a sign.'" She sips her cappuccino. "All the proof I need," she says, "is my baby's laughter and the flowers in the backyard."

"I guess it depends on what you mean by God," he concedes.

"It depends on what you mean by evidence."

That's the story of doubt in a nutshell. It depends on what you mean by God, and it depends on what you mean by evidence.

If you are torn because spirituality seems to be incompatible with science, if you agonize because you can't reconcile religious belief with reason and logic, welcome to the club. But you might want to spare yourself the trouble of trying to come up with satisfactory proof on your own. For thousands of years, great minds have locked horns over these issues, and so far it's a standstill.

Theologians in every tradition have driven logic to the pinnacle of brilliance in pursuit of God. Descartes, Leibnitz, Spinoza and other philosophers have constructed impeccably reasoned arguments demonstrating God's existence. St. Thomas Aquinas assembled a quintet of them, in his *Quinque Viae*, five separate arguments leading to the conclusion that reason can reveal *that* God is but not *what* God is. There are what scholars call cosmological arguments, ontological arguments and teleological arguments; there is the affirmative way and the way of negation. If you can slog your way through them, you will find them all convincing.

That is, until you read the refutations by thinkers like Immanuel Kant. If anything can be said for sure it's that no intellectually honest person can claim to have faith on the basis of reason alone, or to have proof of God on the basis of anything approaching scientific certainty. But that, in itself, is not enough to justify *disbelief*, because it's just as impossible to prove the opposite claims.

We forget sometimes that the tools of rationality are limited and that unrestrained confidence in them is itself a leap of faith. The notion that all worth-while knowledge is discoverable through the scientific method is, to use science's own language, a hypothesis at best. It is an unproven supposition and is probably just as unprovable as the existence of God. The famous incompleteness theorem of mathematician Kurt Gödel proved, in 1931, that it is impossible to construct a logical system that is both consistent (containing no internal contradictions) and complete. The system will always be able to generate a statement that the system itself cannot prove. Like the bald man who says, "Trust me, all bald men are liars," science says, "Our method is the only way to know reality" and also, "All scientific knowledge is tentative and incomplete." In other words, the scientific method can no more prove its omniscience and omnipotence than theology can prove God's.

All of which is to say: 1) Reason and scientific discovery can shed doubt on the claims of religion, but on the ultimate question of God, the jury is deadlocked and always will be; 2) Ultimately, logic can't satisfactorily prove or disprove anything about God's existence or God's ways. That much seems inescapable, whether you are a Christian monk, like Thomas Merton—"We can never fully know Him if we think of Him as an object of capture, to be fenced in by the enclosure of our own ideas. We know Him better after our minds have let Him go."; a sage from India, like Jiddu Krishnamurti—"God is something that cannot be talked about, that cannot be described, that cannot be put into words, because it must ever remain the unknown."; or a professional debunker, like Michael Shermer, editor of *Skeptic* magazine—"God's existence is beyond our competence as a problem to solve."

How Science Inspires Faith

"I was the brainy kid who got all the right answers in class and saw through all the 'malarkey' in Sunday school," says Richard Blaine*, a heart surgeon in Philadelphia. "I always wanted to know how things worked. I would take apart radios and watches. I would ask Santa Claus for microscopes and chemistry sets. I also asked how he covers every house on the planet in one night." By the time he was in high school, Richard had placed God in the same category as Santa—a childish myth, a fairy tale. "I was going to find out the secrets of the universe through science."

He soared through college and medical school on the wings of his prodigious intellect. "I was a classic materialist," he recalls. "The cosmos was this awesome machine that could be understood by figuring out how its parts worked. I worshipped at the altar of reason. Everything else was superstition."

Then a funny thing happened: Richard had a road-to-Damascus epiphany.

"It was the first surgery I participated in, and I was standing next to the senior surgeon when he opened the patient's chest. I was immediately transfixed. The sight of that heart beating, and all the blood vessels entering and leaving, and the living tissue, it was . . . well, I don't know how to describe it, except that what I saw was so magnificent, so astonishingly beautiful, so perfect, that . . . well, I hesitate to use terms like this, but I suddenly knew what was meant by 'the hand of God.' I saw it at work, that's all I can say."

He still regards much of what he hears in church as malarkey, he says, but he has, on his own terms, "cut a deal with God."

If not a glimpse at the wondrous workings of the human body, then perhaps a contemplation of the night sky and the dimensions of the universe, or the whirligig of subatomic particles, or the intricate ballet of weather patterns, or the mating habits of insects and beasts, or the interconnected threads that form the tapestry of earth's ecology—wherever the rational enquirer looks, infinite creativity and orderly design are on display. That may not be enough to *prove* that some form of divine intelligence is responsible; such arguments have been artfully opposed by many good minds. But it might be enough to tickle the fancy of faith, or at least inspire some doubt about doubt.

The ranks of world-class scientists have always included devout worshippers and deeply spiritual independents who had no problem reconciling their profession with their faith. For many, in fact, the two are as compatible as crackers and cheese, and their systematic analysis provokes a kind of spiritual wonder. Said Albert Einstein, the very embodiment of the scientific mind: "A knowledge of the existence of something we cannot penetrate, of the manifestations of the profoundest reason and the most radiant beauty, which are only accessible to our reason in their most elementary forms—it is this knowledge and this emotion that constitute the truly religious attitude; in this sense, and in this alone, I am a deeply religious man."

Science and religion represent different methods of gaining knowledge, but they are after the same prize of ultimate truth, and they are more alike, more complementary, than is generally acknowledged. Especially now. As science advanced, it encroached more and more on the domain of religion. Psychology, which once regarded faith as practically an affliction, has evolved from a science of human pathology to a science of the human spirit. Psychology departments now include the heirs to Carl Jung, who split from Freud in 1912 and took spirituality with him; humanistic psychologists studying self-actualization; and transpersonal psychologists doing systematic research on spiritual development and higher consciousness.

Physics, long considered a universe apart from religion, increasingly resembles *meta*physics. Once upon a time, the focus of its attention was the realm of solid objects that can be seen with the senses and extensions of the senses like microscopes and telescopes. Now physics has penetrated the depths of matter and uncovered a wonderland of subatomic particles that are not really particles in the billiard ball sense, but vibrating waves of energy. The sturdy chair you are sitting on is made up of atoms that are 90 percent empty space. So is the very body you inhabit. Scientific discussions now encompass particles that penetrate barriers that should be impenetrable; that communicate with one another instantaneously when separated by long distances; that simultaneously exist and don't exist; that move along different paths—or along *all* paths—at the same time. And the whole familiar universe is thought to arise from a formless void that physicists call the quantum vacuum, a wellspring of emptiness that unfolds from within itself. Science writer K. C. Cole compared the vacuum to "the strings of an unseen puppeteer," precisely the metaphor that has, for centuries, been used for God. When, in 2000, scientists announced that they might have discovered the Higgs boson, an invisible particle that determines the basic properties of matter, some of them actually labeled it "the God particle."

The universe that science has given us, says physicist Paul Davies, is "nothing but structured nothingness." It does not require much of a stretch to find parallels between concepts like "structured nothingness" and "nonlocal consciousness" and spiritual terms like the Tao, Brahman, *sunyata* and *ein sof*. Way back in the thirteenth century, Meister Eckhart anticipated the physicist's terminology. God, he said, is "the absolute Nothing."

And that structured nothingness is not separate from the substance of human consciousness. Not in the world of modern science, where many experts have stopped viewing consciousness as merely the result of electrochemical reactions in the brain. What Ralph Waldo Emerson stated in the nineteenth century—"I know with certainty that who I am does not end at the top of my head"—was echoed in the twentieth century by neuroscientists like Wilfred Penfield and Karl Pribram. To them and others, consciousness is nonlocal, not confined to specific points in time and space but inextricably woven into the cosmic fabric.

What are we to make of this march of science? The modern philosopher and synthesizer Ken Wilber observed in the 1980s that "the very *facts* of science . . . the actual data (from physics to psychology) seemed to make sense only if we assume some sort of implicit or unifying or transcendental ground underlying the explicit data. [That transcendental ground] seemed to be identical, at least in description, to the timeless and spaceless ground of being (or 'Godhead') so universally described by the world's great mystics and sages." In other words, instead of sucking you into the depths of doubt, modern discoveries can just as easily transport you to new heights of faith, without having to do the math. One person looks at a rainbow and sees the refractive dispersion of photons in drops of mist; another sees proof of God. One person looks through a microscope and sees a minuet of molecules; another sees miracles. And some see both.

Feelings of Doubt;
Doubting Your Feelings

Doubt is thought's despair; despair is personality's doubt. . . .
Despair is an expression of the total personality,
doubt only of thought.

SØREN KIERKEGAARD

Doubt is an intrusion of the mind. It arises when you experience disso-nance between something you hold to be true and thoughts, observations or experiences that seem to contradict that belief. Try as you may, something just doesn't make sense. That is why, of the nine pathways to peace with God, the Thinker is most prone to doubt. The tendency of Thinkers is to use their in-tellects to steer through the tricky waters of cosmic mysteries. They will pon-der and ruminate relentlessly in hopes of settling on a rational solution. When their compasses fail and they get lost in the thickets of paradox and incon-gruity, doubt consumes them. But doubt does not live on intellect alone; it is also fueled by a wide range of emotions. While any combination of factors can tip the scales in someone's mind, each of the nine archetypes is especially vul-nerable to certain ones. Here's when each archetype is most likely to experi-ence doubt:

Reformers: when the imperfections of the world cry out at them; when their efforts at reforming people and institutions, or the planet as a whole are frustrated; when what they think is God's will is thwarted.

Lovers: when the object of their love does not reciprocate; when their de-votional activities fail to elicit the love of God they long for and fully expect to feel.

Achievers: when their hard work fails to bring them the grace of God; when their efforts on behalf of their religion, spiritual organization or worthy cause are not rewarded or appreciated.

Creators: when their creative output dries up for lack of God-given inspi-ration; when their artistry does not measure up to their vision or it fails to earn adequate recognition and reward; when the world seems stale and dreary instead of ecstatically beautiful.

Security-Seekers: when they get hurt by a religious organization to which they've pledged allegiance; when their world becomes unsafe and insecure, and it seems as though God has abandoned them.

Adventurers: when their spiritual pursuits start to feel dull and ritualized; when their passion is stifled by outside influences and it seems that God is forcing them into a routine, circumscribed life.

Bosses: when their attempts to take charge are hindered; when the God they've surrendered to or the religious authority they've been loyal to is not leading them to the Promised Land with clear directives and a firm hand.

Peacemakers: when their efforts to bring people together are stymied; when they can't heal dissension in the ranks of their spiritual affiliation; when they see news reports of carnage and atrocities in the world.

Regardless of your primary archetype, the experience of loss, betrayal, despair, indignation and other powerful emotions can tip the mind into skepticism and incredulity about God. Then the interplay between faith and emotion becomes a complicated feedback loop. Once doubt is ignited, it can trigger a new set of painful feelings or reinforce the old ones. In turn, the persistence of negative emotions serves to hold the doubt in place, blocking all attempts of the intellect to resolve the conflict.

The complex interaction between faith and feeling was compellingly depicted in the movie version of Graham Greene's *The End of the Affair,* in which doubt is reconciled by both love and hate. Maurice and his married lover, Sarah, begin their affair in wartime London as nonbelievers. At one afternoon rendezvous, their bliss is shattered by a German bomb. Sarah, unable to revive the unconscious Maurice, sinks in desperation to her knees and prays to "whatever might be out there." In return for bringing her lover back to life, she offers to give up her adultery and never see him again. Maurice lives. Sarah, awestruck by the apparent miracle, leaves him without an explanation. Later, while struggling to keep her vow against every impulse of her spirit and flesh, she discovers grace in her newfound love of God.

As for the cynical Maurice, when he discovers why the love of his life was taken from him, he declares in a remarkable expression of fierce ambivalence, "I hate you God. I hate you as though you existed."

Eventually, Sarah succumbs to her love for Maurice, breaking her promise to God. The lovers are reunited, but only for a short time. Sarah becomes ill and dies. At the end, in abject despair, Maurice tells God, "I'm tired of hating. Because you're still there. So your cunning is infinite. You used my hate to win my acknowledgment." And he begs God to stay out of his life but to please take care of Sarah.

Are strong emotions fueling your doubt? Which ones are they? Do you feel: Afraid? Lonely? Bitter? Resentful? Vengeful? Defeated? Distraught? Demoralized? Outraged? Envious? Helpless? Frustrated? Are you angry over the persistence of evil in the world? Are you dismayed by all the injustice? Are you disappointed because your prayers have gone unanswered? Are you bitter because you've suffered more than people who are less morally worthy? Are you shocked by the behavior of those who seemed pious and holy? Are you afraid that you are adrift and alone in an indifferent universe? It may seem that the pain of doubt is all in your head. But, as with many headaches, it may be caused or exacerbated by feelings that are hard to cope with. It is vital to identify these emotions, acknowledge their role in your faltering faith and take steps to resolve them. (We will discuss key emotional issues such as anger, fear and guilt in depth in later chapters.)

Grappling with the Dark Side

God is day and night, winter and summer,
war and peace, surfeit and hunger.

HERACLITUS

As a teenager, Ted Turner wanted to become a missionary. According to a *New Yorker* magazine profile by Ken Auletta, Turner was devoted to his younger sister, Mary Jane, who was afflicted with an immune disorder called systemic lupus erythematosus. He spent a good deal of time comforting Mary

Jane, who would vomit frequently and scream loudly from the constant pain. After several years of agony, she died, and with her died Ted Turner's faith. "I was taught that God was love and God was powerful," he told Auletta, "and I couldn't understand how someone so innocent should be made or allowed to suffer so." To this day, according to the article, Turner "alternately describes himself as an atheist and an agnostic." His antipathy to religion is such that when his then-wife Jane Fonda began attending church services en route to declaring herself a Christian, she did not tell her husband. "He would have talked me out of it," she says.

For Ted Turner, the suffering and early death of an innocent loved one jump-started the engine that powers doubt. For others, the catalyst might be a personal illness, financial ruin, the sordid scandal of a religious leader, the loss of love or a deadly disaster of the kind that even the law calls an "act of God." For many, the nightly news is sufficient; the seemingly unending triumph of evil and the persistence of unnecessary torment casts the biggest of shadows on faith.

"I form light and create darkness," God says in Isaiah (45:7); "I make peace and create evil." That would seem to be as solid a case for the prosecution as a videotaped confession. If the prophet is to be trusted, God created evil as well as good. Does that seem incongruous to you? How can a God that is all good and all powerful permit the horrors of the world to continue century after century? That dilemma was summed up as early as 300 B.C. by the Greek philosopher Epicurus: "The gods can either take away evil from the world and will not, or, being willing to do so, cannot; or they neither can nor will, or lastly, they are both able and willing. If they have the will to remove evil and cannot, then they are not omnipotent. If they can, but will not, then they are not benevolent. If they are neither able nor willing, then they are neither omnipotent nor benevolent. Lastly, if they are both able and willing to annihilate evil, how does it exist?"

In other words, we can't have it both ways: either God can't stop bad things from happening, in which case he's not all powerful, or God doesn't care that humans have to put up with unearned misery, in which case she's not all good.

That argument is as reasonable as it is enduring. People who reject God on those grounds are disavowing a deity that is alleged to be an almighty being who keeps an eye on earth and is able to step in like a vigilant parent when his favorites are threatened. He (for it is always a he) is also assumed to be capable of creating an evil-free, suffer-proof paradise on earth, but has, for mysterious reasons, chosen not to do so. But there must be other ways of understanding God, some of which are more consistent with the fact that bad people walk the earth, and children are born deformed and innocents die in earthquakes, floods and wars.

If there are no alternatives, intelligent people must have been fooling themselves for millennia. If the ubiquity of evil means that the only sensible conclusions are either that God does not exist or that God is not good, there would be no Judaism, for all sensible Jews would have given up on the Almighty centuries ago in response to unrelenting oppression. There would be no black churches or gospel music, since the faith of African Americans could not have survived slavery and segregation. Christianity would not have made it past the Roman Empire if smart minds could not find a way to comprehend persecution and still keep their faith. Nor would there be mosques in the occupied territories of the West Bank. And Native Americans, having barely survived attempted genocide, would all be atheists. Somehow, despite the wrangling of the rational mind, faith persists in the presence of pain and spits in the eye of evil.

When the young Martin Luther King, Jr. found himself leading the Montgomery bus boycott, he received a barrage of death threats. One sleepless night, when his fear "had reached the saturation point," he prayed, "I am at the end of my powers. I have nothing left. I've come to the point where I can't face it alone." In the next moment, he writes in *Strength to Love*, "I experienced the presence of the Divine as I had never before experienced him. It seemed as though I could hear the quiet assurance of an inner voice, saying, 'Stand up for righteousness, stand up for truth. God will be at your side forever.'" His fears and his uncertainties passed, he says, and when his house was bombed, three days later, he had the strength and trust to go on. "I knew now that God is able to give us the interior resources to face the storms and problems of life."

What enables some to transcend doubt in the midst of evil and the pain of innocents, while others turn to nihilism or sink into despair? That is as much a mystery as God. Even Ted Turner seems to be keeping his options open. "Although he claims to be an atheist, at the end of every speech he says, 'God bless you,'" Jane Fonda told the *New Yorker* reporter. "He wants to get into Heaven."

Every religion and every philosophy has explained the presence of evil in its own way. If your tradition does not resolve your doubts on these issues, try to look deeper, in scriptures, in commentaries, in discussions with members of the clergy who will not just brush you off with pat answers. And if that fails to satisfy, look elsewhere, to other traditions and more esoteric sources of your own.

But be prepared: you may never be satisfied with what you find. No single answer to the eternal conundrum of evil can satisfy every mind, for logic can always find a way to refute it. It depends, again, on your definition of God and your standard of proof. "The complexities of the question of evil push us to the limits of reason," writes Rabbi David Cooper in *God Is a Verb*. "At these limits, we must extend beyond the mind and draw upon resources that surpass the intellect."

That is one reason why it's called a *leap* of faith. The leap doesn't necessarily carry you to the landing pit of certainty. It may, instead, bring you to a better, more interesting place: acceptance. The "Why?" of evil may always remain a conundrum, but accepting its existence as a necessary companion to good in the mysterious wholeness we call God can, by itself, be a form of doubt-dispelling wisdom. "Good and Evil are the two-forked trunk of the Tree of Life, sprung from a single Seed," wrote Carl Jung. "Or Good and Evil may be viewed as being like twins, offspring of one Father-Mother. They are compensatory, the one to the other, like the right and left ventricles of the heart. They are the two hands doing the work of the Cosmic Body."

The Wisdom of the Mystery: Enlightening Our Mortality

Life is a great surprise. I do not see why death
should not be an even greater one.

VLADIMIR NABOKOV

For most people, one of the strongest inducements to faith is the need to believe that at least part of us is eternal. But we can never know for sure, so in all but the most unshakably devout, a skeptical inner voice snickers, "Don't kid yourself; you're just afraid to accept the reality of your eventual extinction." Add to that mental turmoil the fear and dread that can consume someone who is looking death in the eye for the first time, and it's easy to see why the prospect of dying can rip faith apart like an existential tornado.

"I thought I had the big questions of life and death covered," says Robert Glass*. Propped up in bed in a hospice, he resembles an image of a hermetic saint, with a face so gaunt the skin seems to hug his bones like Saran Wrap, and eyes so luminous they seem to give off more light than they take in. "But I wasn't prepared for this," he admits. "Everything I thought I believed in went out the window as soon as I got the diagnosis."

The diagnosis was colon cancer. A Presbyterian by upbringing, Robert had rejected what he called the "tedious mumbo jumbo" of the church as a young man and turned Eastward for spiritual sustenance. He adopted a Buddhist meditation technique and, from the Hindu tradition, picked up the practice of yoga and certain philosophical convictions, including a belief in reincarnation. "Rebirth made more sense to me than the Christian conception of the afterlife," he explains, pressing the button for more pain medication. When he became a husband and a father, he moved his family to a suburb of San Francisco and once again joined a church. He enjoyed some of the worship services, he says, and the warm, familiar feeling at holiday time. Plus, he and his wife wanted their kids to be exposed to the religion of their ancestors. "That's what I mean by having it covered," he explains. "I had my spiritual practices,

I had a church community and I had given a lot of thought to issues of life and death. I thought that whenever my time came I'd go peacefully."

Instead, terror and toxic doubt flooded his system like the chemicals that failed to kill his malignant cells. "I'm mortal," he recalls thinking. "I'm going to die. This body, this personality, this husband, father, tax attorney, softball player, churchgoing yogi, opera buff, Mercedes owner—this six feet and two hundred pounds of human life is going to disappear. I was stunned. What next? Do I really have a soul that lives on? Will I really come back in another form? Maybe that's all bullshit. Maybe the Christian heaven is also bullshit. Maybe the cynics are right. Maybe the afterlife is just a fairy tale to make us feel better about this vale of tears. Maybe my existence is just an accumulation of molecules, a random accident, no more permanent than a sand castle on a beach, and no more meaningful. What's it all about, Alfie?"

Weary from his monologue, Robert manages a smile as he sips from a cup of water. "It was hell," he continues. "I felt sorry for myself. Was I being punished? Did I have some big karmic debt that I wasn't aware of? I found myself pleading with God to let me live. I hadn't prayed that way in years. I didn't even *believe* in that kind of prayer. I just reverted to this primitive relationship with God, begging and bargaining: 'Can't I just see my kids grow up? Think of my wife! What will she do without me? I promise, if you spare me I'll be a better person.' I was going against everything I believed in about spirituality. Detachment? Forget it! Be in the moment? My moment sucked! It was as if I forgot everything I ever learned. I had no faith whatsoever."

He starts to laugh, but coughs instead, and the jolt to his body is painful. "I don't know about death," he says when he recovers, "but I have to tell you, *dying* is the pits."

He fought for his life on two fronts, says Robert—with cancer and with doubt. Like a fighter behind on points in the late rounds, he tried to land an intellectual haymaker that would solve the riddle of the afterlife before it was too late. All he got was more tired. Then a visiting friend told him a story.

A disciple asks a Buddhist master, "What happens after death?"

"How should I know?" comes the reply.

"But you must know," the student protests. "You're an enlightened man."

"That may be," says the master, "but I'm not a dead one."

Robert laughs when he finishes the tale, then closes his eyes in their hollow shells and sinks deeper into his pillows. "The story had a huge impact," he says. "It made me realize that I'm never going to figure it out. I was only going to wear out my brain trying, and I have other business to take care of before I go. Life, death, God, no God, it's all a fantastic mystery. When I truly accepted that, deep in my gut, I was able to surrender to the awesome magnificence of the unknowable. I could accept the extinction of my body and look at death as the next great adventure: 'Okay, God, I'm ready for the next step!' It's going to be quite a revelation," he says. Then he adds, mischievously, "Or not."

Robert's story illustrates a crucial point about *all* spiritual doubts, not just doubts related to death. He earned his freedom from doubt not with certainty but with uncertainty—or the certainty that some questions are unanswerable and the workings of the Divine are impenetrable by the human mind. By taking his intellect as far as it would go, and then standing, bravely, before the impossibility of knowing, he gained a different kind of knowing. "In the grace of enlightened ignorance," writes James Finley, "we know that we do not know. And in beginning to know that we do not know, we come upon a way of knowing grounded in humility and filled with the mysterious potential of contemplative self-transformation."

Robert resolved his doubt not by willing himself to faith in the conventional sense, but by letting it be OK to doubt—more than OK, in fact, for in the OK was an opening for grace. "When we really worship anything," said G. K. Chesterton, "we love not only its clearness but its obscurity. We exult in its very invisibility." Robert's center of gravity moved from his head to his heart, from trust in his intellect to trust in the essential benevolence of the universe. This shift allowed him to surrender to the ultimate mystery and shout a loud, affirmative "Yes!" to God. That's why it's called the peace which *passeth*—as in goes beyond, or transcends—understanding.

"Though thou hast hidden the truth in darkness," reads Psalm 51:6, "through this mystery thou dost teach me wisdom." Through the wisdom of the mystery, Robert was able to die in peace.

Rethinking God

*Faith will come to him who passionately
yearns for ultimate meaning.*

ABRAHAM JOSHUA HESCHEL

Coming to terms with doubt—and the larger task of making peace with God—often depends on rethinking your understanding of who or what God is. This can be a disturbing process, especially if it puts you into conflict with the belief system in which you were raised. But subjecting your beliefs to scrutiny can be profoundly liberating; the ideas and images to which we are most attached are often the very ones that incite doubt and block our peace with God.

The doubts of a great many people stem from discomfort with the image of God they grew up with—the one depicted by Michelangelo and others as a bearded male figure with a stern countenance, the one portrayed as a divine busybody, an all-powerful ally of his favorites, a granter of worldly wishes and eternal salvation for those who obey the rules, but a jealous, fearsome slayer of enemies who sentences the disobedient to severe retribution.

This anthropomorphic God with the capricious moods is the one that atheists don't believe in and millions of bitter ex-believers have turned their backs on. Discomfort with that image of God has given rise to a flowering of interest in the feminine aspect of divinity. Goddess rites, pagan rituals and the worship of female icons—whether the Christian Mary or the Tara of Tibetan Buddhism or the Hindu's Kali or Saraswati—have exploded, and the language of scripture and liturgy is being altered to include feminine nouns and images of God as Mother. In her book *A Woman's Journey to God*, Joan Borysenko writes, "I do admit to enjoying referring to God as 'Her' or 'the Mother' sometimes, though simply to make the point that this terminology is just as reasonable as viewing God as male and 'the Father,' and that at times a divine motherhood is what speaks most deeply to my soul and provides needed comfort and familiarity."

While there is a political element to some of this trend—a reaction by feminists to the oppression and control of women by patriarchal forms of governance, both secular and religious—a growing number of men are moving in the same direction. It is, in essence, an attempt to upgrade the way we understand God and restore the eternal balance between the masculine and feminine energies in the universe—to have, to put it crudely, a God to hug us not just to discipline us. Without that balance, toxic doubt finds a breeding ground, and it becomes more difficult to locate the God that is beyond gender.

FROM THE PERSONAL TO THE TRANSPERSONAL

The foregoing points to perhaps the most significant way in which one's understanding of the Divine is likely to shift: from a God made in our image (instead of vice versa), to a God of pure spirit that transcends all attributes and forms. Cultural conditioning and the limitations of language work against this transition. Expressions such as "God's will," "the face of God," "God wants," "God loves you" and "God is watching" suggest human qualities. Similarly, we persist in referring to God as "He" even when we know better, because "She" is also a half-truth and "It" seems disrespectful. Despite these hurdles, however, the expansion from personal God to transpersonal God seems to be a necessary component of spiritual maturity and the resolution of doubt. "Once I conceive of God as a person like myself," says Rabbi Harold M. Schulweis in *For Those Who Can't Believe*, "He becomes open to criticism." How can we *not* doubt a God that's like ourselves?

Kate Lutz grew up in a church-going Lutheran family in small-town Pennsylvania. She went to Sunday school and Bible camp and said her prayers every night. She did this not just because she was a dutiful daughter but also because she felt the listening presence of something friendly and embracing. In her early teens, Kate flirted with the idea of becoming a minister. But, it wasn't long before going to church lost its appeal. "It didn't bring me joy, or open my heart," she says. "I believed in God, but it was difficult to have a relationship with God. He was a masculine entity somewhere out there in a place called heaven, and I was just a sinner in a congregation that had to be forgiven. The language of fear sapped my energy as opposed to strengthening it."

As she made her way in the world, the yearning to connect with something bigger and higher than herself kept gnawing at her. The memory of the sweet Presence she felt early in her life would rise up within her, like a grandmother's scent or the melody of a childhood song, and she longed to have it back. Throughout her twenties and thirties, in California, Kate explored various metaphysical ideas. "It was an ongoing process of manifesting an image of God I could relate to in my everyday life," she says.

Eventually, she arrived at a sense of God as a gender-free spirit. "I came to see that God is the vibration of all the energy in the infinite universe, and the vibration of God is love," she explains. "God is like an energy force within my own cellular structure, not a being I'm supposed to live in fear of." Despite the absence of human characteristics in her description, this is a God with whom she can communicate. "I now find ways to cocreate my life with God," she says. "It's a matter of lining up the tuning fork of my own energy with the vibration of love." To remind herself to do that, she created the acronym LIGHT, for Letting In God's Higher Truth.

Perceiving God as boundless, transcendent spirit—or force or energy—is often the single stroke that turns doubt, disbelief or even cynicism into acceptance. Many an atheist has said, "Well, if *that's* what you mean by God, fine." In his classic *The Perennial Philosophy*, the philosopher and novelist Aldous Huxley put it this way: "If God gets to be defined as 'Being itself,' or as 'the integrating principle in the universe,' or as 'the whole of everything,' or as 'the meaningfulness of the cosmos,' or in some other non-personal way, then what will atheists be fighting against?" In other words, the God you doubt may be the God defined by popular lore and religious dogma. But you may still believe in God, even if, like Lisa on *The Simpsons*, you can't quite put your finger on a definition. "I don't know who or what God is exactly," she said. "All I know is, he's a force more powerful than Mom and Dad put together."

FROM THE TRANSPERSONAL TO THE PERSONAL

It must be emphasized that this shift to an impersonal view of God does not in any way require doing away with a personal God. The formless enfolds the form; the form is nested in the formless. The need for a higher power to whom we can relate and with whom we can communicate has always driven human beings to extend their own qualities, motives and feelings to the limits of the imagination and attribute them to God (in some cases, gods). We project onto the Ineffable all our contradictory traits—anger and love, judgment and compassion, etc.—only we stretch them to the nth degree. The danger, of course, is that by fixating on any particular image of God, we automatically box ourselves in.

For most of us, the personal touch completes the picture, whether we turn to an acknowledged embodiment of the Divine—Jesus, Buddha, a saint, a guru—or a vague, intangible sense of an intimate presence, like the radiant Shekhinah of traditional Judaism or something entirely our own. In fact, in many cases, the shift in conception moves in the opposite direction of the one we just described: from the transpersonal to the personal. "I always thought of God as this remote, awesome Force that I could not even think of relating to," says Sharon Peterson*, a commercial real estate broker in St. Louis. "It was as if God was some giant corporation or some faceless government agency, way too big and impersonal to get through to. I would think, 'Why would this entity that runs the whole universe want to hear from a peon like me?'" After realizing that she was projecting onto God her own frustration with Kafka-like bureaucracies, she began to reimagine God as a personal friend *as well as* an omnipotent and benign governing force. This filled her emotional need for a being with whom to communicate, something she could not possibly do with impersonal, Absolute Being.

Feeding our doubt is a deeply ingrained intolerance of paradox and ambiguity, and God is nothing if not paradoxical and ambiguous. "God is both a loving presence, compassionate, wise, kind, and merciful, and an impersonal principle or ultimate condition of consciousness," says Brother Wayne Teas-

dale, a lay Christian monk. It is hard for us to hop the fence of either/or thinking and enter the land of both/and. But faith demands that we try. The danger
of humanizing God is that we subject the Divine to the kind of judgments we
make about ourselves; the danger of thinking of God only as formless and transcendent is to distance ourselves from a higher power with whom to communicate.

Maybe you've gotten God all wrong. Maybe your image of God is somehow incomplete. Maybe what you doubt is not God at all but a misguided
concept you've acquired along the way. Why not rethink what you imagine
God to be? As we mature, we routinely reevaluate a lot of important things—
our values, our attitudes, our views of marriage, career, family and politics—
so why not God? Many people are afraid to take that plunge because they
think it's blasphemous, a fear that is reinforced by many religious authorities,
presumably to protect their flock from heresies. But, while rethinking God
might carry you far from your religious origins, it does not have to result in the
negation of precepts and patterns of worship that work for you. Rather, it can
lead to a broadening of awareness that enfolds the familiar and the traditional
into a more complete whole.

With that advice comes a necessary caveat: getting attached to *any* concept
or model of God can lock the mind into a false sense of certainty and shut
down further growth. No matter how strong your faith may be, leaving some
space for doubt enables you to stand humbly before the eternal mystery.

The Ultimate Proof

The search for God is like riding around
on an ox hunting for the ox.

BUDDHIST SAYING

First she lost the job for which she had moved all the way to Europe. Then
she was dumped by the man she thought was her perfect soul mate. Then her
brother died. This triple play of loss, all in the space of a month, would be

enough to tear anyone's world apart. For Anita, it was especially devastating because she felt that God had sent her both the job and the boyfriend, and she believed that God would heal her brother's illness. She turned to prayer, but not in the way she had been accustomed to in her twenty-seven years as a Christian. She did not ask God for anything, not solace, not strength, not understanding. Instead, she dared God to overpower her doubts with a show of proof.

No such sign was forthcoming. She continued to issue the challenge, however, and one night she finally received what she considered a tentative reply. In a dream, she was told to go to India. Having heard that India was a prime destination for God-seekers, she packed her hopes in her backpack and boarded a plane for New Delhi. On the flight she met a woman who was on her way to an ashram in the Himalayan foothills. Seeing it as another sign, Anita asked to tag along. "I came here to find God," she told the gentle guru who ran the place. He told her she was welcome and assigned her to a spartan room. To Anita, it was the spiritual equivalent of a mansion.

She took to ashram life eagerly, diving into meditation and yoga for hours at a time. Three weeks later, her agitation level had been reduced from raging rapids to rippling stream. Her grief had shifted from frequent convulsive attacks to a calm, bittersweet sadness. At times, she even felt happy. But she was not content. God was still hiding, refusing to dispel her doubt. "Come meditate with me," said the guru when Anita complained that God had not yet taken up her challenge.

Afterward, he asked, "What did you experience?"

"Nothing," said Anita. "I thought about God a lot, but my mind wandered all over the place."

"It never stopped?"

Anita reflected. "Yeah, it did. A couple of times, all the craziness stopped and there was absolutely nothing."

"Nothing?" said the guru.

"Yeah, it was just, like, silent."

"Silent?"

"Yeah."

The guru stared at her and smiled. "He just kept looking at me with this little, twinkly half-smile," says Anita. "Like he was waiting for me see something that was right in front of my eyes. I was like, 'What? Tell me.' It was so weird. Then he said, 'Be still. . . .' and I got it. Like, duh!"

Her guru had never read the Bible, but he had always remembered one sentence from Psalms that someone had recited to him: "Be still and know that I am God."

True faith is less likely to come through thinking than the *cessation* of thinking. Nor is proof likely to come through something seen with the eyes or heard with the ears. God is not a concept to be grasped or a premise to be proved, like an axiom in geometry. God is not a thing. God is not a noun. Buckminster Fuller said that God is a verb, and David Cooper wrote a book with that title. But it could also be said that God is neither a noun nor a verb, but the Noun of nouns and the Verb of verbs, and all the other parts of speech and all the punctuation marks as well. "God is not an object, but the supreme *subject*," asserts Wayne Teasdale. But it could also be said that God is neither object nor subject, but the Object of objects and the Subject of subjects. All of the above and none of the above.

To theologian Paul Tillich, the question "Does God exist?" cannot be answered and should never even be asked. "If asked," he says, "it is a question about that which by its very nature is above existence." That is because God is not a being, says Tillich. "God is being itself, beyond essence and existence." Being itself, as when Moses asks God who he is and the voice from the burning bush replies, "I am that I am." Just Being.

Echoes of God as ineffable Isness ring through the canyons of time and space. "That which makes the eye see but which cannot be seen by the eye — that alone is God, not what people worship," said the sages of the Upanishads. "That which makes the ear hear but which cannot be heard by the ear — that alone is God, not what people worship." And also that which makes the mind think but cannot be thought, and that which makes the tongue speak but cannot be spoken. Which is, it would seem, why Jesus could say, "The kingdom of God cometh not with observation. Neither shall they say, Lo here! or lo there!" Not out there, in other words, not something to be found, like, well, like an Easter egg or the *afikoman*—the matzo that Jews hide at Passover seders—an object to be hunted for in nooks and crannies by children hoping for a prize. Where then? "Behold, the kingdom of God is within you."

Within you, because there, too, is Being itself. There's no Isness like God's Isness, and God's Isness is our Isness.

The Mistake of the Intellect

Ultimately, doubt about the existence of God is traceable to what the Vedas call *pragya parat*, the mistake of the intellect. By identifying with our egoic personalities, we make the mistake of thinking we are separate from the Divine. Only in ending that separation, in realizing that one's self is the Self of the universe, can we truly put an end to doubt. Eons after the Vedas were recorded, and thirteen centuries after Jesus, a devotee of his put it this way: "Some people imagine that they are going to see God as if he were standing yonder, and they here, but it is not to be so," said Meister Eckhart. "God and I: we are one. By knowing God I take him to myself. By loving God, I penetrate him."

Every spiritual tradition contains teachings that say, essentially, God is not hiding; God is present here and now, within and without, always and ever, in *every* here and *every* now. Just as the sun is always shining but we don't see it because of clouds, or the position of the earth or the turning of our heads, the Divine is ever-present, waiting for us to lift the veils from our eyes and the scales from our hearts so we can see and feel that which is right in front of us, right inside of us, practically waving and shouting to get our attention. "Wherever you turn is God's face," said the prophet Muhammad, who also said, "Whoever knows himself knows God." Why? Because God is in us *as* us.

Thirteen centuries after Muhammad and six after Eckhart, in a tradition thought to be at odds with both of theirs, Abraham Joshua Heschel pointed in the same direction for the only proof of God that really matters: direct, intimate experience. Faith comes, he said, not from deliberation, but in the leap from "being overwhelmed by the presence of God to an awareness of His essence." First the profound experience, in other words, then the conviction. That's how the world's religions originated, not with a logical argument or a codified system of beliefs and rules, but with individuals in direct communion with the Holy.

For those whose souls are aflame with God's presence, said Heschel, logical proofs of God's existence are "anticlimactic," an afterthought, just as it was anticlimactic to Einstein when his theory of relativity was finally confirmed. As the rest of the world applauded, Einstein was unmoved; he knew the truth from someplace deep within himself, and the proof was merely a formality he knew would come eventually. As for those whose souls are *not* aflame, says Heschel, "No masterly logical demonstration of God's existence or any analysis of the intricacies of the traditional God-concepts will succeed in dispersing that darkness." To expect it to be otherwise would be like trying to fall in love with someone you haven't yet met. And to jump the gun out of fear would be a contrivance. It would not be true faith but a mere superstition.

When the connection to the Divine is clear and unambiguous, faith rises to the level of knowing. To be with God is to know God is to love God is to believe in God. When asked by a minister how he knows that God exists, a nine-year-old in a Presbyterian church in Los Angeles responded, "I can feel his presence when I'm sad." Out of the mouths of babes. And saints: at the time of his epiphany, wrote St. Augustine, "There was infused in my heart something like the light of full certainty and all the gloom of doubt vanished away."

Keeping the Faith

In the willingness to trust in the midst of perplexity
we begin to taste the peace of God.

JAMES FINLEY

Ah, but here's a Catch-22: until you gain that certainty born of clear and emphatic experience of the Divine, something has to sustain your quest. That's where faith of a different kind comes into play—faith that your doubts can be resolved, and that the outcome, whatever it is, will be good because deep down the universe is benign. That trust keeps the spiritual quest going. Faith and doubt, therefore, are not polar opposites like darkness and light. They are more like dance partners, a dynamic duo whose mutual push and pull keeps you whirling to the music of yearning. The following tips will help you find faith and inspiration when doubt snaps at your heels:

Examine the roots of your doubts. Do your misgivings stem from erroneous beliefs? Fallacies? Misconceptions? The following is a list of "divine illusions" that can give rise to doubt. See if any apply to your thought process.

- God is always supposed to be there for me, to change difficult situations into better ones.
- God is supposed to protect me and shelter me from danger.
- If I do the right things, God will answer my prayers and ensure my happiness and success.
- When things don't go as I wish, God must be punishing me.
- What my tradition says about God must be literally true, or else there is no God.
- Either I believe everything completely or I'm an unbeliever. There is no middle ground.

Ask yourself some questions. Thoughtfully consider your responses to the following:

- On a scale of one to five, how hard is it for you to live with uncertainty in general?
- On a scale of one to five, how trusting are you generally?
- What would it take to resolve your doubts?
- Can you distinguish between disillusionment with religion and a loss of faith in God?
- What emotions might be fueling your doubt? Anger? Frustration? Anxiety? Disappointment? Others?

- Were there influences in your life that created a core of mistrust in you? Were you ignored or abused as a child, for instance? Were you abandoned by a parent figure? As an adult, were you betrayed by a lover, spouse, friend or religious leader?

Turn to your tradition. Is there a cleric to whom you can confide? One who will do more than recite tired clichés? One who can meet your doubt on its own terms instead of trying to talk you out of it? One who can treat your doubt with respect, not disapproval? Such a mentor might be invaluable. Do certain scriptural passages carry particularly potent messages for you? Do certain rituals move you deeply or evoke sweet memories? Returning to them may not convince you to believe what you don't already believe, but it might give you some insight, and it might soothe any emotional agitation that is adding fuel to the fire of your doubt.

Look at other teachings. As we've seen, spiritual truth is not contained like some one-of-a-kind treasure within the walls of any religious compound. You can expand both vertically and horizontally by reaching beyond familiar borders. Don't be afraid that exposure to other sources will pull you away from your own heritage; it is more likely to enhance your understanding and appreciation of it. For example, Kate Lutz, whom we met earlier in this chapter, has a number of spiritual affiliations, but her eclectic path also led her back to her Lutheran roots. She enjoys attending services at a small church where the music and the community feed her soul.

Read about the great ones. The saints and sages of every tradition, and the visionary poets and artists who glorified God, are like experts in any field whose knowledge and experience give us faith in things we can't verify for ourselves. You have faith, for instance, that bacteria exist even though you have never seen them in a microscope. You have faith that eating fiber is good for you even though you haven't done the research yourself. You have faith that beavers build dams even though you've never seen one do so. Think of the enlightened ones as having earned the equivalent of an advanced degree. Their descriptions of communion with the Infinite are so remarkably similar, despite their differences in language, culture and religious context, that they can be considered as reliable as repeated observations in science.

Remember your own experiences. Have you ever had an inkling of God? Have you have felt the embrace of a loving presence? In the silence of the night or deep in the woods, did you ever have a sense of a transcendent other? Did you ever feel at one with nature, or stand in awe before the majesty of the Eternal? Recalling such intimations of the Divine can help revive your faith.

Lean on your spiritual family. It is precisely in moments of doubt and confusion that having companions on the path is most valuable. You might find them at your church, temple or mosque. You might find them among friends of various faiths. You might find them in your family. Wherever they are found, trusted peers who may have had their own crises of faith are in the best position to empathize with your doubt.

Take your doubts to God. Talk it out. Write a letter. Tell God what you doubt and why—even if you doubt God's existence in the first place. Explain what you believe, what you don't believe and what you're not sure about. Spell out exactly why you don't trust God. Even if you feel silly because you're not sure that God is an entity who actually hears your voice or reads your handwriting—or cares—do it anyway. The exercise can help you clarify your thoughts. Don't censor yourself. Let it all hang out. The Almighty can surely handle it. And make sure you end with a request for answers. When you're finished, take a short break and then turn the tables: speak or write to yourself *as if you were God.* Answer your questions as you think God would answer them.

Lighten up. Wrestling with doubt may be necessary on the road to peace with God, but it does not have to be a fight to the death. There are other ways to define the match. Why not wrestle with doubt the way you roll around on the floor with your kids or the way you play around with your lover in bed?

Transmute your doubt. At a certain point, if the same old neurotic doubts and the same sluggish train of reasoning come roaring through your mind for the umpteenth time, you might want to say, "Enough already!" Resolve to stop obsessing over questions that simply cannot be settled by the intellect. When they come up yet again, set them aside, push them out, tell them to shut up. Get rid of them as you would an obnoxious salesman or a toxic substance. If it helps, imagine that the repetitive voice has a form and it's sitting on your shoulder. Reach up, grab it by the throat and throw it aside emphatically: "Get out of here! I don't need you anymore!"

Then take that mental energy and redirect it. Let it propel your personal growth and spiritual development. Beneath your longing to have all doubts removed once and for all are still deeper yearnings: for enlightenment; for freedom from suffering; for wisdom, love, joy and peace.

Shoot for realizing the highest in yourself and you may find that issues of doubt and faith, belief and disbelief, become more like playthings than torments. Perhaps we only stop doubting when we no longer need doubt to push us forward.

4.

WHY, GOD, WHY?

Coming to Terms with Pain and Suffering

The Lord shall be thine everlasting light,
and the days of thy mourning shall be ended.

ISAIAH 60:20

The cry "Why, God, why?" echoes through the canyons of time, from the rending of garments in biblical days to the corridors of high-tech hospitals today; from bloody battlefields and grief-torn graveyards to barren bedrooms and fruitless fields. It may not be a rational question. It may not be an appropriate question. It may not be an answerable question. But it is a necessary question, and when it rises in the throat at times of unbearable pain, it's more than a question; it's a shriek of the soul amplified by harmonic phrases: Why did you do this to me? How could you let this happen? What is the purpose of this agony? I don't deserve this! It's not fair! At such times, "Why, God, why?" demands to be shouted and screamed and hurled to the rafters on wings of rage.

We tend to have an ambivalent relationship with suffering. On the one hand, we are taught that life is a vale of tears and suffering is inevitable. In some religious teachings the only hope for escape is in the next life, and only if we toe the line in this one. Suffering is even romanticized in many quarters, worn as a badge of honor by everyone from would-be saints and self-made martyrs to guilt-inducing parents and shame-based preachers. At the same time, influences as far apart as TV commercials, Sunday sermons and New Age seminars tell us that life can be pain-free, risk-free and discomfort-free—if we do things the right way, whether that means follow religious command- ments, have a positive attitude or use the right deodorant. M. Scott Peck opened his perennial best-seller *The Road Less Traveled*, with the words "Life is difficult" because so many people think there is something wrong with them when their lives are not easy.

Whiplashed between those two extremes, many of us never feel quite right about the world: when things are going great, we either feel guilty about it or fail to enjoy what we have because we're waiting for "reality" to catch up and drop the next shoe on our heads. And when a major tragedy or disappointment strikes, we wonder what the hell's gone wrong, because stuff like this is not supposed to happen when you do everything right. At such times, when the universe seems grossly unjust, we feel as though our soul has separated from its source, and "Why, God, why?" fills our chest.

The Archetypal Spiritual Challenges

The God I believe in does not send us the problem;
He gives us the strength to cope with the problem.
RABBI HAROLD S. KUSHNER

As spiritual beings having a human experience, we are all subject to tragedies, traumas, trials and tribulations. We get sick, we die, we watch our loved ones get sick and die; we have our hearts broken by lovers who leave and friends who betray; we lose things that give us pleasure and get stuck with things that cause us anguish; we get disappointed, defeated and diminished by the turmoil of life. Within that universal framework, of course, we each have our individual crosses to bear. Each of the nine archetypes faces a unique set of challenges to overcome in making peace with suffering:

Reformers suffer most when they can't eliminate evil and imperfection from their world. "Why, God, why do you permit this to go on? Please give me the wisdom and power to make things better." Their greatest frustration comes from not being able to change the people and institutions they think need changing. Ironically, their passion for perfection can actually make things worse; they often get so self-righteous that they create animosity and resistance where they didn't exist before. Their biggest challenge is to learn acceptance — of their own limits and of God's creation as it is, with all its seeming imperfections.

Lovers suffer most when they can't get others to love as strongly as they do — or think they should. "Why, God, why won't she love me like I love her?" "Why, God, why did he leave me?" They want love to be unconditional and unbounded, but few people, if any, are capable of that. Lovers have to learn that human beings love conditionally and selfishly. They also must learn to protect themselves from becoming martyrs to unrequited love. Their challenge is to love themselves as they want to be loved, and to find the ultimate love in the Divine.

Achievers suffer most when their dreams are dashed and their hard work crashes in defeat. "Why, God, why did you let this happen? Why must I be humiliated this way?" Sometimes, it's also, "I did all this to serve you. How could you let me fail?" Their challenges are to learn the lessons imbedded in every setback, to understand that failure is not God's punishment and to realize that grace does not depend on achievement.

Creators suffer most when their passion is squelched by forces seemingly outside themselves, or when their creative drive is thwarted by their own limitations. "Why, God, why am I so blocked?" "Why, God, why don't they appreciate my genius?" They also suffer when their need to escape the bland and commonplace leads to self-destructive behavior and emotional chaos. "Why, God, why did you let me do that?" Their challenges are to find ways to be unrestrained but safe, to stretch their boundaries without breaking them and not get swept away by the allure of pathos.

Thinkers suffer most when they can't comprehend why they and others suffer. "Why, God, why is this happening? Help me to understand. Reveal your reasons!" Their challenge is to accept that the only answer to some questions is, "There is no answer." They have to take things less seriously, learn to re-

spect and appreciate the mysteries of life and make room for the unpredictable.

Security-seekers suffer most when they feel unsafe, and that can occur
when anything important changes or threatens to change. "Why, God, why
can't it stay the way it is? Please protect me. I don't know if I can handle this."
They have to learn that their sense of safety can't depend on outer circumstances and that God helps those who help themselves.

Adventurers suffer most when life gets humdrum, when the thrill is gone
and they feel trapped or bored. "Why, God, why is there no way out of this
stultifying prison? It's not supposed to be this way!" Because their tendency is
to run away from pain and discomfort, they have to avoid falling prey to denial,
addiction or the tendency to constantly look for an exit. Their challenge is to
accept that suffering is sometimes a necessary part of life and it can be used as
an opportunity to grow.

Bosses suffer most when they lose control and can't get things to work out,
or when they can't make the source of pain go away. "Why, God, why am I so
powerless? How did I let things get out of hand?" They have to humbly accept
certain facts of life: that they can't win them all, that they can't control everything, that they can't do it all by themselves and that God is the ultimate authority—and, where God's authority is concerned, they have to take it as it
comes and not try to cut deals: "Help me take control of this mess and I'll do-
nate my next paycheck to the building fund!"

Peacemakers suffer most when others are suffering and they can't help.
Their pain is often compounded by guilt: "Why, God, why didn't I act sooner?
Why can't I make it go away?" They have to stop obsessing about what they
should or shouldn't have done and accept that the suffering of others is usually not their responsibility. Their biggest challenge is to prevent and heal their
own suffering.

As we've mentioned before, we each have all nine personality drives within
us, although we each experience certain tendencies more than others. Regardless of the nature of our individual suffering, however, our task is to *use the
pain as a catalyst for making peace with God.*

The Unanswerable Why

But where shall wisdom be found? and where
is the place of understanding?

Job 28:12

The Judeo-Christian textbook on human suffering is The Book of Job. It is a tale whose spiritual lessons run far deeper than the typical moral drawn from it: to be patient and remain faithful to God no matter what.

The bare bones of the story are as follows: Job is an upright man of high moral standing, who "feared God and set his face against wrong-doing." He plays by the rules, obedient to the religious equation of his time: do right and God will reward you; do wrong and God will punish you. The Almighty is so proud of Job's rectitude that he brags about him to Satan, but Satan replies, essentially, "Sure he's righteous. You've built a protective hedge around him and given him everything he wants. Take away what's dear to him and he'll curse you."

God accepts the challenge, giving Satan permission to take from Job everything but his life. In a short time, Job's children, livestock and home are gone. He grieves, but he remains steadfast: "The Lord gave, and the Lord hath taken away; blessed be the name of the Lord." The stakes are raised. In the next round, Job is afflicted from head to toe with boils so painful he tries to scrape them off with shards of broken pottery. Now, even his wife is fed up with his piety. "Curse God," she implores. But Job replies, "If we accept good from God, shall we not accept evil?"

Enter three of Job's friends, who come to console him. So overwhelmed are they by the sight of their suffering pal that they mourn with him in silence for seven days and seven nights. We are not told what happens to Job during that weeklong retreat, but it must be profound, for he comes out swinging.

What follows is a long, heated exchange between Job and his companions, magnificent in its rhetoric and thorough in its theological argument. In a misguided attempt to soothe Job's anguish, the friends recite the orthodox position: Don't complain. Our heavenly Father is a just God who sees to it that the good prosper and the wicked suffer. For Job, the platitudes are empty and unconvincing. I'm innocent, he insists. I have done no wrong. I have been the most obedient of God's servants. Well, say his friends, if that were true you wouldn't be going through all this agony. Obviously, you have sinned because God does not punish people without good reason. Says Job, I don't pretend to be perfect, but this punishment is undeserved. To which the friends reply, You just proved our point. You're obviously not as pious as you think. You're arrogant, stubborn and disrespectful, so shut up and take what's coming to you.

Job holds his ground. If anything, his righteous indignation only grows stronger. He will no longer accept the common wisdom or cave in to fear. He wants his day in court. He wants to stand before his Maker and plead his case. He wants to let God know what he thinks of his unjust sentence and demand, in turn, an explanation, if not redemption.

Then, in one of the great chapter openings in all of literature, God appears from out of a whirlwind. What follows is not an answer to Job's "Why, God, why?" as such, but a definite and decisive response: an epic depiction of the majesty and splendor of the Divine at work, in both the vastness and minutiae of creation. The awestruck Job is rendered speechless. He stands humbled before God. And in the end, he is blessed with ten new children, greater prosperity than before and a life of 140 years.

It has been said that God's non-answer is a kind of scolding, the equivalent of, "How dare you question my ways!" But if it were a rebuke, why would Job be rewarded in the end? Clearly, the message is not "You are not worthy of knowing," but more like, "Some things are simply unknowable to the human mind." God's response is more profitably seen as a spiritual teaching, for it sparks in Job a profound transformation. What he receives is of far greater value than a direct reply to his query would have been. He is graced by the holy Presence and blessed with a magnificent revelation.

Why Must We Suffer?

What do people mean when they say "I am not afraid of God because I know He is good?" Have they never been to a dentist?

C. S. LEWIS

Two separate questions are enfolded within "Why, God, why?" One is general: "Why does suffering exist at all?" The other is specific: "Why is *this* happening?" The ultimate answer to both is a profound and humble silence.

In the movie *City of Joy*, a resident of the slums of Calcutta says to the doctor played by Patrick Swayze, "The gods have not made it easy to be a human being." Indeed, they have not. Exactly *why* that should be so has been addressed by the same great minds that have tackled the related question of why evil exists. In Western mythology, for instance, human suffering has been viewed as a byproduct of the cosmic confrontation between God and Satan, or the forces of good and evil, and it all started with the Fall, when Adam and Eve disobeyed God, forcing us to pay the price ever since. As for the *purpose* of suffering, all arguments boil down to one basic assumption, succinctly put by C. S. Lewis in *A Grief Observed*: "Well, take your choice. The tortures occur. If they are unnecessary, then there is no God or a bad one. If there is a good God, then these tortures are necessary. For no even moderately good Being could possibly inflict or permit them if they weren't."

In other words, if God is good then suffering must be necessary. As to *why* it's necessary, a host of explanations have been proposed, such as:

- God is a righteous judge who uses reward and punishment to get us to obey his commandments for our own good.
- God created an orderly universe and stepped aside; suffering implies no moral judgment, it simply follows as a consequence of natural laws.
- God left imperfections in the world as a challenge to humans to heal it and make it whole.

- Suffering is the price we pay for free will and the freedom to choose between right and wrong.
- God can't do everything, but he is always there when you need him.
- While it may not seem evident at the time, suffering always clears the way for a higher good.
- Suffering is a teaching tool for soul growth, which is our purpose on earth; without it we would not learn what we need to know.
- Just as we need darkness as a contrast to light, if not for pain and suffering we would not appreciate pleasure and joy.
- Suffering is to the soul what physical pain is to the body, a signal that we have to stop doing what we're doing.
- Suffering turns us away from the futility of worldly pursuits and toward the love and grace of God.

Some combination of those explanations may satisfy you. Or maybe not. Ultimately, the "Why?" may be unanswerable. But if you are angry with God for creating a "no pain, no gain" universe, it might be worth pondering what life would be like without the stain of darkness in the light.

In a memorable episode of *Ally McBeal*, a brain disorder turns a ruthless tycoon into a teddy bear who is happy all the time. His son, afraid that his kinder, gentler father might run the family business into the ground, wants him to have the surgery that would restore his curmudgeonly personality and competitive edge. The father—supported by his wife, who likes her cuddly new mate—would rather keep his don't-worry-be-happy brain. Then the dilemma takes an unexpected twist: the wife dies. Not even that loss can dent the man's giddy happiness. Knowing that there is something profoundly wrong with a life in which he can't feel grief over the death of his beloved, he decides to have the operation. He trades perpetual happiness for the messy complexity of being human.

A PERFECT HELL

The moral of the story above is echoed in the wisdom traditions. In *God Is a Verb*, Rabbi David Cooper asserts that human life cannot be perfect because "our purpose is to continuously perfect ourselves and the universe." If we were to somehow achieve collective perfection, he adds, "we are finished and the universe would cease to exist." In other words, God alone is perfection, and God's perfect creation includes the imperative for humans to strive for perfection. Therefore, our imperfections are part of the larger perfection. Cooper relates a story from the Kaballah, in which a recently deceased man finds himself in a lovely garden where everything he desires instantly materializes. Perfect house, ideal spouse, luxury upon luxury, pleasure upon pleasure, all his for the asking. After a while, everything seems stale and flat, and the man can't think of anything else to wish for. Finally, he hits upon an idea that might end the boredom: he asks to see hell. And he is told, "Where do you think you've been all this time?"

Buddhists say that human life is preferable to the domain of the gods because here, on earth, we are driven to evolve higher and higher, whereas the god realm is marked by complacency. The possibility of suffering prohibits complacency, and, "It is better to find God on the threshold of despair," wrote the Trappist monk Thomas Merton, "than to risk our lives in a complacency that has never felt the need of forgiveness." Suffering can jolt us to a new level of spiritual orbit. It allows the human condition to be a schoolhouse for the soul. It forces us to ponder the big questions, to examine ourselves and strive for wholeness. "If there were no imperfections, no primordial defect in the ground of creation," wrote Carl Jung, "why should there be any urge to create, any longing for what must yet be fulfilled?"

Life without evil and suffering would be like a drama without a villain, an adventure story without a difficult challenge for the protagonist to overcome; there could be no character development, no growth, no learning, no suspense to keep us interested. Without pain, loss, betrayal and misfortune, there could be no heroism, nobility, mercy or redemption. Metaphorically, life nails us to a cross on a regular basis. But for every resurrection there must be a crucifixion, and for that there must be a Judas, even if the Judas can't be identified—and even if the Judas, like the Christ, is within us.

Why Is This Happening to Me?

My God, My God, why hast thou forsaken me? Why art thou so
far from helping me, and from the words of my roaring?

PSALMS 22:1

Each in its own way, every spiritual tradition posits this basic formula for suffering: *we suffer in direct proportion to our distance from the Divine.* In the West, we are urged from every pulpit to line up behind God and do as the Lord commands, or else we cannot hope to find salvation. The story of Job would indicate that there is more to it than obeying the rules. In the beginning, Job is depicted as a perfect servant of God. So concerned is he about not offending God that when his sons visit he gets up early to make offerings on their behalf, just in case they have sinned or "committed blasphemy in their hearts." Yet, despite his rectitude, he suffers mightily. Is that because God is testing him? An alternative interpretation is that Job has some distance to traverse before he is truly close to God. As Stephen Mitchell points out in his provocative translation of The Book of Job, when we first meet Job, he is "a good man, not a wise one." He is, says Mitchell, "as far from spiritual maturity as he is from rebellion."

The view from the East, where the emphasis is less on behavior than on consciousness, is instructive in this regard. The first of Buddha's Four Noble Truths is often translated as "Life is suffering." A more accurate, less pessimistic, rendering would be something like, "Life as it is normally lived invariably gives rise to discontent." Why? Because, as the Second Noble Truth tells us, we seek happiness in that which is transitory and impermanent. Everything in the realm of the mind and senses is constantly changing, ever dying, never the same from one minute to the next. The world as we experience it, said Buddha, is like "a star at dawn, a bubble in a stream, a flash of lightning in a summer cloud, a flickering lamp, a phantom and a dream." No pleasure can last forever, no person, situation or object can last forever. Therefore, loss and pain are inevitable—unless we heed the third and fourth of the Noble Truths and turn toward the state of liberated awareness called *nirvana.*

The Hindu version of that diagnosis is essentially the same. Because we are ignorant of—and therefore disconnected from—our own divine nature as *sat-chit-ananda* (absolute bliss consciousness), we identify with our individual egos and try to achieve happiness by satisfying a never-ending stream of needs and desires. After each pleasure fades, as it must, we suffer the pain of its absence and attach ourselves to the next craving in hopes of returning to the enjoyable end of the pleasure-pain spectrum. And so it goes, on and on, in a futile search for permanent happiness in the realm of relativity and change, where permanence simply cannot be found. "When the senses touch objects, the pleasures therefrom are like wombs of sorrow," says the Bhagavad Gita. "They begin, they are ended: they bring no delight to the wise." That is why, like the Eastern sages, Jesus advised us not to lay up treasures on earth, "where moth and rust doth corrupt," but rather in heaven (which, don't forget, is within you).

In other words, suffering is the absence of divine bliss, just as cold is the absence of warmth and darkness is the absence of light. Disconnection from God brings pain, sorrow and dissatisfaction; union with God brings joy, love and all that is good. Our task is to the end the illusion of separation by removing the obstacles that obscure the Presence (we'll return to this theme later in the chapter).

With regard to the specifics of individual suffering, every tradition posits some kind of cosmic judicial system. The codes and procedures vary from culture to culture, but every system agrees that we are accountable for everything we do and even for everything we think. In the East, the mechanism through which our actions and their consequences play out is *karma,* which is similar to the biblical system of reward and punishment, but without the intervention of a judging deity. Karma, whose literal meaning is "action," operates in an orderly way, like a vast organism of interconnected parts and energies, governed by natural laws. The basic karmic rule resembles a principle of physics: every action (and thought) has an equal and opposite reaction. Right actions lead to positive returns and wrong actions lead to negative returns. In Judeo-Christian terms, we reap what we sow, sooner or later, in this life or another.

It is always tempting to ascribe a larger meaning to unpleasant events. For some, that entails speculating as to God's intentions: "It was God's will because . . ." or "God wanted it this way because . . ." Doing this makes the universe seem more comprehensible when life is harsh. Those who prefer the doctrine of karma do it in their way, e.g., "It's my karma. I must have done such and such in a previous life." But the Bhagavad Gita comes down on the side of the author of Job: don't waste your time speculating. "Unfathomable is the course of action," it declares. In his commentary on that verse, Maharishi Mahesh Yogi writes: "Every thought, word or act sets up waves of influence in the atmosphere. These waves travel through space and strike against everything in creation. Wherever they strike they have some effect. The effect of a particular thought on any particular object cannot be known because of the diversity and vast extent of creation. This complexity goes beyond the possibility of comprehension."

In a reverberating universe of crisscrossing, overlapping energy waves, trying to fathom the causal links of an event of any complexity is like trying to calculate both the position and velocity of a subatomic particle, something that the famous uncertainty principle of Werner Heisenberg proved to be impossible. In the midst of inexplicable suffering, we are left, like Job, to accept the Unknowable.

Accepting the Unacceptable

Be in a realm where neither good nor evil exists. Both of them belong to the world of created beings; in the presence of Unity there is neither command nor prohibition.

ABU YAZID AL-BISTAMI

That there is no final answer to "Why, God, why?" may seem unsatisfactory, but it is not something to be taken with a shrug of resignation. It is best accepted with eyes ablaze in wonder. That is where Job ends up. Like a Zen novice struggling with a koan (a conundrum used as a teaching tool, such as the classic "What is the sound of one hand clapping?"), Job racks his brain to make sense of his suffering. His frustration turns him into a perfect receptacle for mind-transcending wisdom.

God addresses Job directly with statements such as, "Where were you when I laid the earth's foundations?" "Did you proclaim the rules that govern the heavens, or determine the laws of nature on earth?" "Dare you deny that I am just or put me in the wrong that you may be right?" Again, these rejoinders could be taken to mean, "Don't you dare question me. Shut up and take it." But the more likely intention, as suggested by God's evident love of Job, is, "Throw away your preconceived ideas about right and wrong and good and evil. Give up all your concepts and beliefs about me. Behold! I am eternal, infinite and ineffable."

In language as elegant as Shakespeare's and rhythms as thrilling as Beethoven's Ninth, God reveals the thunderous energy of divine intelligence at work. Exploding with images of primordial nature in the raw, it is a vision in which the morning star is lit and the shoreline of the sea is drawn, where beasts devour beasts and death is as essential as life. As Stephen Mitchell puts it, Job is given a "God's-eye view of creation *before* man, beyond good and evil, marked by the innocence of a mind that has stepped outside the circle of human values." In its sublime and terrifying grandeur, it is comparable to the sequence in the Bhagavad Gita when Lord Krishna reveals himself to the awestruck warrior-prince Arjuna. Within the body of Krishna, Arjuna sees the entirety of the universe in all its multitudinous diversity. Like Job, he is shown not just the magnificent beauty of creation but also its necessary partner, the colossal might and relentless energy of destruction, "devouring all the worlds." He sees that both the Spirit in whom "the cosmos rests in safety" and "the Lord of fire and death" are part of one God. Job and Arjuna alike surrender in wonder to the Unity that transcends concepts and polarities.

Implied in God's nonanswer to Job's entreaties is a different kind of answer: in a universe in which stars are born and extinguished every moment, in which creatures are predator to some and prey for others, in which birth and death occur thousands of times per second, in which cries of horror and shouts of joy echo through the heavens as voices in a single choir, how can we comprehend the meaning of one human being's suffering? God tells Job that the laws of the universe are eternally just but also unfathomable to the human mind. "Give up the demands of your ego for justice on your terms," the message seems to be. "Give up your craving for certainty. Give up your narrow standards of right and wrong. And while you're at it, give up your despair." In yielding to the ineffable Isness of God's creation, Job surrenders in pure amazement and says "Yes" to the divine mystery.

KNOWLEDGE IS STRUCTURED IN CONSCIOUSNESS

Behold the light beyond right and wrong.

CHUANG-TZU

Early in the story, in what we can think of as a reflection of Job's state of consciousness at that time, God is portrayed as a distant potentate who keeps a watchful eye on earth and passes sentence on human behavior, doling out rewards and punishments as he sees fit. Because he saw God as the protector and benefactor of those who follow the rules, Job's suffering was unbearable. He felt adrift in the cosmos as well as nailed to the earth. But, a verse in the

Vedas says that knowledge is different in different states of consciousness. By the end of the story, Job's consciousness has been raised. Now we don't see a humanlike God of judgment but a disembodied voice describing a universe so miraculously complete that it must include the possibility of evil and suffering—along with intelligent creatures who are free to choose goodness and grace instead.

Job may be less certain of God's ways at the end but he is closer to God—and who among us would not choose divine intimacy over false certainty in a New York minute? Job himself acknowledges the shift. "I have spoken of great things which I have not understood, things too wonderful for me to know," he admits. "I knew of thee only by report, but now I see thee with my own eyes."

Job's last line, "Wherefore I abhor myself, and repent in dust and ashes," can easily be taken as the words of a mortified man. But it is possible, instead, to see Job as a *transformed* man, not brought to his knees in humiliation but kneeling in humility. In Mitchell's translation, that final statement is, "Therefore I will be quiet, comforted that I am dust," dust being a symbol of mortality and therefore a recognition of the insignificance and impermanence of the individual self. "I abhor myself" has also been interpreted as "I melt away." That melting is similar in spirit to Arjuna's response to his revelation: "Therefore I bow down and prostrate my body before Thee, the adorable Lord, and seek Thy grace." Mitchell describes Job's transformation this way: "He has faced evil, has looked straight into its face and through it, into a vast wonder and love. He has let go of everything, and surrendered into the light."

Job has gone from a believer to a mystic, from one who merely performs the deeds supposedly required by God to one who communes directly with God, from one who submits to one who surrenders. The surrender he achieves is not a fearful capitulation, but a conscious yielding of individual will to Divine intelligence. And that, not just the property he acquires and the length of his life, is why Job is truly more blessed at the end of his days than at the beginning.

Cosmic Chutzpah

Let nothing disturb you,
Let nothing dismay you.
All things pass.
God never changes.

ST. TERESA OF AVILA

Suffering always entails a sense of loss. It might be the loss of a loved one, the loss of health, the loss of certainty, the loss of faith, the loss of safety or the loss of any number of things. As with all losses, healing requires that we go through three distinct phases: 1) shock and denial ("This can't be happening!"); 2) anger, fear and sadness ("Why, God, why?"); and 3) understanding and acceptance. To make peace with God over our own suffering and that of others, we not only need to accept that the big "Why?" may be unanswerable, but we need to accept what is for what it is and give up wishing it were different. Problems arise when we get stuck in phase two, clinging stubbornly to our anger and sorrow and refusing to move on. Problems also arise when we get stuck in the first stage because we're afraid to go through the turmoil of powerful emotions. Sometimes, what passes for acceptance is really denial.

Acceptance does not mean acquiescence. We are not called upon to give up our standards or become passive, submissive or apathetic. The pain is real. The outrage is real. Attention must be paid.

In a sense, Job is a prototype for anyone who is tempted to settle for a false or premature acceptance in times of pain. He could have shrugged in empty resignation: "What are you gonna do? That's life. I must deserve this." His friends urge him to do exactly that. But Job is heroic not because he stays loyal to his religious precepts, but because he has the courage to question those assumptions, face his pain squarely and work through his rage. In doing so, he paves the way for an acceptance so profound it is transcendent.

Skipping ahead to a superficial acceptance is a pitfall faced by religious people and spiritual seekers of every persuasion. Mother Teresa once told of the time she tried to console a little girl who was afflicted with a painful illness. "You should be happy that God sends you suffering," she told the child, "because your sufferings are a proof that God loves you much. Your sufferings are kisses from Jesus." The child's response was, "Please ask Jesus not to kiss me so much." In her refusal to settle for a saccharine acceptance, that girl was a soul mate of the Yiddish writer Shalom Aleichem, who said of the suffering of Jews, "God, I know we are your chosen people, but couldn't you choose somebody else for a change?"

As for those who seek Buddha-like detachment, the story is told of a guru whose child had recently died. A disciple, seeing his teacher in tears, is astonished. "But Master," he says, "why do you cry? You taught us that life and death and all the things of the world are merely illusions."

"Yes," acknowledges the master, "and the saddest illusion of all is the death of a child."

Anne Cushman learned that lesson in the agonizing aftermath of losing her child during pregnancy. In an essay in *Yoga Journal*, she writes, "I used to think that spiritual practice would be a way of lessening the pain of grief; that I could escape into some Self, some detached witness consciousness that is beyond the world, from which I would watch my life dispassionately, like a movie I could turn off at any moment." She found, however, that her grief was too overwhelming. To her credit, she did not try to bypass it. Instead, she allowed herself to feel the full measure of pain. "I would never want to be so detached, so cut off from that primal pulse that I did not mourn my daughter's death," she wrote. "And I don't think that's what the yogis meant—that we should use practice as a kind of spiritual epidural to anesthetize us from the pain of our lives."

No, the yogis would probably say that the goal of someone who lives in the world, as opposed to a cave or monastery, is to be in the midst of turmoil and pain and at the same time hold fast to the bliss and boundless awareness of the Divine. This would be like having a steadfast anchor on a choppy sea. On the way to that blessed state, however, suffering is not to be denied or sugarcoated. It is to be acknowledged and felt, and, paradoxically, used as a catalyst for the very transformation that will do away with itself. The horrors of life, says religious scholar Andrew Harvey, are here to "compel us to the highest level of love, which flowers from acceptance." And, he adds, "You can only get to that level of acceptance if you give up trying to explain anything and instead just open your heart in immense, 'blind,' all-embracing love."

During rough times, you might, like Job, hear so many platitudes you feel as if the world has become a giant Hallmark greeting card. "It's God's will." "There must be a higher purpose to this." "It's your karma; you must accept it." "It's all an illusion; don't be attached." "God has something better in mind for you." Of course, those voices may be inside your head, echoing religious precepts and spiritual teachings you've absorbed but possibly misconstrued. The voices may tell you it's unseemly to argue with God, that it's spiritually weak to feel bitter or resentful. They may remind you that you believe in reincarnation or life eternal, so there is no sense grieving over someone's death. They may urge you to be more "spiritual" and love the enemy who's trying to destroy you, or to rise above your troubles. They may point out that the treasures of earth are as nothing compared to those of heaven, so there is no reason to mourn their loss. Paying heed to those voices can lead to "mood-making"— deceiving yourself and others by contriving a mood of calmness, detachment, love, compassion or other qualities you think of as spiritual, when in reality you want to howl at the heavens.

Three days before Easter weekend one year, William Grimbol, the minister of a Presbyterian church on Shelter Island, New York, learned that his wife had died in a freakish mishap during surgery. Some of his parishioners, in a well-meaning attempt to soothe his anguish, told their pastor what they thought he would tell them under such circumstances: "Christine is in a better place now." While the love and concern of his congregation were vital in getting Grimbol through his crisis, comments like that were irrelevant to him. "We have to accept life on God's terms," he says. "God's will is for us to be human." And he was a human being who would never see his beloved again.

In an effort to avoid pain, we can use religion the same way many of us use alcohol, drugs, food, sex or work—as anesthetics. In the name of acceptance, we can cut ourselves off from our feelings and turn ourselves into spiritual imposters. Reverend Grimbol compares it to caterpillars who resist entering their cocoons. Metaphorically, we often do the same thing—avoid the dark places that seem foreboding, but which actually hold out the promise of vital transformation.

Job refuses to do that. His willingness to face his pain with brutal honesty ignites in him a passionate longing for higher wisdom and true knowledge of God. This transforms him from a goody-two-shoes caterpillar into a bold butterfly who has what the Talmud approvingly calls "chutzpah even to heaven." As a result, the acceptance he achieves contains the power of deep humility. It is an act of appreciation, of glorification and of magnificent trust, because it says not only that the Creator is great but that, in the final analysis, Creation is basically good.

Feel the Pain

"People should not try to run away from their suffering," says Vietnamese Buddhist master Thich Nhat Hanh. "In fact, you have to hold the suffering and look deeply into it, because that is the only way to discover the true nature of your suffering. And when you have seen the true nature of your suffering you have a chance to see the way out."

There is nothing "unspiritual" about feeling deeply. In fact, when pain, grief, horror, despair or other difficult emotions are stirring in your breast, it is a good idea to sit down and allow yourself to really feel them. For that period of time, let your attention rest on the physical sensations attached to those feelings. Let yourself be with the pain. Note that this is very different from dwelling on your problems or wallowing in your status as a victim. Don't ponder your feelings; don't label them; don't contemplate the situation or people that you think caused them; don't worry about how to fix things. Just feel what is going on without resistance and without anticipation. At the same time, see if you can pull back a bit and watch, like a silent witness. See if you can relax into the pain instead of resisting it, breathing with it like a mother going through natural childbirth.

At first, the intensity of the feeling may tempt you to stop. Your mind may tell you, "This is ridiculous." Your body will want to get up and do something to distract your attention. This is normal; our survival instincts are geared to *avoid* pain, not focus on it. For that reason, it's a good idea to commit to a set period of time, say ten minutes, and treat this as a spiritual exercise. You will find that before long the intensity begins to diminish.

Allowing yourself to feel the pain accomplishes three things: 1) it ensures that you won't fall prey to the trap of denial; 2) it helps you move through the agony more quickly; and 3) it removes, at least temporarily, the element of suffering. Why that last benefit? Because suffering is more than pain—it is pain plus resentment, blame, resistance and other accessories we attach to the reality of our condition. When you are fully in the moment, even if the moment is painful, suffering is suspended because you are not busy lamenting, regretting or wishing that anything were different from what it is.

Sometimes, when you give your full attention to what you are feeling, a surprising thing happens: the agony becomes more like labor pains, an opening to a blessing. You have stopped, at least for the moment, the incessant mental chatter that perpetuates the anguish. You have stopped rewriting the past and plotting for the future. You have stopped blaming God or other people. Instead, you have surrendered to the truth of the moment. And *the peace of God is in every moment*, whether you've made peace *with* God or not. "There is a crack in everything," sang Leonard Cohen. "That's how the light gets in." By fixing the radar of consciousness fully on the present, you may very well locate the crack where divine Presence shines through.

It would be a mistake to anticipate a flood of holy radiance each time you allow yourself to be fully attentive to your pain. But, at the very least, feeling it is the beginning of healing it. (Of course, for severe intractable pain, or the emotional anguish of major depression, allow yourself to accept God's gift of appropriate therapy and, if needed, prescribed medication.)

Divine Rage, Outrageous Spirituality

I will speak in the anguish of my spirit; I will
complain in the bitterness of my soul.

JOB 7:11

Divine rage is a long and honorable custom, understood by many traditions to be not only healing but also a privilege of those who are intimate with
the Infinite. In India, the story is told of a man who wanders through his village every day, cursing at God. The townspeople regard him as an offensive
blasphemer, but they can't get him to stop. One day he clambers onto the roof
of a temple and announces that he is going to die. He sits down, closes his eyes
and peacefully leaves his body. As if that weren't astounding enough, just then
magnificent music fills the air. So enchanting is the sound that all the villagers
stop what they are doing and listen. "Who is making this celestial music?" they
wonder. "Who in the village has such a gift?" But no one is playing an instrument and no one is singing. When the music finally stops, the people run to
the wisest man in town: "Did this music come from the heavens? Could it possibly have been for that obnoxious madman who profaned God all the time?"

"Yes," affirms the guru, "the angels were welcoming him to their presence."

"But how can this be?"

"He chanted the name of God more than all of you put together," says the
holy man. "If you could remember God one tenth of the time he did, you too
would be liberated."

The person who told us that story is Gurutej Kaur, a yoga teacher in Los
Angeles who grew up Catholic in the Midwest and became a Sikh nearly
three decades ago. She's been fighting with God for years: "Ever since I got
over the fear that I'll be punished for doing it." Ordinary prayer could not satisfy the demands of her personal relationship with the Divine, she says. It was
too complacent. Now, when she feels the need, she might scream and holler
out loud, or argue with God in the sanctuary of her mind or let loose in writing. The battle might last two minutes or five hours. "The main thing," she

says, "is not just to rant, but to listen. Fighting with God is a form of communication, and I want answers."

The value of engaging God in this way hit home for Gurutej several years ago, when she had her own Job-like experience. "It was a very difficult time," she recalls. "My relationship ended. The business we had started together fell apart. My daughter left home. Everything was falling to pieces. I had nowhere to turn except to my altar. I said, 'Okay, God, either I'm deaf or you need to talk to me more clearly. I can see everything that's leaving, but I can't see what's coming. Couldn't you be using me better?'" The answers eventually came. In the meantime, the sacred connection kept her going. "If I didn't fight with God, I'd have lost my life spark," she says. "It kept the fire ignited." Ever since, "Couldn't you be using me better?" has been her most frequent challenge to God.

Some people are reluctant to rage at God because it doesn't make sense to them. They think, "Why would God want to hear about my problems? He has more important things to deal with." Or perhaps they don't see God as a humanoid figure that pays attention to the details of their lives, but rather as a transpersonal force. In the face of injustice and senseless suffering, they feel the urge to shout at the heavens because there is nowhere else to direct their fury—and then they stop themselves because they feel foolish. But rage is not about making sense; it is about giving vent to a buildup of negative psychic energy. If it is not released in a safe, appropriate manner, it will poison the mind and body and eventually find an outlet in some destructive behavior. Moreover, suppressing the anger amounts to getting stuck in the first stage of grief resolution: denial.

To get to full acceptance, it makes sense to stop making sense. Sometimes you have to override the voice of reason and let out the fury inside. After earning a doctorate in education and building a successful career in organizational development, Kikanza Nuri Robins felt the calling and entered divinity school. After blitzing through seminary training, she approached her ordination exams, which most candidates fail the first time around, with the confidence of someone who had always excelled. She failed the theology test. "I was devastated," she recalls. "I felt totally humiliated." She cried for days, unable to comprehend what had gone wrong. Her way of climbing out of that pit was to let herself get angry with God. To do this, she had to temporarily set aside her own theology. "I know God is not a person or an object," she says. "God is all that is, and our sense of separation is a misperception. But I was hurting, and I had to make noise. I had to let myself feel like a victim. So I gave myself permission to fabricate an anthropomorphic God and put him in a box so I could beat up on him."

Having allowed herself to vent her anger, she listened for a response. One message was predictable: take responsibility for your own failure. The other was an unexpected flash of light in the darkness: you had never experienced failure before; now you can be a better pastor because you will have compassion for those who fail. Reinspired, she buckled down and passed the exam with the proverbial flying colors. Now a Presbyterian minister in Los Angeles, Reverend Nuri Robins lets her parishioners know that it's OK to be mad at God, even as she urges them to accept the gift of life, warts and all, and to use neither God nor Satan as a scapegoat for their troubles.

If it's not our intellects telling us it's stupid to express our rage, the resistance usually comes from guilt ("I'm awful to harbor such terrible feelings toward God") or fear ("The Almighty will strike me down"). But to hold back for such reasons would be a discredit to the Divine. Thinking that God would not approve, or would get testy over your impertinence, is tantamount to calling him a petty tyrant who can't handle confrontation and won't tolerate the challenge of one small human being. If you're going to attribute human qualities to God, isn't it better to assume that she has the wisdom to know you're in pain and the compassion to allow your agony to have an outlet? So far, all the evidence indicates that God can handle it. After all, a fervent argument is a form of connection, and most mature relationships can withstand a little commotion once in a while. "Wouldn't you rather have a passionate lover who occasionally offends you than someone who tiptoes around?" asks Gurutej Kaur.

At the beginning of his story, Job relates to God from a distance. His righteous behavior is rooted in fear-based obedience. Then a new Job is forged in the flames of catharsis. Despite the pious warnings and cogent arguments of his friends, who *don't* change, Job refuses to let God off the hook. He engages

God passionately, courageously, like a lover who feels betrayed and will not rest until he gets his beloved to set the record straight. Is he punished for his temerity? No, he is blessed by tangible riches and a newfound intimacy with God. As if the mere appearance of the divine Presence were not evidence enough, Job's attitude is explicitly vindicated when the voice in the whirlwind admonishes the three friends, "Ye have not spoken of me the thing that is right, as my servant Job hath."

The Alchemy of Suffering

Life is like photography. You use the negative to develop.

SWAMI BEYONDANANDA

Once the pain is felt, once the rage has been released and the reality has been accepted, the opportunity arises to use what life has presented us. This is where human choice enters the equation. We can wallow in despair, feel sorry for ourselves and curse God for the rest of our lives. Or, we can, like martial artists who absorb the energy of an attack and turn it against their opponents, grab hold of pain and turn it into a blessing.

Wayne Dosick, a San Diego rabbi, returned home with his wife one night to find that his house had burned to the ground. In his memoir of that event and its aftermath, *When Life Hurts*, he writes, "Standing in the ashes of my house, I could not see beyond the immediate destruction; I could not feel beyond my immediate pain. . . . But I could sense that I did not know all there was to know; I could imagine that somewhere deep in mystery there was an explanation that was not mine to grasp." Nothing happens by chance, he contends. "There is a Divine plan. There is a reason and—even though we do not know it now—an ultimate explanation for what happened to us."

Is he simply saying what a man of the cloth is expected to say? Is he rationalizing out of a need to believe that his tragedy was part of the blueprint of a higher wisdom? Perhaps the good that eventually came from the fire was part of the Grand Design. Perhaps it was the specific intention of a beneficent deity. Or maybe it arose solely from the positive actions of Dosick, his wife and their community. Ultimately, these questions are unanswerable. We've all seen unexpected blessings rise from the ashes of disaster. We've all seen things turn out beautifully when they appeared to be headed in the opposite direction. Nancy Peddle, founder of the Lemonaid Fund, a Chicago nonprofit organization that works with childhood victims of violence, calls such auspicious turns of events "Godincidences." If they happen often enough, you might begin to sense that a benevolent stage manager is working behind the scenes. But sometimes things just seem rotten, and there's no Godincidence in sight. What do you do then? "You have to assume that God's intention is for you to do something about it," says Peddle.

There may or may not be a divine meaning behind your personal suffering. Your pain may or may not have been given to you for a specific purpose. Some unrevealed good may or may not have been intended. But one thing is certain: you can *make* it meaningful, you can *find* a purpose and you can *create* something good. For the gift of having that ability, perhaps we ought to thank God.

"Till the bread is broken, how can it serve as food?" asks Rumi. "Till the grapes are crushed, how can they yield wine?" Sufi mystics in the tradition of Rumi regard heartbreak as a treasure. "They have realized the mastery of pain," says Andrew Harvey, "which is to accept and embrace it, and suck the dark juice out of it, and to taste in the deepest suffering that most outrageous possibility: that the deepest suffering is also the source of the deepest grace." The Sufis would find kinship with whomever in the Jewish tradition was the first to say, "God is closest to those with broken hearts." To the Talmudic rabbis, God was not just the sweetest of the sweet but the bitterest of the bitter, and sometimes, they said, the sweetness is unbearably bitter and the bitterness is unbearably sweet. That pain can be converted to grace was also evident to the early Christians, who referred to the "alchemy of the soul," a process by which the fire of suffering transmutes the heart's impurities into spiritual gold.

We might not know "God's purpose" for our suffering, or whether it even makes sense to think in those terms. But if we accept that the Grand Plan is for each of us to grow toward God-realization and fulfill our soul's potential, we are virtually compelled to use everything that is put on our plate—joys and sorrows alike—to consciously move in that direction. Any life experience can be a catalyst for spiritual growth—not just the birth of a child but also a death; not just buying a dream house but seeing the house destroyed by fire; not just the fulfillment of a cherished goal but also a devastating failure; not just a walk on a beach but lying in bed too ill to walk to the bathroom. We can ask "Why, God, why?" but the more important question is one we ask ourselves: how can I use this dark night of the soul for a higher good?

"A true dark night of the soul is a powerful vehicle of transformation," says Reverend Michael Beckwith, the senior and founding minister of the Agape International Spiritual Center, in Los Angeles, "and my inclination is to take full advantage of it. I give thanks for it, because I know it has come into consciousness to take me to another level of spiritual maturity. This kind of spiritual experience draws me prayerfully, meditatively inward, beyond mere silence to stillness, where I listen and commune with the Spirit."

Karmic Lessons

The times when God seems absent are also the times God is close, tangible and real.

REVEREND WILLIAM GRIMBOL

The law of karma may be immutable, but it should not be confused with fate. Karma is a call to action. At every moment, the cosmic mail service is leaving self-addressed envelopes on our doorsteps, for better and for worse. We get to decide how to respond to the content. Each action we take with our free will creates new karma. This freedom gives us the power to cushion the blow of painful deliveries and act in such a way as to create *good* karma in the future—not necessarily in a future life, but the next moment, the next hour, the next day, the next year, however long it takes for the ripples to reverberate through the cosmos and trickle back to meet us. To deal effectively with karma is to free ourselves from the constrictions of the past and move toward higher states of awareness.

None of which means that suffering is good. It is not a virtue. It is not noble. It is not, in itself, a path to God. It is what it is, and the entire thrust of evolution is to rise above it. The remarkable paradox of human freedom is that suffering can be used for the very purpose of defeating itself, just as we might ride the floodwaters to carry us away from the flood zone.

When asked who his greatest teacher was, the Dalai Lama answered, Mao Zedong. Mao? The Chinese leader who ordered the invasion of Tibet and forced the Dalai Lama into exile? Why him? Because the unspeakable suffering Mao unleashed on the Tibetan people, and the wanton destruction of their ancient land and culture, forced the Dalai Lama to learn about patience and compassion at a depth he might never have penetrated otherwise.

Asking, "What can I learn from this?" is a crucial step in converting suffering into a blessing. In fact, it is so important that many people regard the seemingly negative events that come our way as deliberate attempts by God to teach us something. Those who don't think in terms of an interventionist deity prefer to look upon earth as a vast blue-green classroom, in which each of us has a personal curriculum and every package of karma that comes our way contains a lesson plan. Either way, it seems that our task is to read the clues and figure out what we need to know in order to take the next step in our soul's evolution.

Another well-known figure who has shown how to sculpt vital lessons out of the rubble of pain is Ram Dass, whose celebrated journey from Harvard professor (Richard Alpert) to psychedelic pioneer to avid seeker to mature spiritual teacher hit an unexpected road block in 1997, when he had a stroke. Still suffering from complications that require him to sleep with a respiratory machine, Ram Dass is confined to a wheelchair with one side of his body virtually useless and his ability to speak limited. "What happened to my body was far less frightening than what happened to my soul," he says. "The stroke wiped out my faith." In time, however, this thought arose: "Maybe the stroke is a form of grace." That possibility initiated a process that brought him closer to God. "And that's grace," he says. "Fierce grace." Among the blessings he says he's gleaned from his condition are greater compassion, a more authentic humility, heightened appreciation of silence and insight into how suffering can be "a stepping-stone toward a spiritual goal."

It's not just the famous, of course, who profit from using pain as a stepping-stone for growth. For anyone willing to probe deeply, the lessons to be derived can be profound. Shortly before her fortieth birthday, Maria Gallo's husband of twenty-one years left her for another woman. She found herself in rural Canada, thousands of miles from her native Argentina, with three children, hardly any money and a huge gaping wound in her heart. Raised Catholic, she worked her rosary beads feverishly and prayed every chance she could: "What do you want from me? Why did you let this happen to me?"

Maria's despair grew darker than the Canadian winter. "At one point, I didn't care to live anymore," she says. She had been to church almost every Sunday of her life. Now, she associated church with pain. "I was so mad I had to break up with God."

She grew to miss her connection to the Divine, however, and so initiated an urgent search for a new way to relate to God. "Before, God was up there," she says, "and I would denigrate myself by pleading with him and asking for things. Now it's more like a conversation."

As her spiritual quest progressed, so did her perspective on her years of agony. "I saw that the purpose of life is the growth of the soul, and I had been given a wonderful opportunity to grow up. If all that hadn't happened, I'd still be dependent and weak. I say, 'God, if you chose this way to make me grow up, thank you very much. It could have been something worse.'"

What lessons are screaming out for you to learn? What does your suffering tell you about your values? Your expectations? Your relationship to a higher power? Finding the diamond of wisdom in the mud of despair is not always easy. But it is essential if we are to achieve genuine acceptance and make peace with God.

Gaining Perspective

Oh Lord, won't you buy me a Mercedes Benz.

JANIS JOPLIN

In an episode of the TV series *Chicago Hope*, an anesthetized patient sees the spirit of a departed friend. He asks him what God wants from us. "He wants you to feel joy" is the reply. "It really offends him when people don't do that."

"How are we supposed to feel joy in a world full of pain and suffering?" asks the patient, who had lost both his son and his wife. "The suffering in this life is enormous."

The spirit replies, "So is the beauty, my friend, but you wouldn't know it. You're not looking for it."

Making peace with God on the issue of personal suffering demands that we step back and get some perspective. How bad is it really? Are you compounding your pain by feeling sorry for yourself? In the larger picture of human suffering, is what's happening to you really unjust? Are you blaming God because your desires have not been fulfilled or your prayers have not been answered? Are you seeing only the worst and losing sight of your blessings? "The ungrateful man overlooks ten gifts from God," said Guru Arjan Dev, a sixth-century Sikh leader, "but when one is withheld, loses his faith."

Janet Taylor* lived a sheltered life in a suburb of Phoenix. One night she was awakened by a call from an emergency room. Her housekeeper's car had been rammed by a drunk driver. The housekeeper had facial injuries and a broken ankle. Her husband, who had done handiwork for the Taylors, suffered a severe spinal injury that would leave him paralyzed from the waist down. In the ensuing weeks, as Janet visited her housekeeper in the hospital, in her small apartment in the barrio and at the county facility where her husband was getting rehab, her eyes were opened. "I realized that I'd been pissed off at God my whole adult life," she says. "I was constantly complaining that I wasn't getting what I wanted, always wishing I could have what someone else had." The meager conditions in which her housekeeper's family lived, the agony of the patients in rehab, the distress of families who could not pay their medical bills—it all made her realize how lucky she was and how trivial her complaints had been. "God must have been really annoyed at this spoiled brat," says Janet.

In America, where envy is as ubiquitous as designer sneakers, every day brings another reason to feel deprived when you ought to feel thankful. Everywhere you turn, some lucky stiff seems to have something you want: "Why not me, God? When do I get mine?" It's worth examining whether your conflict with God is rooted in a sense of cosmic entitlement, or an image of God as a Santa Claus figure who's supposed to give you what you ask for if you're not naughty. Maybe we get what we need, not what we want, and maybe, at every moment, God is offering you a great deal more than you're asking for: joy, love, freedom and wisdom, to name just a few possibilities. Maybe our challenge is to love God for what we have, not keep asking for more. "When a man prays to God, 'Give me this, and give me that,' it is not love," said the nineteenth-century Vedanta master Vivekananda. ". . . it is mere shopkeeping."

Holy Humor

Humor is a prelude to faith, and laughter
is the beginning of prayer.
REINHOLD NIEBUHR

Someone once complained to the Indian sage Ramakrishna that one of his disciples was drunk. "But don't you think God is drunk?" asked Ramakrishna. "How else would the universe be so crazy if God wasn't drunk?"

If not drunk, at least a cosmic comic. That's what Voltaire thought. He saw God as a comedian playing for an audience that's afraid to laugh.

Recognizing that it is indeed a crazy universe opens the door to one of the best catalysts in the alchemy of pain: laughter. Needless to say, humor is not always appropriate in the midst of suffering, but at times it is as soothing to the troubled spirit as a good massage is to a worn-out body. In fact, some of the best jokes are leavened by pain, which is, perhaps, why so much of American humor has come from Jews and African Americans. At the saddest moment in *Fiddler on the Roof,* when the Jews are ordered to vacate their beloved village, a man says, "Our forefathers have been forced out of many, many places at a moment's notice."

"Maybe," says Tevye, "that's why we always wear our hats."

It could be said that a great deal of human suffering comes from taking ourselves too seriously. A good laugh at our own expense is, if nothing else, a reminder not to do that. No holy book has been taken more seriously than the Koran, but in it is the statement, "He deserves Paradise who makes his companions laugh." Perhaps we can think of humor as an offering.

As our offering to the altar of humor, here is a joke on the relevant theme of gratitude. Fed up with the emptiness and clamor of modern life, Tom quits his job at the ad agency and enters a monastery where the monks are permitted to speak only two words a year. He settles into a barren room, dons a woolen robe and settles in for a life of silence, study and ascetic discipline. After one year, he is taken to see the abbot. The abbot smiles and gestures for Tom to speak the two words allotted to him. "Bed hard," he says. The abbot nods and waves for two monks to escort Tom back to his room.

Another year of rigorous silence passes. This time, Tom tells the Abbot, "Food cold." The abbot nods as before, and once again Tom is escorted back to his room.

One more wordless year with the cold food and the hard bed, and Tom has had it. His tells the abbot, "I quit."

"Well, good riddance," says the abbot. "All you ever do is complain."

Forgiving God

Normally, it is we who ask God to forgive us. But if you've been harboring resentment toward God for all the unjust pain you've been forced to endure, perhaps it's time for *you* to forgive.

If you're having trouble taking that step, remember that the one who benefits most from any act of forgiveness is the forgiver. Think of forgiving as "for giving"—not to someone else, but to yourself. Forgiving God will liberate you from the bitter blame that poisons your body, corrupts your mind and stifles your spirit. However, you can't achieve genuine forgiveness unless you first give voice to your pent-up rage. Faking it will only exacerbate your internal conflict and result in incomplete healing. So, before you dismiss the issue with a quick, "OK, God, I forgive you," make sure you have completely expunged your anger. Here are two safe ways to find release.

WRITE A LETTER TO GOD

Write God a letter expressing all your outrage, all your fury, all your indignation. Don't hold anything back. Don't be concerned with spelling, grammar or even coherence. Don't be concerned with truth either, except for your emotional truth. The purpose is to vent your anger, not to make sense. No one but you need ever read this letter; you can tear it up as soon as you're done if you like.

Be sure to use strong, explicit language. Cite examples of why you're mad. Explain why you think you deserve better. Tell God how you think the universe should be run.

No matter how ridiculous you may think it is to be dumping on God, keep going. Don't stop the first time you think you've said it all—or the second, or the third. Go deeper into your feelings, and deeper still. Wherever there is anger, there is hurt beneath it. Dig down and tap into your innermost pain, so you can get it out of your system. You may be surprised by how deep the well of your bitterness runs. If you need to take a break, do so. But come back to the writing, and don't stop until you feel spent.

RELEASE THE ENERGY OF RAGE

Sometimes, we need a more muscular release than writing permits. For the extra healing that a physical catharsis affords, place some thick pillows or a mattress in a private place, where you won't disturb anyone or attract unwanted attention. Arrange the target so that you can comfortably bash it with your fists or with a child's wiffle bat made of plastic or foam.

Assume a balanced stance—standing, sitting or kneeling, whichever you prefer—so you can swing your arms easily without falling. Take a few deep breaths and let loose. Pound away with all your might. And, while you're flailing away, unleash your anger verbally as well. Yell at God. Roar. Curse. Shriek. Throw a tantrum. "Why, God, why?" "How could you let this happen to me?" "I don't deserve this!" If you're concerned about being heard, put on some loud music to drown out your voice. Just don't suppress anything. Bash until you are exhausted, and when you're done, pamper yourself and get plenty of rest.

You might find yourself resisting this exercise. It might feel blasphemous to use God as a punching bag and to shout God's name in vain. If you truly regard this as offensive to your religious precepts, by all means do not do it. But if you're resisting only because it feels foolish, consider fighting through that self-consciousness. If you're resisting because you're afraid God will punish you if you go ahead with it, why not take a chance? Remember, this is to help you heal your conflict with God so you can trust the universe again. Finding out that it's OK to be angry at God may, in itself, be a big step toward making peace.

One caveat: If you find the exercise too physically taxing, or if you have heart disease, back pain or any other condition that would make it risky, do something less demanding, such as squeezing a stuffed doll, stomping on a cardboard box while seated or throwing something against a wall. Also, if you are feeling emotionally unstable, do the exercise in the presence of a psychotherapist or a trusted friend.

Declare Your Forgiveness

If you are ready to forgive God, you will benefit from doing so in a formal manner. You can say it out loud, you can voice it in the silence of your mind or you can write it out in the form of a letter. You might also want to create a ritual to accompany your statement of forgiveness: light a candle, ring a bell, bang a drum, make an offering to the wind or a body of water, whatever seems appropriate to mark the occasion.

It bears repeating that you are doing this for the sake of your own mental, physical and spiritual health. Therefore, express yourself completely. Say what must be said, and say it in your own personal style. To help you think your statement through, here is an example of a forgiveness letter written by a man named Terrance, whose journey from rage to acceptance began when multiple sclerosis robbed him of his livelihood as a graphic artist, along with the pleasures of tennis and dancing and romping with his grandchildren:

Dear God,

I forgive you. I was mad at you for afflicting me with a terrible disease and taking away the things I thought were most important. I felt sorry for myself. I cursed you. But I have gotten past my anger now, and I have come to accept that I was wrong about you. I thought you were some mean old man sitting around heaven, tossing lightning bolts on your creatures whenever you got bored, or felt offended or just wanted to scare us into submission. I see you differently now. I don't understand you, but I never will, and I feel humbled by that limitation.

I don't know why I have MS. I don't know if there is any purpose to it. I don't know why anything happens. But I've already learned an awful lot about myself and life, and for that I'm grateful. I don't feel like a vic-

tim anymore. I'm ready to take responsibility to handle whatever comes my way with all the strength, dignity and wisdom I can muster—and use it all to further my spiritual growth.

I realize that it's kind of bigheaded of me to say I forgive you. Who am I to presume such a thing? I'm the one who should apologize, I know that. But I need to do this for my own healing. I'm sure you understand, so I hope it gives you a good laugh. Meanwhile, I'm determined to make the most of my life with the time I have left. Can we work together on that? I'll be in touch a lot more often from now on.

With love,
Terrance

Reconciling with God

Though he slay me, yet will I trust in him.

JOB 13:15

Forgiveness is one thing, reconciliation is quite another. When relationships are disturbed by conflict, it is entirely possible to forgive, and to resolve the dispute to everyone's satisfaction—and still not reconcile. Resolution is always possible; it is an inner process by which an individual comes to terms with the issues involved. Reconciliation, however, is *not* always possible. It requires that *both* parties be willing to take whatever steps are needed to put the conflict to rest. For that to happen, the one who feels injured must feel safe enough to trust again. It is very similar when you're at odds with God—only where God is concerned, the only obstacle to reconciliation is you. Are you willing to trust again?

Albert Einstein once said that there is only one real question: Do we live in a friendly universe? If you are still not ready to reconcile with God, it might be because you suspect that the universe is unfriendly. Why not have a candid conversation with God as a step toward restoring your trust?

Set aside fifteen or twenty minutes when you won't be disturbed. Sit in a comfortable chair or on a meditation pillow. Lower the lights, or perhaps burn a candle. Loosen your belt and your collar. Close your eyes. Use whatever form of relaxation you are familiar with—meditation, deep breathing, prayer or any other practice that enables you to quiet your mind and calm your body.

When you feel deeply relaxed, begin to speak to God. You can do it out loud or internally, whichever feels more suitable to you. You may want to lift your head and speak your words as if to heaven, or kneel with folded hands or simply sit in a comfortable position. You may choose to mentally focus on an image of the Divine—Buddha or Jesus or a favorite saint or spiritual master— or place an image before you and open your eyes to speak to it. Or you may simply speak to the formless, boundless God in the chapel of your soul. However you elect to communicate, do it from the heart. Speak your deepest thoughts and your deepest feelings. Tell God why you're having difficulty trusting. What do you fear might happen if you were to let down your guard? Why does the universe appear to be unfriendly?

You might become aware that you are saying more about yourself than you are about God. This is, of course, one of the purposes of the exercise: to unveil the emotional roots of your mistrust and the misconceptions you may be harboring. You may, for example, realize that you have trouble trusting anyone or anything, perhaps because your childhood was marked by unpredictability, danger or abuse. You might discover that you've had an immature view of God. Continue to speak until you have unburdened your mind and heart.

When you feel you have said enough, pose a question to God. Ask if it is safe for you to trust.

Now sit still, with eyes closed, and wait. Without trying to control or manipulate your thoughts, keep your attention on the area around your heart. Be as receptive as possible. In time, you might hear an inner voice that sounds different from your own—or one that sounds exactly like your own. You might not hear words at all. Instead, you might sense some kind of presence, or notice physical sensations in different parts of your body, or find that various emotions arise in a trickle or a flood. Consider whatever comes up to be a response to your remarks—whether you view it as a direct communiqué from

God or a bubbling up of your subconscious. Whatever you choose to call it, look for the sense of the message. Is it telling you that it's OK for you to trust because the universe is, at its core, a friendly place?

Pain Is Inevitable;
Suffering Is Optional

Cast thy burden upon the Lord and He shall sustain thee.

PSALMS 55:22

Pain, sorrow and loss may be inevitable. Suffering can be useful and purposeful. But we are not *meant* to suffer. It is not necessary, and it need not be a permanent feature of our lives.

It may seem at times that the universe is not only unfriendly but cruel. However, if the mystics and masters who have penetrated the depths of reality are to be believed—and if the ordinary individuals who have tasted union with God can be considered reliable—then we have to conclude that the universe is not only friendly but radiant with love and peace, even as the surface whirls in apparent chaos and destruction. You will recall that God does not answer Job's questions about suffering. Rather, God *is* the answer. The sages have told us this in no uncertain terms: our suffering is not caused by God's volition like a fire is caused by an arsonist's match or the cry of a child by a parent's spanking. On the contrary, God is both the peaceful refuge to which we all have access and the source of the strength and wisdom we need to deal with life's pain.

It bears repeating that we suffer in direct proportion to our degree of separation from the Divine. It is when we are disconnected from our spiritual essence that the agonies and tragedies of worldly life overshadow the bliss that is our birthright. "Men are not in hell because God is angry with them," wrote the eighteenth-century British theologian William Law, "they are in wrath and darkness because they have done to the light, which infinitely flows forth from God, as that man does to the light of the sun who puts out his own eyes."

In short, if the cause of darkness is the absence of light, the remedy is its presence; the closer we move toward the source, the greater the light. In the view of every wisdom tradition, the essence of the universe is love and light and goodness. Our grand purpose is to awaken to our essential nature, which is the very same love and light and goodness.

Buddha's Third Noble Truth is that the suffering described in the First and Second Noble Truths can be overcome through the eradication of craving and attachment, in the state of supreme peace called *nirvana*. The Fourth is the Buddhist formula for achieving it, known as the Eightfold Path. Similarly, Hindus would say that suffering ends with the achievement of *moksha*, or enlightenment, in which the ego-self with which we've identified gives way to the Self we share with all that is, and whose very nature is bliss. Because we live in the realm of change and duality, life will offer up a mix of joys and sorrows, pleasures and pains. But the *suffering* that comes from identification with the ego and attachment to the objects of desire can be dissolved in the pure light and love of the Divine.

The holy ones, the saintly ones, do not know suffering as we do. They age, they ail, they lose, they fail, they die, but their inner core is never anything but at one with the Holy Essence. They dwell in the bosom of an all-encompassing bliss that both transcends and includes the ups and downs of relative existence. They are, in the metaphor of the Bhagavad Gita, like candles in a windless place, immovable in their inner peace and incorruptible by loss and gain, pleasure and pain. Secure in the protective embrace of divine love, they bear silent witness to the tribulations of life even as they respond to them.

There are, of course, degrees of attainment, and the path to enlightenment can be long and sometimes rocky. It would be naive to assume that devotion to God, or the use of spiritual technologies, will dispel the darkness overnight or guarantee a quick end to suffering. Turning to the light will not bring back the dead spouse, the burned-down house, the lost fortune or the once-healthy body. Nor will it instantly obliterate the grief of those losses. But peace can be found in the moment, and the existential despair that turns temporary pain into long-term suffering can be ended. The miracle is that, even in the midst of immense distress, human beings have managed to find the light.

Even in the horror of horrors that was Auschwitz. "In spite of all the enforced physical and mental primitiveness of the life in a concentration camp, it was possible for spiritual life to deepen," writes Viktor Frankl, a Holocaust survivor who became a well-known psychiatrist. He observed that certain inmates "were able to retreat from their terrible surroundings to a life of inner riches and spiritual freedom." Those fortunate souls, he adds, were able to endure the torment of the camps better than the other inmates. Frankl describes his own moment of epiphany, during forced labor in a trench, as he searched his soul to find a reason for his suffering: "In a last violent protest against the hopelessness of imminent death, I sensed my spirit piercing through the enveloping gloom. I felt it transcend that hopeless, meaningless world, and from somewhere I heard a victorious 'Yes' in answer to my question of the existence of an ultimate purpose."

5.
AM I GOOD ENOUGH, GOD?

Accepting Our Sins and Imperfections

Help me to banish from myself whatever is mean, ugly, callous,
stubborn or otherwise unworthy of a being created in your image.

YOM KIPPUR PRAYER

Eventually, God brings us all to our knees. The question is, will you sink to your knees in humiliation, or will you kneel, gently and gracefully, in humility? Will you turn toward God with eyes lowered in guilt or with eyes upraised in trust?

It is a sad commentary on modern religion that there is far more humiliation than humility in our pulpits and pews. All too often, institutions that were intended to lead people to the peace, love and freedom of the Divine have, instead, herded them into cages of guilt, shame and fear. In the cacophony of contradictory messages—unconditional love versus harsh judgment; forgiveness versus punishment; mercy versus wrath—the punitive chorus has outshouted the music of love.

We are told what God expects of us and how a good and righteous person ought to behave. Unfortunately, the descriptions never look like us. What *does* look like us is the list of offenses that are said to provoke a divine slap on the wrist or a card that says "Go Directly to Hell. Do Not Pass Go." Not just the Ten Commandments, and not just the seven deadlies of pride, covetousness, lust, envy, gluttony, anger and sloth, but a cornucopia of sins and transgressions so comprehensive that anyone who does not check off at least a few is certainly guilty of lying. At a recent prayer service at a mainstream New England church, for example, the congregation called upon God to deliver them from the following: cowardice, laziness and arrogance; lack of reverence; trite ideals and cheap pleasures; vulgarity, cynicism, intolerance and cruel indifference; being dull, pompous or rude; selfishness and self-indulgence; greed, apathy, bigotry and bloated pride; addiction to achievement and accumulation; idolatries of pleasure and youth; hopelessness; lack of faith in times of crisis; and "everything in us that may hide your light."

At a Yom Kippur service in California, the congregants asked to be forgiven for, "The sin we have committed against You, under duress or by choice . . . consciously or unconsciously . . . openly or secretly . . . in our thought . . . with our words . . . by the abuse of power . . . by hardening our hearts . . . by profaning Your name . . . by disrespect for parents and teachers . . . by speaking slander . . . by dishonesty in our work . . . by hurting others in any way." The prayer went on to name a few dozen sins, including: pretending to emotions we do not feel, using the sins of others to excuse our own, denying responsibility for our own misfortunes, turning a deaf ear to the cry of the oppressed, poisoning the air and polluting land and sea, confusing love with lust, malicious gossip, gluttony, fraud and falsehood, arrogance, insolence, irreverence, hypocrisy, passing judgment, exploiting the weak, giving way to hostile impulses and "running to do evil."

All religions, of course, feature codes of behavior. The holy Koran contains nearly a hundred terms for offenses against God, and every Muslim is taught the principal guidelines for walking "the straight path" that earns a soul a good accounting on the Day of Judgment. In Judaism, there are 613 *mitzvoth* (commandments) specified in the Torah, of which 365 are prohibitions and 248 are positive actions. Hinduism's "six enemies of the soul" are close to the West's deadly sins: lust, anger, covetousness, inordinate affection, pride and envy. These are complemented by the five *yamas*, or virtues: truthfulness, nonviolence, non-stealing, continence and detachment from possessions and desires. The "five hindrances" of Buddhism are sensual desire, hatred, sloth, restlessness and doubt; the basic obligation of a Buddhist layperson ("right behavior") is to follow the "five precepts," which boil down to refraining from the following: harming any living being, taking anything not given, misconduct involving sensory pleasures, false speech and the abuse of alcohol or drugs.

Religious standards lift our gaze to the best in us. They lend cohesion to society and structure to individual behavior. As Tevye says in *Fiddler on the Roof*, "Because of our traditions, everyone knows who he is and what God expects of him." Unfortunately, the heavy-handed methods by which the codes have often been imposed have led to widespread guilt, shame and fear.

Missing the Mark

Sin is whatever obscures the soul.

ANDRE GIDE

It could be argued that the original intent of religious do's and don'ts was spiritual pragmatism: to bring an individual closer to union with the Divine by encouraging behaviors that enhance that connection and discouraging those that foster separation. The word "sin" derives from roots meaning "to miss," or "to be off the mark," as in missing the road or shooting off target in archery. To sin, therefore, is to do things that detract or deviate from the direct path to God-realization. Even prescriptions that were clearly intended to promote family and social cohesion — rules against adultery, for example — can be seen in that light, as creating a stable framework conducive to spiritual engagement. The Bible is fairly consistent in describing God as turning "his face" away from sinners and toward those who atone or repent. Indeed, those two words, atone and repent, are suggestive of getting back on the mark. The Middle English root of atone is *atonem*, to reconcile, which comes from "at one." Repent has been said to derive from either the Hebrew word meaning "return" or the Greek root for "change of mind," hence returning to God or shifting the mind's orientation from the profane to the sacred.

Seen in this way, sin is like a plug in the permeable membrane between individual consciousness and its divine source, a self-created barrier to spiritual progress—like driving recklessly or failing to service your car before a road trip. Most religious edicts focus on rejecting the cravings of the lesser self and embracing the promptings of the Higher Self. They mean to turn us away from ego-centered thoughts and actions, away from attachment to personal desires, away from the feverish pursuit of sensual pleasures and worldly possessions. "There is no greater trouble for thee than thine own self," said the Muslim mystic Abu Sa'id, "for when thou art occupied with thyself, thou remainest away from God." We are directed to perform actions that are in accord with "the will of God"—or, in Eastern terms, in line with *dharma*, the evolutionary direction of life—and to not do that which bumps us out of line. Because they keep us apart from the sacred, sins are, in effect, their own punishment; we are punished *by* sin more than *for* sin. "On thy heart is rust on rust collected," says Rumi of one who sins, "so that thou art blind to divine mysteries."

Somewhere along the way, however, the concept of sin itself got off the mark. For one thing, the notion was advanced that human beings are not only capable of sin but *born* in sin, thanks to our disobedient forebears, Adam and Eve. A creation story rich in symbolism and pregnant with possibilities for uplifting interpretations became instead a tale of disobedience and banishment, of debt incurred through disrespect and passed down in perpetuity generation after generation. As a result, millions were taught as children that we are inherently corrupt and can be saved only by the grace of a deity who monitors our every thought. This stands in striking contrast to teachings—often from the very same traditions—whose core premise is that we are blessed beings, eternally embraced by divine love.

SIN AND SEX, SHOULDS AND SHOULDN'TS

Another funny thing happened on the way to the twenty-first century: sin became virtually synonymous with sex. How this came to be is a matter for historians to determine. In addition to the obvious function of stabilizing families, one possible origin of religious sexual codes was to encourage followers—monks and nuns in particular—to direct their sexual energy upward, away from the instinctual urge for procreation and physical gratification to the higher centers of love and spiritual awakening. Various Tantric and Taoist sexual practices are designed to do exactly that. So are, less directly, meditative disciplines in other traditions. Over time, however, sexual rules became ends in themselves, turning into moral obligations whose violation was considered a grave offense against God and elevated to special status as carnal sins, often accompanied by harsh reprisals. Such is the alchemy of repression that religious institutions trying to regulate the reproductive drive and the natural desire for pleasure became obsessed by sex, like individuals trying to diet who can think of little else but food.

The sad result of that legacy is that millions of people have suffered the torment of ostracism or private hellfire because they engaged in forbidden sexual relations or acts that were regarded as depraved or perverted, or merely had thoughts and fantasies that are now portrayed with impunity on MTV. In some cases, simply "touching yourself" damned you to the flames of hell unto eternity. The shame attached to these most natural of God-given urges may have contributed to the social epidemic of depression. And it continues to this day. Despite the sexual revolution, women's liberation and years of lusty in-your-face exposure of body parts, a significant percentage of those who seek psychotherapy are dealing with guilt, shame and various dysfunctions surrounding sex. Ironically, it could be argued that the sexual excess that so troubles the religious community is, in large part, an unintended consequence of the linkage of sex and sin, a massive acting out. It is only natural for pleasure-seeking, passionate spirits in human form—especially young ones—to counter repression with expression, oppression with obsession and forced compliance with forceful defiance.

The end result, for both conservative moralists and licentious sensualists, has been a break in the wholeness of being. Except perhaps for monks and nuns, a body-denying spirituality is not a complete spirituality. "Spirituality must also be sensuous," Deepak Chopra has pointed out, "because a spiritual person is one who lives fully in the present moment, which means living fully in the body." Somewhere between suppression and obsessive indulgence is a sensible middle way for every sensual seeker of peace with God.

Such has been the fate of many shalt and shalt nots, sexual and otherwise. Dr. Karen Horney called it "the tyranny of the shoulds." The rules may once have been guidelines for social harmony and spiritual advancement, but over time they were converted into legal codes and backed by the threat of draconian enforcement: Do as you're told, or else you'll be punished. Why? Because God allegedly wants it that way. The uncompromising severity of domination and damnation has overshadowed the unconditional love at the heart of the religious impulse. Sadly, instead of drawing people closer to the Divine, this punitive approach shreds them with shame and guilt, driving millions away from religious participation and preventing many who feel the calling from entering the clergy. "The best that can be said for ritualistic legalism is that it improves conduct," said Aldous Huxley. "It does little, however, to alter character and nothing of itself to modify consciousness."

The Fear of God

"Fear of God" and "God-fearing" have been used as terms of praise for centuries, far more so, tragically, than "God-loving." In a moral universe, a certain amount of holy dread is a useful defense mechanism; when we're tempted to cross the line, it's good to remember that we reap what we sow. Certainly, society as a whole stands to benefit; without a medicinal dose of cosmic fear, the dark side might run amok. But when trepidation gets implanted in the psyche like an artificial organ, causing widespread apprehension, the universe turns into a giant police state. As a rule, spiritual awareness does not have room to soar in a police state.

Fear can be understood as an acronym: False Expectations Appearing Real. The dominant religious voices have made the expectation of punishment appear more real than love, and if the holy ones who have become intimate with the Divine are to be believed, that is false, because God's very essence is love. How can we open up to the Sacred when we're afraid that the universe is not safe and that God can't be trusted unless we're perfect? How can we welcome the Divine when we are hiding, like Adam in the garden? Instead, we contract our spirits like slugs compress their bodies when they sense danger. We dig moats around our hearts. We bar the doors and windows of our senses. We turn our minds into watchdogs. This perpetual vigilance floods the system with the chemistry of anxiety and drowns the music of the soul like an alarm bell in a concert hall.

Evidence suggests that the original meaning of the phrase that has come down to us as "fear of God" was something more like *awe*. And awe, wrote Abraham Joshua Heschel, "enables us to perceive in the world intimations of the divine, to sense in small things the beginning of infinite significance, to sense the ultimate in the common and the simple; to feel in the rush of the passing the stillness of the eternal." In the presence of that kind of vision, what can we possibly be afraid of? Instead of awe, however, we have trembling. "The most important moment in my spiritual life," said a former nun who is now a social worker in Seattle, "was when I went from God-fearing to God-revering. I realized that God is not a threatening figure but one that I can turn to with trust and openness."

If God can be said to have a parental personality, do we really think our Heavenly Father wants us to spend our precious time on earth walking on eggshells rather than dancing for joy? Do we truly believe that our Divine Mother wants us to be paralyzed by apprehension rather than electrified by wonder? Is that what you would want for *your* children?

"Am I Worthy?"

Perhaps the victory of religious legalism came about because of honest misinterpretations by well-meaning authorities. Perhaps it was the result of a paternalistic belief that weak-willed humans had to be protected from their base instincts. Or perhaps, as many believe, it was a cynical attempt to control populations of believers and sustain the power of religious institutions. That issue is best left to historians. What is not debatable is that structures that ought to be sanctuaries of love and kindness are often factories of anguish, where millions of worshippers are told that they are depraved by virtue of their very existence, and that every natural urge, wayward thought and ungenerous feeling is an offense to God.

This mocks the Creator as either cruel or irrational. Why would the Great Designer make us imperfect only to punish us for not being perfect? In the film *Devil's Advocate*, written by Jonathan Lemkin and Tony Gilroy, the Devil, played by Al Pacino as a high-powered New York attorney, accuses God of being a prankster. "He gives man instincts," he bellows. "He gives you this extraordinary gift, and what does he do? I swear, for his own amusement, his own private, cosmic gag reel, he sets the rules in opposition. It's the goof of all time: look but don't touch; touch but don't taste; taste, don't swallow. And while you're jumping from one foot to the next, what does he do? He's laughing his sick, freakin' head off. He's a tight-ass. He's a sadist. He's an absentee landlord."

Of course, that over-the-top appraisal is missing the other half of the religious equation: that God loves and forgives us all. It is a sad truth, however, that despite that promise, millions continue to feel unworthy. "I don't deserve God's love," they tell themselves. "I don't measure up to God's standards. I blew my chances of getting to heaven." Why does this self-disdain persist? For one thing, the religious emphasis in the West has been works oriented: to earn God's love and approval you must do good works and obey the commandments.

Another reason for the persistence of self-recrimination is that people just can't forgive themselves, no matter how much they are told that they are forgiven. They feel they have to pay a high price for their sins, and they can't quite believe that God would let them off the hook that easily. Perhaps they are repeating to themselves the threats they heard from clergy and God-fearing parents, who projected their own private torments in messages such as, "You can't hide anything from God," and "God will punish you for that." But perhaps the most important reason, one we will return to later in the chapter, is that for most believers, the love of God is merely a concept, an article of faith, not their actual experience. They hope to receive it one day, when God decides they deserve it; they were never told that it's closer than their breath.

Religion has certainly kept many people sane who otherwise would not have been. It has helped to regulate some of our baser instincts. But when you're asked to live up to role models like Moses, Muhammad and Jesus, it's easy to drive yourself crazy trying to get it right. Love my enemies? Do good to those who hate me? Speak well of those who speak badly of me? No problemo. Piece of cake! That burden is a principal reason why many God-seekers have drifted from the religion of their birth. Some find a new home in a kinder, gentler parish. Others switch denominations or convert to a new religion entirely or adopt an offbeat path. One reason that so many Americans are drawn to the East, for example, is that the message they hear is refreshing: that we all possess—indeed we all *are* at the core of our being—buddha-nature or *sat-chit-ananda* (absolute bliss consciousness), and sins are mistakes we make because we're evolving souls for whom earth is a place to grow.

The absence of judgmentalism is one reason why millions have found homes in 12-Step programs. There, they are told not that they're evil but merely powerless; they see that no matter what they've done, they are accepted; and they learn that the Higher Power they turn themselves over to forgives, understands and helps them to gain strength. "I got tired of feeling worse after church than before I got there," says Suzie Baker*, who grew up in a Congregational church in Ohio. As a child, she saw the horizontal limb of the cross as a symbol of God's open arms. By her late teens, she came to see it as a "Keep Out" sign, as if the church were a barrier to salvation not the entryway. "At the time, I was secretly in love with an older boy," she recalls, "and the sermons made me feel dirty." Her urge to flee took wing when the minister turned out to be having an affair. There is nothing like clerical hypocrisy or a juicy scandal to prompt a worshipper to take her doubt and discontent elsewhere. Nearly twenty years of personal turmoil later, Suzie found a spiritual home that suited her: Overeaters Anonymous. "That's where God is," she says. "In the twelve steps, in the turning over, in the people—men and women who suffer like me, who teach me what humility is and accept me totally as I am."

Regardless of one's affiliation (or *non*affiliation), everyone who takes spirituality seriously has at some time felt undeserving or inadequate. We all know what it's like to be off the mark, to feel that our actions are slowing down our progress or keeping at arm's length the peace and bliss we seek. We all struggle to tame our venal thoughts and egocentric instincts and to align ourselves with the noble values of our Higher Selves. No matter what your chosen path, therefore, it is not always easy to measure up to its highest standards—or your own standards—and the common result is self-punishment.

Certainly, there is spiritual advantage in trying to live up to elevated values. And it is certainly important to hold ourselves accountable for our actions. But without self-compassion and self-forgiveness, we can't change in a meaningful way. If sin is that which keeps us separate from the Divine, then shame is a sin, and guilt is a sin and fear is a sin, for they build walls between us and all that is holy. For many of us, therefore, it is necessary to rid ourselves of the emotional baggage we're hauling around before we can raise our eyes to God in the spirit of peace and reverence.

The Lie of Shame

It is time to forget the shame of your younger days.

ISAIAH 54:4

You may be thinking, what's wrong with shame? Isn't it useful? Doesn't guilt serve a purpose? To fully understand why those emotions take us further from peace with God, it is important to define exactly what they are and what they are not.

When we speak of the virtues of shame or guilt, we are usually thinking of something that has a better name: remorse. Remorse is a healthy emotion. Rooted in moral conscience and triggered by a sense of distress over a wrong we've committed, it enables us to feel regret, apologize for our actions and make amends. Without the capacity for remorse, we would not be able to recognize our mistakes and learn from them.

Guilt is similar to remorse in that it stems from the conscious acknowledgment of a misdeed. However, in psychological terms, remorse is constructive whereas guilt is nothing more than self-inflicted punishment you don't deserve. In many cases, the sentence is so severe that it amounts to emotional incarceration for life.

Shame is even more penetrating. We feel it not for what we've done but for what we *are*. Shame doesn't say you made a mistake; it says you *are* a mistake. It says, "You're a sham. You're despicable. You're flawed, worthless and unlovable."

Like all emotions, shame exists on a continuum. To some extent, it is part of the human condition; like the common cold, it afflicts even the healthiest of us on occasion. For others, shame is more like a chronic disease that never quite goes away and flares up frequently, with disabling symptoms. And for far too many, shame is an emotional cancer, a painful malignancy that eats away at the spirit and gnaws at the soul. At its worst, shame inflicts a self-loathing so intense that you feel you don't deserve the respect or concern of anyone, not even God.

The difference between remorse and shame is similar to that of self-esteem and self-worth. We measure our self-esteem by our deeds. It is something we earn, and it rises and falls depending on how we assess our impact on the world. Self-worth, on the other hand, is a measure of our intrinsic value. It is something we deserve by virtue of our very existence as beings born with the spark of the Divine. When people with a healthy sense of worth make mistakes or cause pain to others, their self-esteem may suffer a temporary blow, but their fundamental worth does not budge an inch. Not so those who are wrapped in the shackles of shame. They not only have a deficiency of self-worth, they have accepted the lie that they are worth*less*. They can't forgive themselves for even minor misdeeds, and if they're religious, they are sure that God won't forgive them either, no matter how much they repent. Shame-based people can't accept God's love because deep down they feel they don't deserve it.

The seeds of shame are usually planted early in life, long before we can even discern the word "God," let alone imagine what a supreme being might be like. When an infant's needs are not attended to, when he is unwanted or resented, when she does not receive the all-embracing love she deserves and needs, the primal pain of having been yanked from the blissful womb is compounded. At around eighteen months, when we start to become aware that we are unique individuals with our own thoughts and feelings, we comprehend the word "No" for the first time. From then on we get scolded or punished for doing things the wrong way. If a child is cared for properly, the pain of those inevitable moments of negation is like the prick of a vaccination—short-lived, soothed by the balm of parental love and ultimately strengthening. Those inoculations of medicinal shame form the bedrock of self-discipline and moral responsibility. But if the required lessons are dispensed harshly, with threats or abuse, the result is not a protective immunization but a weakening dose of toxic shame.

Children personalize everything. If they don't feel safe, loved and attended to, they know something is wrong. But they can't attribute blame to the omnipotent parents who are supposed to protect them; that would mean they are totally alone, and the sense of danger would be unbearable. Therefore, they conclude, "It must be *me*. If Mommy and Daddy are upset, it must be *my* fault." Because they can't distinguish between what they do and what they are, children interpret a parent's angry disapproval not as, "I shouldn't do that," but rather as, "I'm bad."

If this happens often enough, and with sufficient intensity, a deep, abiding sense of shame takes root in the psyche. As a child matures in self-awareness, the internalized shame gets reinforced every time something goes wrong: "I'm no good. I'm worthless. I don't deserve love." The deeper those early impressions are etched in memory, the more vulnerable we are to the onslaughts of shame that come later on, as we develop our sense of individuality and more is expected of us. In late childhood, as our understanding of right and wrong matures, the rules of the game become more explicit and more exacting. Some parents have reasonable expectations, and lovingly and patiently help their children learn from mistakes. But demanding parents with unrealistic standards respond to disappointments harshly, as if their own well-being depended on their child's perfection. That kind of treatment, especially if accompanied by rage or abuse, reinforces the child's sense that he or she is fundamentally defective.

The pummeling of a young psyche with fistfuls of shame can, of course, take place perfectly well in the absence of religion. Secular families are quite capable of inflicting psychic damage. But when God is part of the family portrait, the children of shame project their feelings about their parents and, in some cases, religious authorities, onto the Almighty. God becomes a frightening figure who must be obeyed, appeased and placated at all cost. This is especially true if God is used as a disciplinary tool: "Don't do that. God won't like it!" "God will send you straight to hell if you keep that up." "You can't hide from God, he sees everything." If such parental messages are supplemented by fire-and-brimstone sermons or Sunday school lessons that underscore the high price of disobedience, the image of a punitive God can hover over a maturing psyche like the sword of Damocles.

With the onset of puberty and adolescent angst, the opportunities for shame to perpetuate become endless. The pressure to measure up gets more and more intense, and the comparison to peers is relentless. We want to tell those dumb adults what they can do with their moronic rules and their invisible God, who's stricter than the minister and the school principal combined, and a whole lot more powerful. But what if they're right? What if God is marking down everything I do on my permanent record? At the same time the hormone hurricane whips up shameful urges, disgusting thoughts and forbidden fantasies—selfish, aggressive and, above all, sexual—every one of which God, that omnipresent Peeping Tom, can see as clearly as we see a TV screen.

To alleviate their pain and fear, shame-driven teens make one of two basic vows to themselves: either to do exactly what is expected of them to earn love and acceptance or to get revenge by doing exactly the opposite. Unfortunately, neither alternative brings them freedom from shame. Quite the contrary, in fact. It makes them slaves to a psychic contract that does not resemble their true selves.

If the waves of shame have been moderate and we've been able to ride them safely to a more loving shore, we land in adulthood with confidence, self-respect and inner strength. When we commit an unethical or immoral act, we accept responsibility, face the consequences, forgive ourselves and move on, having learned another valuable lesson. But if we land on the beach of independent life battered and bruised by tsunamis of shame, every subsequent setback, every rejection, every failure, every questionable act and sinful thought will reactivate our self-disdain and our fear of divine wrath.

THE WOUNDING WAVES OF SHAME

The effect of shame on every aspect of the Quintessential Self can be enormously damaging. *Physically*, the stress of each new collision, whether inflicted by others or self-imposed, unleashes a flood of adrenaline, cortisol and other substances that can, in excess, lead to a variety of illnesses later in life. The altered biochemistry can also create a state of agitation that disallows the inner peace we associate with the presence of God.

Mentally, the stress chemicals from chronic shame can alter the brain, even to the point of killing neurons and lowering IQ. Excessive amounts of adrenaline and cortisol not only reduce learning ability, memory and other higher functions, but they bend the direction of our thoughts toward fear, hostility and self-loathing. To every legitimate desire, the voice of shame whispers, "Forget it. You don't deserve it. You're worthless." That voice can easily be mistaken for the voice of God.

Emotionally, internalized shame is crippling. In an effort to protect ourselves from the pain of feeling defective, deficient and despicable, we numb our feelings. That numbness, however, also shuts us off from pleasure, happiness and love. It can lead to chronic depression or perpetual anxiety, or both. Gratitude, veneration and other emotions associated with devotion to God may be attempted and displayed, but they can't be authentically felt when deep down we don't feel worthy of such exalted feelings.

Relationally, the messy tension of human interaction, and the spotlight that relationships shed on our weaknesses and flaws, serves to reinforce the shame-based person's sense of inadequacy. They either become meek doormats or tyrants who project their self-loathing onto others and lash out at the slightest provocation. It is difficult, if not impossible, to treat others in accordance with the highest ideals of spirituality if you can't treat yourself with kindness. How can you see the divinity in others if you can't see it in yourself?

Spiritually, shame is toxic to the soul. It stifles the capacity for awe, wonder, joy and reverence. It not only shuts the door on peace, it can force you to shy away from the Divine altogether, like a naughty child who's scared to face her parents. Shame makes you afraid to be seen by God, and that is a crying shame, because home sweet home for the soul is to be face-to-face with the Holy.

FROM COMPLIANCE AND DEFIANCE TO ALLIANCE

To practice a religion can be lovely.
To believe in one is almost always disastrous.

TOM ROBBINS

With respect to religious involvement, shame (and chronic guilt as well) typically leads first to compliance and then to defiance. Shame-based people tend to cling to the bosom of an institution, either because its welcoming social climate alleviates some of their internal pain or because they see it as their only hope of salvation. Within the church or temple community, some may also become obsessive do-gooders in an attempt to expiate their shame. But if the shame is deeply ingrained, they find ways to confirm their lack of worth even in the most accepting circumstances. In their minds, they can never live up to the moral standards they internalized from their upbringing and their early religious training.

In many cases, shame takes the person in the opposite direction: rebellion. Some reject the entire package, cutting themselves off not only from the soul-enriching properties of their own traditions but also from *everything* spiritual. Some become perpetual cynics or crass materialists, contemptuous of faith, God and anything resembling religion. Shame-based defiance can even carry a person so far off the mark as to pose a serious danger.

Babak Sayadi's* response to shaming took him to the edge of death, and only something resembling a miracle spared him. When he was born, in London, his prosperous parents were thrilled to finally have a son to go with their three daughters. Earmarked at birth to take over the family business and provide for his extended family in Iran, Babak's preparation included a rigorous education and a solid grounding in morality and discipline. The family was not particularly religious, although Allah was given token recognition in everyday Farsi expressions that meant "God willing" or "God be with you." However, Babak's father had an unbending sense of propriety rooted in Muslim precepts. Believing that his son would grow strong and virtuous if he taught him the rules at an early age, he hammered those principles home relentlessly. His idea of preparing his son for leadership was to constantly push him to do better and never let him rest on his laurels. He could not have known that what he was really telling him was, "You're never quite good enough."

Babak excelled in college, earning degrees in international relations and business management. He had complied at every step, walking the straight and narrow and straining to meet impossible standards. Now, with apprehension, he assumed the position of heir apparent. For a year and a half he performed well by any measure—except that of his father. The absence of paternal approval made Babak increasingly resentful. Then something pushed him over the edge. In an effort to keep an impressive accomplishment from going to Babak's head, his father humiliated him in a board meeting by calling him useless.

Babak left the company, cashed in his trust fund, and used the money to pursue every wicked pleasure he could think of. He flew to rock concerts all over world, consumed every drug he could obtain and cavorted with high-priced call girls and common hookers. He didn't realize it at the time, but his highly visible behavior was a subconscious attempt to give back to his parents the shame they'd inflicted upon him. He also could not have known the terrible price of his debauchery. At one point, feeling weak, he had a physical exam and discovered he was HIV positive. As his T-cell count plunged and opportunistic infections cropped up with alarming regularity, he grew progressively weaker and more and more hopeless. In the mid-1980s, there was not much by way of treatment for AIDS. When he was diagnosed with cancer, he was given three months to live.

Babak put his affairs in order and flew to an island off Thailand to die. He had not given a thought to God since childhood. But now, alone on a remote Asian shore, he vented his rage for being robbed of his life in such a crushing and painful way. The screams he directed at God soon turned 180 degrees: he cursed himself for being selfish and careless, for failing his father, disgracing his family and soiling the moral precepts by which he'd been raised. With tears pouring from his eyes, he pounded the sand with his fists. One of those blows uncovered something buried just beneath the surface. It was a book by the Indian spiritual teacher Bhagwan Shri Rajneesh. That night, in his hotel room, Babak read about a spirituality of inner development vastly different from the piety he equated with religion. Captivated by what he'd read and by the book's discussion of reincarnation, he decided to hold off death as best he could and explore his own spirituality while he still had time.

As he prepared to fly to the Philippines to see a psychic healer, Babak made another fortuitous discovery. While browsing through the books and audiotapes left behind by previous hotel guests, he was drawn to one item: a self-help tape on shame by Lazaris. Within minutes of popping it into his cassette player, he was struck by the lightning of recognition. He saw himself in everything the narrator said. His whole life, he realized, he had been made to feel worthless, not special; debased, not privileged; deficient, not gifted. "I'd been emotionally abused," he says. "The shame was like an ice cold shower running through the center of my being, and all the drugs and sex and jet life was an attempt to break through the numbness." He changed his plans and flew to New York, where he found experts to help him heal his shame. He thought he was preparing spiritually for his next incarnation. He was, but not quite the way he thought. To his astonishment, he was actually beginning a new life in his current form. Now, seventeen years later, the body he expected to lose is still intact, with normal blood counts.

The grateful Babak now sees his entire saga as the work of God, with whom he has developed a working alliance. As part of his healing, he promised that he would dedicate whatever time he had left to doing some good in the world. He is keeping that vow by working with abused children to help them heal their shame.

Whether chronic shame leads to obedient compliance or insolent defiance, the end result is to block access to the most desirable state: alliance. Not necessarily through conformity to a spiritual institution—although reconciliation with your heritage might certainly be part of it—but through the experience of being aligned with God, as befits your birthright.

Smashing the Shackles of Shame

Because we all share in the same humanity, there is
nothing inhuman in sinning, hence nothing to be
ashamed of or to be despised for.

ERICH FROMM

The good news is that shame is a sham. It is not who you are. It is not natural. It is not God's punishment. The voice in your head that says you are shameful is not God's voice. Like everyone else, you may be imperfect, but you are not worthless. Your existence has value and purpose. You deserve the love of the Divine and all of life's blessings.

You may have trouble accepting the statements in the previous paragraph. Shame itself will tell you that they're false. It will find reason after reason, proof after proof, to convince you that you are not good enough. That is the real lie, and it must be countered by the voice of acceptance and love—over and over again if necessary, until that positive, life-affirming message antidotes the toxicity of shame.

If you need a regular reminder of the truth, consider doing what Linda Vincent* did. A flight attendant in the San Francisco area, Linda posted on her front door a note that reads, GOD LOVES YOU. As a convert to Catholicism, she feels that love when she's in church and in private talks with her priest. But she also struggles with "the tension between my current reality and the vision

I have for my life." That vision, for which she has ardently prayed, includes a husband and children. As she inches toward age forty with her dream unful-filled, she sometimes slips into an old habit, rooted in a painful childhood with an alcoholic mother and a workaholic father: she thinks she is not getting what she wants because she's not good enough. Intellectually, she knows that unanswered prayers are not God's punishment for doing something wrong. Still, that shaming voice comes through. The note on the door helps to silence it. "In that moment," she says, "I remember that no matter what may happen as I pass through that door to the outside world, I am a child of God and good enough as I am. How can I not love myself if God loves me?"

GIVING IT BACK

Unlike anger or grief, shame is not a feeling that can be processed and worked with. It has to be expunged from your system by identifying its sources and sending it back to from whence it came.

When you were a child, who implied that you were worthless? Who made you feel unwanted or unlovable? Who neglected you? Abused you? Aban-doned you? In what ways were you humiliated, belittled or demeaned? Who told you that God didn't like you? Who said God would punish you if you weren't good? Later in life, who taunted and teased you? Who told you that you were useless? Who ridiculed your spiritual beliefs or values?

List all the sources of your shame. Include the major perpetrators and the minor offenders; those who gave you the shame virus in the first place and those who subsequently kept it alive. Mother? Stepmother? Father? Step-father? Siblings? Extended family? Clergy? Friends and neighbors? School-teachers? Sunday school teachers? Peers? Bosses? Don't let anyone off the hook.

Once you've identified the origins of your shame, it is extremely important to find a safe way to speak about the shame-inducing experiences of your past. One way to do this is to find someone you trust implicitly—a friend, a pastor, a psychotherapist—and ask for an hour of their time. Your confidant should be someone who will honor your request for confidentiality and never use what you say against you; someone who cares enough to listen patiently and attentively without the need to solve your problems or give unsolicited advice; someone with whom you won't feel inhibited; someone who can let you be emotional without judging you. Tell that person something like this: "I need to share something very personal with you. If I ask for feedback, please give it to me honestly. Otherwise, please be quiet and make it safe for me to share my feelings. Afterward, if you would like to have the same opportunity, I'd be honored to listen to whatever you'd like to share." If you get the go-ahead, find a comfortable, quiet place to tell your story as openly and thoroughly as you can.

If it is at all possible, and only if it can be done in a safe, unthreatening way, expressing your feelings directly to the *source* of your shame can be extremely healing. Brad Hathaway's* story illustrates the value of doing this. As a child in western Pennsylvania, much of Brad's life revolved around the Catholic Church. At age ten, at a Church-sponsored summer camp, he entered the locker room after a swim one day and was greeted by one of the Brothers who ran the program. The Brother told Brad he was special. He caressed him and kissed him, and pulled down his swim trunks. That began a month of molestation. Brad was told that he must keep the encounters a secret. Implied in that demand was both the promise of unspecified favors and the threat of brutal punishment. Confused by how a representative of God could commit what he felt in his bones was a sinful act, Brad convinced himself that he must have done something to deserve it. He buried the memory, but he could not block the numbness and constant nausea. "I had already been taught by serious people dressed in serious black that there are no secrets from God," he says. "I carried the shame with me like a brick around my neck."

That winter it got worse. A priest at school began fondling Brad and other boys while helping them dress for sports and altar boy duties. "Everyone knew what was going on, but no one could say anything," Brad recalls. Eventually, someone must have spoken up, because the priest was suddenly reassigned. His replacement was an exemplary pastor whose loving presence taught Brad that not all priests were dangerous and he could participate in church activities without fear. But the damage was done. "Something had shattered inside of me," says Brad. "I never felt normal after that, and I was too ashamed to speak about it. My denial was a prison of silence."

For the next thirty years, Brad struggled through many failed relationships, two broken engagements, attenuated careers and a nagging, constant depression. "My shame complicated my love life," he says. "I was driven by sex, but I was terrified of commitment and very co-dependent." One night, while driving, he heard a woman on the radio speak about her childhood molestation at the hands of her own father. Her story convinced Brad that he had to deal with his past. Psychotherapy opened the door to healing. "I was able to see the web of shame and self-deceit that had bound me for so long and had consumed so much energy."

When he was in his mid-forties and living in New Mexico, he took another crucial step toward healing his shame. In a letter to the archbishop of the diocese where he grew up, he described his childhood ordeal. The bishop replied with heartfelt concern and offered to have the diocese pay for some of Brad's therapy. Brad was grateful, but he wanted something more: to meet with the men who molested him. The summer camp Brother could not be located, but the priest, now old and contrite and himself in therapy, agreed to a supervised meeting. "It was extremely valuable," says Brad. "I expressed my anger and told him how what he'd done had affected my life. The adult Brad was able to walk into the room with the little child Brad, who was still traumatized and scared, and say to this priest, 'I know what you did to this little boy.'" The priest admitted what he'd done and expressed remorse. "To stand up to him at last and have *him* be the one who was scared—that was all the retribution I needed," says Brad. "I took back the power that had been taken from me as an innocent child."

Brad's healing continues to this day. His spiritual pursuits have given him an alternate vision of who he really is, and therapy has enabled him to work out his anger toward those who presume to represent God on earth. But his successful encounter with the tormentor of his youth was a crucial turning point. It helped to free him from decades of internalized shame.

Before you attempt to face your sources of shame, think it through clearly and seek out expert advice. Make sure you can do it in a way that heals instead

of exacerbates your pain, and make sure it won't cause trouble for innocent by-
standers such as your family or the family of the shamer. If it is impossible to
confront the perpetrator, or if you decide not to do so, it can be just as effective, if not more so, to purge your shame safely with the following exercises. (It
is also extremely helpful to do these *before* an in-person encounter, to vent
some of your fiercest emotions.)

Purging Your Shame

It is vital to release your long-suppressed feelings of rage toward those who
shamed you. The healing power of catharsis has been understood ever since
the word was coined in ancient Greece, and in recent years, scientists have
confirmed its value. Studies show, for instance, that patients who write about
their feelings heal faster from diseases such as asthma and arthritis.

Try writing a letter to each of the shamers in your past. As in the previous
writing exercise, don't hold back; don't censor yourself; don't worry about
spelling, grammar or coherence. The letters are not meant to be read by anyone but you. The purpose is not to hurt anyone or get revenge, but simply to
give you the chance to let out painful feelings that have been festering inside.

Some of the individuals who shamed you may have done so unintention-
ally. They may be otherwise wonderful people who felt they had your best in-
terests at heart. For now, set aside the aspects of their personalities that you love
and respect. You are writing to the parts of them that made the mistake of
shaming you. Give yourself permission to use words you would never speak
aloud. Take on the voice of the child or adolescent who was injured, and accuse them, condemn them and curse them in the strongest possible terms.
Tell them how their actions made you feel at the time and the effect they had
on the rest of your life. Go into as much detail as you can; there is healing
value in specificity.

Write first to the shamers about whom you feel strongest and work your
way down the list. Set aside enough time to complete each letter without feel-

ing rushed or cutting yourself short. You don't have to accomplish it all in one sitting.

Once your letters are done, you may feel the need for a more physical catharsis. As before, discharging your rage can be accomplished safely by pounding a pillow or another soft target with your fists or a plastic bat. Again, separate out the negative aspects of the people who shamed you. Imagine the person's face on the surface of the bashing target (place a photo there if you think it will help) and let loose. (Go back to page 139 for a reminder of other instructions.)

The Ravages of Guilt

Of course [God] will forgive me; that's his business.

LAST WORDS OF HEINRICH HEINE

Like remorse, guilt begins with the conscious recognition of having done something wrong. But, whereas remorse transforms the energy of that awareness into positive, useful action, guilt turns it into a self-destructive force. With guilt, you assign yourself the roles of prosecutor, judge and jury, and sentence yourself to contempt. In most cases, it amounts to cruel and unusual punishment.

As children, we look for signals from our parents to let us know when we're doing right and when we're doing wrong—not just to avoid punishment, but to stay safe in the big, scary world and get the things we want. When parental disapproval is used properly, it builds in the developing child a sense of conscience and the habit of recognizing mistakes and correcting inappropriate behavior. It also installs an internal warning system that tells them when they're about to do something wrong so they can stop themselves in time. However, when parents and others criticize excessively, guilt becomes a coercive means of control. Guilt-trippers tell children, through word and gesture, that if they don't do as they're told, they are, in effect, punishing their parents.

If religion is part of the equation, they might also imply that they're hurting God. As a result, many children carry into adult life a habit of self-blame. They convict themselves of crimes they didn't commit and dish out harsh sentences for minor offenses.

Depending on their religious code, the guilt-prone constantly feel the need to apologize to God for something—if not for selfish or immoral actions, then for the unacceptable thoughts that flash through their minds and which an all-knowing deity must surely overhear (including doubts about that very deity). Guilty thoughts are particularly insidious, since only saints—and probably few of them—escape the spontaneous eruption of hate, greed, envy, lust and other presumable sins. With every transgression—real or imagined, small or large, acted out or merely thought—the habitually guilty project onto God the message they got from their parents: "Look what you've done. How could you let me down like that?" By way of penance, they deprive themselves of life's pleasures and forbid themselves the satisfaction of desires. It's as if making themselves feel guilty were the only way they can convince themselves— and God—that they are worthy of redemption. After all, only a genuinely good person would punish him- or herself for doing wrong.

The propensity to feel guilty before God is often compounded by distorted thought patterns. These include the following:

Self-blaming: You think everything that goes wrong is your fault, and you don't want to be confused by the facts.

Negative scanning: Your radar is always on the alert for sins; positive actions are off the screen.

Exaggeration: You always assume the worst, and you believe that your transgressions are more awful than they actually are.

Either/or thinking: Everything you do is either saintly or sinful; there's no room for shades of gray.

Shoulding: Your self-talk is dominated by words like *should, shouldn't, must* and *mustn't*; the rules you internalized to earn the approval of your parents or God overshadow the voice of your authentic self.

By recognizing these distorted thought patterns, you can often stop guilt in its tracks. But the habit of self-blame and self-punishment may be so entrenched that more work is required before you can give yourself the compassion and forgiveness you deserve. Rebecca Glazer's* parents were Polish Jews who survived the Nazi concentration camps. The rest of their families had not. Strict adherence to Jewish law gave the Glazers a sense of order amid the chaos of post-Holocaust life in a new land and helped to soothe their endless grief. Rebecca was made to observe every ritual and obey every commandment. The message was, "If you don't follow the rules to the letter, God will be angry and you will not be protected from the Outsider." Her adolescence was one of strict compliance, enforced by self-imposed guilt. Then, in the early 1970s, she went away to college. "For the first time in my life, I went a whole week without hearing the words, 'God forbid,'" she says. It wasn't long before she decided that her parents' ways were antiquated. By her sophomore year, compliance gave way to defiance. "Philosophically, I became an agnostic, a woman of science." She was so secular that when a God-like figure in a dream told her, "Look for the light," she saw it as a sign—and went out the next day to buy a new floor lamp!

One thing Rebecca did not drop was the habit of guilt she had internalized from her parents. She merely transferred it to her own moral code. An uncompromising inner voice constantly nagged her to work harder and do more. She took it personally that her lab had not found a cure for cancer. Sometimes that voice in her head said, "You're killing your father," just as her mother had when Rebecca failed to do things in the prescribed manner.

Then her father did die. Rebecca found herself doing something she could not believe at the time: she fell to her knees and begged God to forgive her for not being a good enough daughter. "What I was really asking for was some sign that I had tried my best and done enough." At synagogue to perform the traditional Kaddish ritual for the dead, she found something she had longed for without realizing it was missing. Moved by the rhythmic cadence of the Aramaic chant and the words of praise for God, she felt, once again, the ineffable Presence she had known as a child. "It was like God was hugging me," she says.

The guilt-prone Rebecca evolved from compliance to defiance and now to alliance: "My contempt for certain aspects of religion had deprived me and my children of something valuable." She could not return to orthodoxy, but she could join a synagogue and participate in the elements of her tradition that carried meaning for her. To deal with what she came to realize was chronic low-grade depression brought on by internalized guilt, she started seeing a psychiatrist. And, in hopes of making that loving hug from God a permanent feature of her life, she learned meditative practices from the mystical tradition of Kaballah.

The mere fact that you are capable of guilt is a sign of your innate worth; it means that you have a working conscience and an active sense of morality. But conscience has to be modified with a realistic self-appraisal and an acceptance of who you are. By the same token, it is also possible that some of your guilt has been earned. You may, indeed, have done things that are worthy of self-reproach. In which case, specific steps must be taken before your inner judge is able, in good conscience, to transmute your sentence from guilt to remorse and finally free your incarcerated spirit.

Bringing Your Shadow into the Light

The face of the holy is not turned away from but towards
the profane; it does not want to hover over the profane
but to take it up into itself.

MARTIN BUBER

A crucial aspect of spiritual maturity is accepting the totality of our flesh-and-blood humanness. We all want to move toward the light. Unfortunately, we think that means we have to keep our backs turned to the darkness. We want to let our Higher Selves run the show. Unfortunately, we think that means stuffing our lesser selves into the closet of the unconscious. But it is vital to accept that, just as we have the spark of the Divine in us, we also have the capacity for evil—what Mother Teresa called her inner Hitler.

The shadow is where we hide the parts of ourselves we would prefer to disown: the envy, the greed, the lust, the vanity, the jealousy, the hostility, the rage—all the qualities the ego mobilizes for its own survival and glorification. But we pay a price for repressing what we would rather not see. As long as unwanted traits remain unexplored, they feed the lie that we are not worthy in the eyes of God. Unexamined, they can never be understood, corrected or tamed. They are also, as Jung said, "liable to burst forth suddenly in a moment of unawareness," at which time we can't control them or guide them toward appropriate expression.

Just as important, the shadow does not hide only our undesirable and destructive qualities. It also obscures tendencies that frighten us or appear to be sinful, but that, when properly channeled, can serve our highest and most godly aspirations: passion, ambition, charisma, idealism, creativity, excitement, rapture, even the very yearning for transcendence that drives us toward God. Like children afraid to turn off the lights, we imagine that horrible monsters are lurking in the dark. However, not only are the actual demons less frightful than we imagine, but the darkness also holds shelves full of toys and enlightening games that make life worth living and enable us to grow.

Making peace with the shadow is an imperative for making peace with God. We may not want to look at our dark side, but denying the fullness of our humanity dishonors our Creator. To restore wholeness—to atone and make all the parts of ourselves *at one* again—we need to reach into the dark recesses of our psyche and, like teaching a child to walk, gently, wisely and compassionately lead our dark side into the light.

MAKING PEACE WITH YOUR SHADOW

As long as you have not made peace with your shadow, you will keep finding reasons to feel unworthy before God. It might be because you feel you don't hold your religious beliefs strongly enough, or because you harbor doubts about the doctrines of your heritage, or because you have not followed the letter of its laws. You might feel contemptible because of something you've done, such as lie or cheat, or because of something you *haven't* done, like tithe to your church or help the poor. When something bad happens, you might think you're being punished for your sins. One person we interviewed, for example, suffered for months from excruciating nerve damage incurred during cosmetic surgery. She was convinced it was God's retribution for the vanity that made her want to do away with wrinkles.

The "evidence" of your lack of worth might be that your prayers have not been answered or the miracle you asked for was not granted. Or it might be because your prayers *have* been answered; maybe you feel you don't deserve your good fortune and fear that God will come to his senses and take it all away. In an interview with the *Los Angeles Times* in 1999, Jim Carrey, whose rise from living in a car to wealth and adulation would count as an answered prayer in anyone's book, said, "I'm constantly at odds with what you acquire in life and . . . whether you deserve that much." He says that some mornings he looks at his beautiful garden and tells himself, "Remember how good this is. Because you can lose it."

Whatever pushes the button of guilt, shame or self-disgust in your mind, it is either a flaw that genuinely needs to be worked on or a trait that you falsely label as sinful and whose depravity you exaggerate. In either case, it has nothing to do with God but only your projection *onto* God of your own fear and self-contempt.

What monsters lurk in your shadow? To help shed light on your dark side, take a look at how the issue of worthiness affects the nine archetypes:

Reformers can be such perfectionists that if God were to hand them the keys to Paradise they would say, "Wait, there's something you should know about me." The "sin" they are most susceptible to is being critical, judgmental, controlling and self-righteous toward others. But they also turn those tendencies on themselves with a vengeance. Guilt-prone Reformers are never good enough in their own eyes—and therefore, they believe, in God's eyes. Inclined toward absolutism and fanaticism, they feel they've come up short when they are not able to transform their families and friends, the spiritual institution to which they belong, society in general or, in some cases, the world. "I'm sorry, God, for not fixing things. I'll try harder from now on."

Lovers are often plagued by the feeling that they don't love well enough, purely enough, compassionately enough — and therefore don't deserve to be loved in return, by another person or by God. They feel sinful when their ego needs get in the way of total surrender. "Forgive me, God, for not loving you completely." Lovers can be manipulative and possessive in their drive to be loved, but the "sins" to which they are most prone are anger and hate. They'll hide it from themselves because they think a true lover should not feel such emotions, but when they don't get the love they want, they will cry out in their martyrdom, to God or human, "I've given you so much, and you give me so little love in return." Of course, the rage will be followed by self-contempt for being so needy when their love should be selfless and unconditional. Unfortunately, Lovers' need to be loving obscures their ability to acknowledge their own shadows.

Achievers beat themselves up because they haven't accomplished enough. They see failure where others see progress, and humiliation where others see a mere setback. "I'm sorry, God, I have not served you well enough." Achievers' weak spot is their greed for grandeur and glory. They might work hard to accomplish something worthy, but along the way fall prey to self-aggrandizement, exploitation or unethical behavior. Some even have the delusion of being more important than God. Then it's, "Forgive me, Lord, for my vanity."

Creators are their own worst critics, berating themselves for not birthing enough beauty, in either quantity or quality. The religious ones might cry, "I'm sorry, God, for not using my talent to fully express the inspiration you shine through me." They'll also attack themselves for the sin of hubris: "Who am I to think I could create something like that? Who am I to think the world should shower me with recognition?" However, they are far more likely to curse their excesses than their narcissism. When, in search of ecstasy, Creators plunge into the underworld of drugs and sensuality, they usually end up hating themselves in the morning.

Thinkers can spend an evening impressing a crowd with their knowledge and go home feeling like imposters who don't really know anything. When they find that their most exquisite thoughts bring them only to the doorstep of the great spiritual mysteries, they feel that they've fallen short. Thinkers have

trouble leaving the ivory tower of the mind and taking the leap to direct experience of the sublime—and that makes them feel inadequate. Thinkers can be
arrogant know-it-alls, stingy and emotionally distant—and they're often smart
enough to know it. "I'm all brain and no heart. Forgive me, God, for not caring for others, and for all my doubts about you."

Security-Seekers see others whose lives appear to be more blessed than
theirs and ask, "What have I done wrong, God? I tried to follow the rules."
Fearful, often to the point of cosmic paranoia, they are always trying to com-
ply, and they judge themselves harshly when they fall short of the standards
they think will grant them entry to the kingdom, however they define it.
Sometimes, Security-Seekers will pin their safety needs on material affluence.
But, after working hard to build a nest egg, they'll feel guilty for rendering too
much unto Caesar. "I'm sorry, God, for doubting that you'll provide for me
like the lilies of the field."

Adventurers can be so hell-bent for excitement they fall prey to restlessness,
impulsiveness and self-destructive extremes. In the aftermath, their usual al-
lergy to negativity may give way to self-recrimination. They're first in line to
confess on Monday morning ("I'm a terrible sinner, God. I have strayed from
the path."), but they're also first in line to "sin" again the next weekend. Adventurers often genuinely want to serve God, but only if they can keep the adventure going and feel special. When those terms are not met, they might
either rebel or give in to their tendency toward sloth—and then feel lousy
about themselves for lacking discipline.

Bosses feel unworthy when they don't live up to their high standards of
leadership. They'll assume personal responsibility for the well-being of their
family, company, congregation or community—which gives them lots of opportunity to blame themselves when something goes wrong. Religious Bosses
hold themselves to high moral and ethical standards, and when they betray
those values in their lust for power and control, they hate themselves. "I failed
you, God. I've lied and cheated and abused others to serve my selfish ambition. Please give me another chance to prove I'm worthy." Often, they'll promise to do things God's way, only to start renegotiating before the cosmic ink is
dry. Then they feel unworthy for lacking faith.

Peacemakers feel that they've let God down when they can't put an end to conflict. When people they care about are suffering and they can't heal them, they think they're lazy and inept—even if they've worked so hard that they're close to burnout. Because they tend to look outside themselves for rules to live by, Peacemakers take quite literally the codes of their religion, only to feel like sinners when they fall short. Many will appeal to the Divine for instructions— "Show me what to do, God, I need your guidance."—and if a clear response is not forthcoming, they'll take it as a sign that they're out of favor with God. They'll guilt themselves for any bitter, hostile or jealous thought that creates an absence of peace inside them.

CONFRONTING YOUR DARK SIDE

What do you feel guilty about? What makes you feel unworthy? The following questions will help you honestly evaluate where you stand on these issues. Take your time to contemplate them thoroughly.

1. What is it about you that makes you feel you don't deserve God's love?
2. Which of your personal traits do you think God disapproves of?
3. What evidence do you have that God disapproves?
4. Are you being arrogant in assuming you know how God feels about you?
5. Could you be projecting onto God your own feelings about yourself?
6. Are the standards by which you evaluate yourself your own, or have you adopted them from other sources, such as your parents or religion?
7. Have you carefully examined those standards to see if they are consistent with your personal values?
8. What specific actions do you feel guilty about? (Make a complete list.)

9. For which of those have you punished yourself enough — or too much — already?

10. For which specific incidents do you crave forgiveness?

The Healing Power of Confession

Wash away all my guilt and cleanse me from my sin.
For well I know my misdeeds . . .

PSALMS 51:2–3

Every evening, from coast to coast, millions of people enter church basements and community rooms, spiritual settings as far removed from the splendor of cathedrals as Britney is from Bach. There, in a uniquely modern way, they do what people struggling with inner demons have done for millennia in the context of traditional religions: they declare their willingness to turn over their will to a higher power; they confess their personal weaknesses and past misdeeds; and they promise to make amends to those they've injured. Those are among the key ingredients behind the extraordinary success of Alcoholics Anonymous and other 12-Step programs. (See "The Twelve Steps" on the next page.)

One of the millions who attends 12-Step meetings on a regular basis is Charles Verde*, a New York investment banker. Charles led an outwardly observant life all through college, but the minute he removed his graduation gown, he headed straight for the home of mammon: Wall Street. "I believed there was a higher power that vaguely affected my life," he says from his Upper East Side co-op. "But I was convinced that *I* was the real god of my life. I could control my destiny with intelligence, discipline and will. I was a self-absorbed narcissist whose religion revolved around money and power."

Calling that personality of twenty-two years ago arrogant, Charles says he was compelled to be bigger and better than everyone else. "My life was a zero sum game," he says. "If I won, you lost. I was a user. I was dishonest, irresponsible, manipulative, deceptive and disrespectful."

THE TWELVE STEPS

1. We admitted we were powerless over alcohol—that our lives had become unmanageable.
2. Came to believe that a Power greater than ourselves could restore us to sanity.
3. Made a decision to turn our will and our lives over to the care of God as we understood Him.
4. Made a searching and fearless moral inventory of ourselves.
5. Admitted to God, to ourselves and to another human being the exact nature of our wrongs.
6. Were entirely ready to have God remove all these defects of character.
7. Humbly asked Him to remove our shortcomings.
8. Made a list of all persons we had harmed, and became willing to make amends to them all.
9. Made direct amends to such people wherever possible, except when to do so would injure them or others.
10. Continued to take personal inventory and when we were wrong promptly admitted it
11. Sought through prayer and meditation to improve our conscious contact with God as we understood Him, praying only for knowledge of His will for us and the power to carry that out.
12. Having had a spiritual awakening as the result of these steps, we tried to carry this message to alcoholics and to practice these principles in all our affairs.

As he recounts his history, it is clear that Charles is comfortable with self-disclosure. That wasn't always the case. He used to be sly and secretive, he says, a closed book even to his girlfriends and close pals. His candid self-awareness is one of the benefits of working the 12-Step program diligently. But it took a long time to reach that point, and a great many dizzying ups and downs. By twenty-seven, Charles was earning over a million dollars a year. Every night he ushered friends from bar to party to bar in his limousine. Weekends were sleepless orgies of getting high and having sex with strangers. "The theme was more, more, more," he says. "More booze, more drugs, more women, more money, more power—and more insanity." Predictably, it all blew up: relationships, friendships, job—all destroyed by his addictions. "Every time I hit bottom, I would beg God to pull me out. I was praying in the foxhole: 'Please, God, if you help me out I'll never do it again.' And after he saved my ass for the umpteenth time, I would renege on my deal."

His real God was drugs, Charles admits, and his savior was his dealer. "The only times I wasn't high was when I'd pass out for a twelve or fourteen hours. When I woke up, with my brain un-medicated, I'd be overwhelmed by feelings of guilt, shame and hopelessness. I felt that I'd ruined my life, and I could never salvage it." Until he got high again.

After ten years of this, he overdosed. He remembers regaining consciousness in the ER, and hearing a nurse say, "We lost you several times, but God was watching over you. You are a lucky man."

"At that moment," he says, "I felt for the first time a strange, yet strong connection to God. I prayed to him and thanked him for saving my life."

The lesson didn't hold. Over the next ten harrowing years, he was in rehab five times. Eventually, reality overcame his prodigious capacity for denial. "The only way I could recover was by relying on God." Staying sober, he says, is a daily battle, but his AA sponsor and the daily meetings, along with prescribed medication for clinical depression, keep him on top of his addiction.

The chief value of the 12 Steps for him, Charles believes, was acknowledging he was powerless over his addiction and turning over his will to God. Also of immense value was making what AA calls a "searching and fearless moral inventory of ourselves," and admitting "to God, to ourselves and to another human being the exact nature of our wrongs."

The benefit of owning up to our weaknesses and transgressions has been understood for millennia. In recent years, the healing power of confession has been exemplified by the public apologies of world leaders on behalf of entire nations and powerful institutions. Early in the new millennium, for example, Pope John Paul II asked forgiveness for the historical sins committed in the name of the Roman Catholic Church against Jews, women, fellow Christians and various indigenous populations.

Consider taking such a step yourself. Whether in a formal setting or on your own, you will find it tremendously healing to release your self-contempt, along with all the guilty memories of wrongdoing that may be keeping you from making peace with God. Apologizing directly to those you've hurt is perhaps the most powerful form of confession, and the most challenging. Be aware that this must be done with true humility and contrition. If your apology comes across as self-serving or inauthentic, it could exacerbate the damage already done to the relationship. Give careful consideration to whether a face-to-face apology will truly be healing for you and the other person or whether it might merely create new sources of pain. If you go ahead with it, choose with utmost care the best possible timing and location for your confession, and, most important, the tone and language you use.

Another possibility is to write your confession in a private journal. If it helps you to focus, imagine you are writing to those who were hurt or disappointed the most by your past behavior—or *would* have been if they'd known what you'd done. Alternatively, you might imagine writing the letter to someone, living or dead, who would surely understand and forgive you. Or write it to God.

You might also want to bring your confession to a wise individual whom you can trust with your deepest feelings, perhaps a close friend who will honor your confidentiality, or a spiritual counselor who can be counted on to listen with compassion, not judgment, no matter what you reveal. You might also consider seeing a trained psychotherapist, preferably one with a spiritual orientation who can understand your desire to make peace with God. With an experienced professional, you will be able to release your painful emotional burden, work on deeper issues and heal the psychic wounds that your past actions may have caused.

Making Amends

Create in me a clean heart, O God; and renew
a right spirit within me.

Psalms 51:10

A vital ingredient in Charles's recovery, and the 12-Step success in general, is the combined energy of steps eight and nine, which call for naming everyone you've harmed and making amends. If you feel guilty because of damage done to others, verbal release may not be sufficient. You might never fully forgive yourself until you do something concrete to make up for it.

"You have done wrong? Then counteract it by doing right." Simple, profound advice from Martin Buber, a twentieth-century philosopher of Judaism. But it's not as easy as it sounds. It can be hard to decide exactly how to make amends. It may be impossible to predict how the other person will react to your gesture. You may have to conquer the fear of rejection or retaliation. A voice in your head will say, "Don't bother; it's way too late. Nothing you do now will make a difference." It may indeed be true that you can't heal hurt feelings or restore a broken relationship at this point. But the crucial issue in our context is how to redeem yourself *in your own eyes* so you once again feel deserving of God's love. When done in the spirit of a sacred offering, any attempt to make amends is worthwhile and healing.

Put yourself in the other person's shoes, completely and with no reservations, and ask yourself what would it take for your actions to be forgiven. In some cases, a heartfelt confession, accompanied by an apology and a promise not to do it again, will be enough. But, if you've hurt someone badly, you may have to *show* you're sorry with some form of tangible restitution—either something of material value or actions that balance the emotional scale. For example, if you were selfish, make an extra effort to put the other person's needs first. If you were stingy, be a bit extravagant. But only if you can do it sincerely. You'll know if you're just being self-serving, and you'll know that God knows.

Sometimes, making amends to those you've injured is impossible because of distance, time, resistance or even death. In such cases, the best approach is to do something that only you and God know is a heartfelt offering of restitution. In the spirit of ritual sacrifice, give up something you value, whether it's a financial donation or a significant investment of time, effort and human kindness to those in need. Only when you are able to forgive yourself in the privacy of your own heart, knowing you have made your best effort to make amends, can you stand tall before God and breathe in the divine forgiveness that is, like oxygen, always present.

Religious Faith and Depression

If feelings of unworthiness, guilt or shame have been your constant companions over a long period of time, it would not be surprising to learn that your agony has left you feeling depressed. Clinical depression is both a common consequence of self-contempt and a common *cause* of it. Depression leads to shame leads to depression leads to shame in a tortured downward spiral.

In the face of depression, the power of faith crashes and burns. When you're depressed, the most uplifting sermons and the most inspiring words from cheerful friends can make you even *more* depressed. In fact, perhaps the least helpful thing one can say to a depressed person is, "Cheer up!" or its spiritual equivalent, "Count your blessings," or "Don't worry, God loves you." Yeah, right! Like the farmer who casts his seed upon the rocks, your best spiritual intentions cannot bear fruit when planted in a depressed mind, because depression biologically interferes with the brain's ability to maintain positive thoughts for any period of time. This state of mind was captured by the nineteenth-century minister Henry Ward Beecher: "There are joys which long to be ours. God sends ten thousand truths, which come about us like birds seeking inlet; but we are shut up to them, and so they bring us nothing, but sit and sing awhile upon the roof, and then fly away."

On one level, psychiatry now understands depression as the product of a biochemical imbalance in the brain, along with a corresponding psychological imbalance often called "faulty thinking." Certain people may have a genetic predisposition to clinical depression, just as some are predisposed to diabetes or heart disease. Any number of factors can trigger the symptoms: a painful childhood, a major loss, unresolved grief, excessive stress, a serious illness, troublesome relationships, substance abuse and many more. And, in reverse, depression makes every one of those situations more likely to occur.

If you regularly experience any of the following symptoms (compiled by the National Institute of Mental Health), you might very well be clinically depressed:

- Persistent sad or "empty" mood
- Loss of interest or pleasure in ordinary activities, including sex
- Fatigue and decreased energy
- Sleep disturbances
- Eating disturbances
- Difficulty concentrating, remembering or making decisions
- Feelings of guilt, worthlessness or helplessness
- Thoughts of death or suicide; suicide attempts
- Irritability
- Excessive crying
- Chronic aches and pains that don't respond to treatment
- Decreased productivity
- Alcohol or drug abuse

If you have led a religious or spiritual life, the symptoms might be accompanied by persistent thoughts such as, "God doesn't love me," "I'm not worthy of salvation," or "I'll never make spiritual progress, let alone get enlightened." Your customary form of worship might be dispiriting rather than uplifting. Your spiritual practice might feel dull and stale rather than energizing and inspiring. You might feel that you are incapable of meditating or praying correctly, or undeserving of grace. You might be convinced that the possibility of making peace with God is hopeless, like everything else in your life.

You might think you are doomed to a bleak and Godless future, but many depressed individuals have managed to lift themselves out of despair. Consider how depressed the man who wrote this must have been: "I am now the most miserable man living. If what I feel were equally distributed to the whole human family, there would be not one cheerful face on earth. Whether I shall ever be better, I cannot tell. I awfully forebode I shall not. To remain as I am is impossible. I must die or be better it appears to me." The author of that was Abraham Lincoln. Somehow, he mustered the faith to go on and keep not only himself but the nation intact. And that was long before science understood the biological nature of depression.

Depression is now easily treated with medication—both natural and synthetic—and/or psychotherapy, preferably both. Seeking treatment for it is no more of a stigma than getting help for arthritis or diabetes. Nor is it in any way "unspiritual" to seek help from a physician or mental-health expert. It does not imply a lack of character, discipline, strength or faith in God. It is nothing to be ashamed of or feel guilty about. Depression is no one's fault, not yours, not your parents', not society's, not God's. Get the help you need, preferably from an expert psychiatrist who not only empathizes with your pain but also fully understands the medical, psychological and spiritual dimensions of your condition.

Bring It to God

Among the attributes of God, although they are all equal,
mercy shines with even more brilliancy than justice.

MIGUEL DE CERVANTES

If your past behavior has caused your soul to cry out, "Am I good enough, God?" why not pose the question directly? Why not unburden yourself to the ultimate listener, the ultimate counselor, the ultimate healer?

In 1980, Dr. Larry Lea started an evangelical church in Texas with fourteen congregants. Ten years later he was the head of the mother church with over 10,000 active members, more than 300 affiliate churches and a television ministry that reached millions. At the age of forty, having also published the religious best-seller *Could You Not Tarry One Hour*, the "Apostle of Prayer" left the empire he created in the hands of others so he could answer the call to preach around the globe. In the world of evangelical Christianity, Larry Lea was a superstar. Flying his own plane from one preaching engagement to the next, serving as dean of the seminary at Oral Roberts University, he had it made by every standard, material and spiritual. Then came the fall.

Lea's marriage of twenty years was falling apart. He and his wife sought counseling within the evangelical community, where divorce was abhorred, but the couple's differences only grew wider. During a trial separation, Larry fell in love with a woman in San Diego. Now he was pulled in two directions at once: his Christian values, his duty to his family and the threat of scandal pulled him toward home, but his heart was California dreaming. He returned to Texas to give the marriage a final chance. After fourteen months, he and his wife agreed that they had done all they could. The California woman, whom he had been unable to forget, had waited for him, and the minute Larry's divorce was finalized, they were married. Shortly thereafter their child was born. For most people, this would have been a happy ending to a difficult ordeal. Lea's ex-wife forgave him. His three grown children forgave him. But, in the eyes of the evangelical community, the man who had been called "Gospel's Golden Boy" and "the next Billy Graham" was fatally tarnished. His fellow evangelists *would* have forgiven the divorce and remarriage, but they could not forgive the scandal of an extramarital affair.

Reverend Larry Lea was a pariah. Booked for years in advance, he now saw cancellations pouring in from around the world. He was asked to resign from all the boards on which he served. "I could totally understand their need to say, 'Larry, step down for a while,'" he says. But he did not expect ostracism without the possibility of redemption. "The most painful aspect was that their response was so unlike Jesus Christ," he says. "The overall teaching of the Bible is redemption, love, acceptance and forgiveness. I was open to reconciliation at any cost, but there was never any kind of olive branch. I thought I would die from the personal sadness and the professional assassination."

Reduced to second-class citizenship in the community that had once adored him, shunned by close personal friends, Larry took his case directly to

God. It was, he says, like asking for a second opinion. "In the Book of Proverbs it says, 'Trust the Lord with all your heart; lean not only to your own under- standing; in all your ways know him; He will direct your path.' It doesn't say 'in all your *good* ways know him,' it says 'in *all* your ways.' Most people only want to bring the good things to God. They're afraid that if they get alone with God they'll be squashed like a bug." Lea chose to bare his neck. "Every morning, as the sun came up over the Pacific Ocean, I would sit on my prayer bench and bring it to God, again and again." He prayed for an hour or two a day, ex- pressing his guilt and shame, offering thanks, expressing contrition, asking questions and waiting for answers. What he received, he says, was a clear mes- sage that God was not angry with him. "He never cast me away," says Lea. "It was the sweetest, most wonderful thing, because his voice said, 'Neither do I condemn you. Now go and offend no more'"—the famous line that Jesus speaks to the adulteress whom he saved from being stoned.

Dr. Lea has so far been unable to make peace with his religious brethren. But he *has* made peace with God. He says that when he turned to God, he felt a healing forgiveness and "unmitigated, unlimited, relentless love."

Sometimes, during his prayer sessions, when the emotional pain was in- tense, he would shift from worship to a visualization process. "While feeling love for the people who hurt me," he says, "I took the shaming darts they had sent into my soul and visually pulled them out. I would envision throwing those darts before the throne of God with a violent motion. I cast them before God because the pain was too heavy to bear alone." At one point, the exercise led to a powerful catharsis. What Lea calls "a holy scream" rose up from deep inside of him. Allowing it to break through his resistance, he released "into the presence of God" a loud, guttural shriek. "It helped me break through the bondage that had held me captive," he says. Afterward, he nestled in the lov- ing forgiveness of his God's embrace—and continued to abide there as he re- built his life. He is now counseling individuals and working on a book called *The Holy Scream*.

You don't have to be seminary trained to take your shame and guilt directly to God for a second opinion. It requires only the courage to stand alone before the eternal void and bare your soul. You might recite a traditional prayer of repentance. You might, in your own personal way, say you're sorry for what you've done. You might ask God for the forgiveness you can't quite give yourself. You might confess that you're not even sure you did wrong and you need to know if you have. You might ask what you can do to make up for it. You can scream your pain, you can admit your doubt, you can curse yourself, your accusers and even God. You can say anything, ask any question. What you might *not* want to do is bargain with God. Why cheapen your dialogue by turning it into a negotiation? Go ahead and make promises if you think that doing so will help you move ahead in your life, but don't ask for anything in return—no miracles, no material blessings, not even guidance, love or peace. You already have that coming to you.

When you're finished speaking, in the silence that remains, shut up and listen. Don't expect a clear voice or some concrete sign. Pay attention to the faint stirring in your bosom and the whispers in the corners of your mind. If, in your quiet receptivity, nothing comes by way of revelation or discovery, give it a rest and go about your business. But keep paying attention. Messages can come when least expected. And if all your efforts bring you is a bit of calm or a semblance of comfort, don't be disappointed; that's not chopped liver, it's a spoonful of divine forgiveness.

The Love of God

It is here . . . that love is to be found—not hidden away
in corners but in the midst of occasions of sin.

St. Teresa of Avila

The question "Am I good enough, God?" implies that God loves some and not others, loves sometimes and not at other times, parceling out love like a human being, only when moved to do so. But, do we really have to earn God's love? Do we have to do our chores and mind our manners like children with undemonstrative parents? Is God's love like an item held in a pawnshop until we have enough moral currency to redeem it? Not if, as we're told, God *is* love. In that case, the love of God is eternally present, like gravity or electro-magnetism. We don't have to earn it; we have to awaken to it.

The question of deserving God's love is relevant only in this regard: as long as you believe you're not worthy of it, you won't allow yourself to receive it. That is one of the wages of sin: by doing things that make us feel ashamed, guilty and afraid, we deprive ourselves of the love and peace that is rightfully ours. Similarly, doing things right doesn't motivate God to love you; it con-vinces *you* that you're deserving, which allows you to open up to what has al-ways been yours. God does not withhold rewards because we've been naughty, like a dog trainer who keeps a biscuit in his fist until the puppy obeys his com-mands. "God does not punish sin," said the fifteenth-century mystic Julian of Norwich. "Sin punishes sin." By definition, sin separates us from God. The punishment is the separation; the healing is the at-one-ment.

God's love is the cosmic glue that binds us, one to the other and all to the One. It is here, now. It is there, then. It is. Love emanates from existence itself, like heat emanates from fire. Just as we get warmer as we inch closer to the flame, we feel loved in direct proportion to our intimacy with the Divine. "He that dwells in love is dwelling in God, and God in him," declared the apostle John. The corollary is also true: he that dwells in God is dwelling in love. For in union with God, fear is gone, shame is gone, guilt is gone. Everything about the "I" is gone, and all that remains is Love with a capital L.

If we accept that God is love and God is infinite, then we are forced to con-clude that the very stuff of the universe is love. As Dante said, love "moves the sun and the other stars." We also have to conclude that the only thing stopping us from experiencing that love is our own inability to receive it. It can't be be-cause we're unworthy. Think of it this way: If God can be said to have expec-tations of us, would he expect us to be perfect? If God can be said to bestow love only on the deserving, would her standards be so high as to make that love available only to saints? Listen to the passionate wisdom of James Kavanaugh, a dissident Catholic priest, from his book *God Lives:* "My God understands all, forgives all, loves me with an unconditional love, and asks universal for-giveness of me. He does not have to save me because there is nothing to save me from except my separation from His presence. . . . Nor does His love depend on what I do or don't do, say or don't say! . . . He does not demand that I change before He offers me His love. . . . He does not terrorize me with His laws and punishments. . . . He does not call me an unworthy son since He has fashioned me through the miracle of millions of years of growth and change. . . . He does not want me to be instantly perfect, only to be honest and alive and growing. He does not want me to live in fear of Him or to be saturated with guilt; He wants my freedom which is His own."

But you've no doubt heard "God is love" and "God loves you" before, perhaps hundreds of times. You've been told that you are the beloved of God and that you were created in the image and likeness of God. You have been told that you are forgiven. Do you believe it? Why should you? The proof is in the pudding, after all, and if you do not taste God's love, it's probably because you've been rummaging in the refrigerator when the pudding is in the cupboard of your own heart. "Though the inner chamber of the heart is small," said the Muslim mystic Mahmud Shabestari, "the Lord of both worlds gladly makes His home there."

Out with the Old God, in with the New

Before he could arrive at the above conviction, Father Kavanaugh no doubt had to struggle with much of the theology he'd been taught. Doing so is often a necessity on the path to God's love—to overcome the internalized messages that portray us as unworthy and God as punitive and judgmental.

When Carol Schaefer was a college freshman, she got pregnant. As the year was 1965, the school was in the South and Carol's family was Catholic, the options of abortion and single motherhood were both unthinkable. She was sent to a home for unwed mothers to complete her pregnancy in secret humiliation. After several months in isolation, she spent Christmas pondering a bitter irony: she and her sisters in shame were celebrating the most beloved birth in history, but *their* pregnancy was a mortal sin, and when they gave birth, they would immediately hand their children to strangers. Carol, who had never missed a Sunday Mass, prayed to God for a way to keep her child. No answer came. Five days after giving up her son, she was back in school, making up stories to explain her absence.

She turned away from God and the Church. "I had been somewhat skeptical already," she says, "but now I was mad." Despite her crushing pain, however, a kernel of faith remained. She prayed every day, only not to God, whom she no longer trusted, but to the Blessed Virgin. "The only thing that kept me sane," she says, "was praying to Mary to protect my son and let him know I loved him."

Having been let down by the disciplinarian Father God she was raised to believe in, Carol turned to the Divine Mother, who loves unconditionally and nurtures and protects her children. "My prayers to Mary evolved into a broader exploration of the feminine energy in the universe," says Carol. "That enabled me to eventually make peace with God."

In a mysterious way it also helped her find her son. Eighteen years after his birth, Carol initiated a search for him. Shortly thereafter, while gazing at a famous statue of Mary in a Paris church, she suddenly had a vision of her child. She lit a votive candle and wept. Six months later, she and her son were reunited. "Deep inside, I always felt that we had somehow remained connected," says Carol, who wrote about her experience in a memoir, *The Other Mother*, which was later made into a TV movie. Now she realized that the bond was not just in her imagination and that its very substance was love. The experience ignited a search for a deeper, more inclusive spirituality. "I came to understand myself as an evolving soul, and to see God as a force, not a figure. I can trust God now, because I can feel the female energy of the Goddess as a source of love." The feminine aspect of the Divine led to a reconciliation with the masculine God she had spurned. And why not? What would any mother do if her child had turned her back on her father except to bring them back together?

Often, rising above stigma and guilt to embrace the grace that is always present necessitates a process similar to Carol's: purging the mind and heart of naive, incomplete notions of God, and replacing them with a more mature, more complete understanding. One woman we spoke to went so far as to fire God. That's right, she wrote a formal letter of dismissal to the God she had been afraid of since childhood. "Dear God," she wrote in part, "It is not easy to say this since you have been with me my entire life, but your services are no longer required. I have no further need of a God who watches over my life and judges everything I do. I no longer wish to live in fear and shame. I will now be interviewing candidates to replace you." And she boldly set off in search of a new spirituality.

You too may need to formally divorce the God of your past. Or, perhaps you might prefer a more conciliatory approach. How about facilitating a reconciliation between God as the Authoritarian Father and God as the Divine Mother? That sacred marriage has been torn apart by centuries of patriarchal ignorance. As offspring of the union of God and Goddess, we deserve better than a broken home. "I have said, Ye are gods; and all of you are children of the most High" (Psalms 82:6).

You Are More Than Good Enough in God's Eyes

*The world contains no man so righteous that he can
do right always and never do wrong.*

ECCLESIASTES 7:20

There is an old joke that is set in a synagogue but could just as well take place in a church, a mosque, an ashram or a 12-Step meeting. A congregant, moved by the power of God, falls to his knees and shouts, "The Lord is great and I am but a speck of dirt. I am nothing!" Not to be outdone, another worshipper falls to her knees and shouts, "God is mighty and powerful, and I am nothing! Nothing!" And as they display their superior humility before God, a man in the back falls to his knees and wails, "Oh, Lord, you are infinite and vast. You are all that is and ever was. You are love and mercy, and I am but a filthy sinner. I am nothing!" The first two turn and see that the voice from the back is the janitor's. One turns to the other and sneers, "Look who thinks he's nothing."

Those people evidently never heard the saying of the Baal Shem Tov, the founder of Hasidism: "We must bend down, but not too low and not too often. For in bowing too low and too often, we may forget how to raise our heads." Of course humility is a desirable trait. But false humility is an ego trip, and self-flagellation, no matter how sincere, is not humility; it's humiliation. Embracing your innate self-worth does not constitute the sin of pride. Nor does whipping yourself with the chains of self-criticism bring you any closer to the ego death that Eastern teachings urge us to achieve. Awakening to the divine Self does not come about by battering the small self into submission with insults. It comes from dissolving our sense of individual identity in the unity of all that is. In a sense, convincing yourself that you are unworthy can be just as egotistical as boasting about how accomplished you are. It's still your ego at work, only it's a weak ego, a defeated ego, and from a spiritual perspective, that's no better than an inflated ego. It's still separate from God.

You are not perfect. Who is? Certainly not the heroes of the world's sacred scriptures. The Bible is filled with reprobates and connivers, self-centered fools and slayers of innocents. But their stories are timeless because they contain great lessons and most of the characters grow and change. Like everyone else, the authors of this book also fall short of our highest ideals and the standards we believe God holds for us. One of us, Harold, went through the lowest and most excruciating period of his life while this book was being completed. In his words: "Following a botched elective surgery, I became progressively more addicted to prescription pain medications. With my judgment seriously impaired, I made some very unwise professional and personal actions, which I now regret. Spiritually, I suffered a complete tear in the fabric of my being. My cherished connection to God seemed to be suddenly and irrevocably severed. I felt abandoned by, and ashamed before, God. But it was not until I became broken and went through unimaginable darkness that I began to truly make peace with God. That ongoing process, and the task of piecing together my life, has been painful and challenging. But, by living the principles we write about in this book, I am emerging a better person, and feel closer to God."

To Buddhists, the lotus flower has always been a symbol of enlightenment because it is able to grow out of dark muddy water—not in spite of the mud's impurities but because those very impurities contain nutrients that are essential for the lotus's growth. Like that, we have to use our inner mud to nourish the growth of our souls. Sin, as in being off the mark, and repentance, as in getting back on track, can be seen as crucial elements in the evolution of consciousness. As Ken Wilber puts it, "An acorn is not a sin; it is simply not yet an oak."

The paradox is, to really transform you first have to accept that who you are now is, in its own strange way, perfect in its imperfection. It is today's starting point in the marathon trek toward God-realization. We have no choice but to stretch toward the perfection of our godliness, even if that goal seems unreachable, just as plants must reach for the unattainable sun. That's what we signed up for when we enrolled in the University of Earth. But we are not denied the blessings of creation just because we make mistakes. "For he makes his sun rise on the evil and on the good," said Jesus, "and sends rain to the just and to the unjust" (Matthew 5:45). When we beat ourselves up, we are being cruel, harsh, critical and judgmental—all the things we don't want to be to others. Maybe the Golden Rule should be amended to "Do unto yourself as you would have yourself do unto others."

The nineteenth-century Rabbi Bunam of Pzhysha said that "everyone must have two pockets, so that he can reach into the one or the other, according to his needs. In his right pocket are to be the words: 'For my sake was the world created,' and in his left: 'I am earth and ashes.'" What bridges those two messages is the answer to Einstein's question: we *do* live in a friendly universe. In God's eyes we are always good enough. Taking in God's love as a conscious daily practice can help you heal your emotional wounds and arrive at a place of internal peace.

6.

WHERE ARE YOU, GOD?

Reuniting with the Divine

Lead us from the unreal to the real. Lead us from darkness to light.
Lead us from death to immortality. Peace, peace, peace.

BRIHADARANYAKA UPANISHAD

If, in some distant galaxy, an intelligent species has been monitoring thought waves from earth, they would probably conclude that "Where are you, God?" is the central concern of the human spirit. Cries of "Show me your face, Lord! Why do you hide from me?" have reverberated through space and time in a thousand tongues, from the secret caverns of the heart; from temples, churches and mosques; from desert canyons, Himalayan caves, jungle clearings and monastic cloisters. That eavesdropping civilization might marvel at the game of hide-and-seek that the God of earth has played with its creatures; or, if they are wiser than we are, they might pity us for not seeing what is right before our very eyes.

So far, the emphasis of this book has been on surmounting the most troublesome psychological and emotional barriers to making peace with God. But peace on that level opens the door to something far more sublime. Throughout, we have reiterated the fundamental truth that the ultimate peace is the peace *of* God, to be found only when we shatter the illusion of our separation and discover that, in the words of St. Francis of Assisi, "What we are looking for is what is looking." Now we return to the eternal yearning with which we

began, to explore ways to achieve a relationship with God that is more intimate than conversation, more profound than a covenant and more transformative than emotional resolution.

The Seven States of Consciousness

Where are you searching for me, friend? Look! Here am I
right within you. Not in temple, nor in mosque, not in
Kaaba, nor Kailas, but here right within you am I.

KABIR

Just as the body evolves from fetus through infancy, childhood, maturity,
old age and its eventual return to dust, the soul can be said to grow through
natural stages of conscious evolution. The spiritual pursuit begins as a journey
to God, becomes a journey *with* God and culminates as a journey *in* God.

As with every journey, having a map is useful. Models of spiritual development have been proposed by outstanding thinkers in psychology and religion,
from both the East and the West. Some are quite complex, incorporating research on moral development, psychological maturity and other factors in
addition to spiritual awareness. Here, we are using the seven states of consciousness as outlined by Maharishi Mahesh Yogi and rooted in India's Vedic
tradition. The model is simple enough to present in our context and profound
enough to illuminate the fundamental stages of growth toward full realization
of God.

The first three states of consciousness are those with which we are all familiar: waking, sleeping and dreaming. Each of these "normal" states is characterized by a unique mode of awareness and perception. In the waking state,
we perceive the world through the five senses. The material objects of which
we are aware, along with the subtler objects we call thoughts and feelings, constitute what we consider reality. In deep sleep, of course, awareness is shut
down entirely, and there are no objects of perception at all. In the dream state,
perception occurs, but what is perceived is unconscious and illusory. The

three states are also marked by different ways of defining who we are. In ordinary waking consciousness, we identify ourselves as specific individuals with distinct personalities, roles and bodily forms. In dreaming, we might be aware of that identity, but our knowledge is distorted and capricious. In sleep, no self-awareness exists. We also know from scientific research that the three states of consciousness can be distinguished physiologically by various metabolic factors and measures of brain function.

So much for ordinary reality. The fun begins when we move on to the other four states of consciousness. These too represent distinct modes of awareness, perception and self-identification, along with significant differences in neurophysiology. While they are as natural as trees or waterfalls, these higher states are far from ordinary. They constitute the very essence of spiritual experience, as recorded by the mystics, saints and sages who have explored the inner realm of consciousness with the kind of rigor that scientists employ when probing matter. The development of higher awareness is a movement from the prison of ordinary consciousness to the radiant ecstasy of the sublime; from relative dullness to complete aliveness; from illusion to reality; from agitation to peace; from discontent to bliss; from ignorance of our true nature to ultimate knowledge of who we are. It can also be seen as a progressive movement toward intimacy with God, culminating when divine union is realized and every corner of manifest creation is perceived as holy.

TRANSCENDENTAL CONSCIOUSNESS

The Consciousness within, purged of the mind, is felt as God.

RAMANA MAHARSHI

Imagine you are in a movie theater. Watching ordinary films is analogous to life in the waking state: you are having a series of sensory experiences that fit together in a coherent way to constitute your "story." As in the movies, the content of the waking state is highly variable; sometimes it's funny, sometimes exciting, sometimes tragic, sometimes romantic, sometimes suspenseful, sometimes farcical. The *quality* of experience also varies. Just as some movies are better than others, waking consciousness fluctuates, depending on your energy, your mood, the acuity of your senses, your alertness and myriad other factors.

Now suppose what appears on screen is a surreal, whimsical series of images and sounds that lack any sense of linear coherence. That would be analogous to the dream state. Then suppose the screen went dark. That would be the equivalent of deep sleep. Three cinematic experiences; three states of consciousness. Now consider the experience of seeing the screen by itself, fully illuminated but with no images projected upon it, as if the projector were to run without any film in it. That would be analogous to the fourth state: transcendental consciousness (TC).

Waking consciousness can be seen as an interaction of three elements: the experiencer, the objects of experience, and the process of experiencing (alternatively, knower, known and knowing). Most of the time, as when watching a gripping film, we are unaware of the experiencer, for we are lost in what appears on the screen of our awareness. We identify, in other words, with the changing perceptions of which we are conscious. In TC, however, all sensory and perceptual experience is transcended. The chatter of the mind, the feelings, perceptions and sensations that normally grip our awareness as we move through time and space—all left behind. What remains is the pure light of the knower or experiencer, alone in the timeless silence. And, says Meister Eckhart, "There is nothing so much like God in all the world as silence."

Another way of looking at it is this: normally we are conscious *of* something; in transcendence we are conscious of conscious*ness*. More accurately, we *are* consciousness. Stated yet another way, consciousness is conscious of its own pure, unadulterated essence, devoid of content. That pure consciousness has been called the Self—the Self we share with all of creation and is at one with the transpersonal aspect of God, what Eckhart called, "God beyond God, utterly without numeration or distinctive marks."

Transcendental consciousness has been glimpsed, and in many cases sustained, by so many individuals in so many cultures that it is safe to call it the ground of Being, the universal substrate of existence. It is from such an encounter with the Divine within that the prophet could declare, "Hear O Israel: the Lord is God, the Lord is One." It is toward that state of consciousness that Jesus pointed to when he said, in the Gospel of Thomas, "When you make the two one and when you make the inside like the outside, and the outside like the inside, and the upper like the lower, and when you make male and female into a single one, then you will enter the kingdom." That extinguishing of duality points to the same state of unified, content-free awareness that Buddhists call *sunyata* (most commonly translated as "emptiness") and Hindus call *samadhi*, or *turiya*, which is characterized as sat-chit-ananda (absolute bliss consciousness). The Zen master Shunryo Suzuki said that experiencing pure consciousness is like being with God before God said, "Let there be light." Or, since it is in this state that the ego's sense of "I" dissolves into the infinite "I's," we can look at it with the thirteenth-century Muslim mystic Ibn Arabi: "When you know yourself, your 'I-ness' vanishes and you know that you and God are one and the same."

It should be noted that while transcendental consciousness is experienced most commonly in deep meditation, it has been stumbled upon spontaneously by a great many people (whether to attribute these occurrences to chance or divine grace depends on one's beliefs). Take, for instance, this description by the poet Alfred, Lord Tennyson: "All at once, as it were out of the intensity of the consciousness of individuality, individuality itself seemed to dissolve and fade away into boundless being, and this not a confused state but the clearest of the clear, the surest of the sure, utterly beyond words — where death was an almost laughable impossibility — the loss of personality (if so it were) seeming no extinction but the only true life."

It is also important to note that this fourth state of consciousness seems to be characterized by a uniquely discernable state of physiology. As reported in numerous media sources in recent years, scientists in the emerging field of neurotheology have begun to map out the changes that occur in the brain during absorption in deep meditation or prayer. The early findings indicate that as thought and sensory awareness dissolve, the areas of the brain that give us our sense of boundaries and orient us in time and space essentially switch off. This leaves the individual with a sense of boundlessness in which the usual distinction between self and non-self disappears. The brain, write researchers Eugene d'Aquili and Andrew Newberg in *Why God Won't Go Away*, perceives the self "as endless and intimately interwoven with everyone and everything."

An older body of data expands that portrait of transcendence. For nearly thirty years, researchers have been studying the physiological correlates of Transcendental Meditation in an attempt to map out the fourth state of consciousness. Significant changes mediated by the autonomic nervous system have been found to occur, especially in the deepest stages of meditation when pure consciousness is experienced. Heart rate, for instance, diminishes markedly, as does the rate of breathing. "Respiration slows to essentially a nonactive state," says Dr. Alarik Arenander, director of the Brain Research Institute at Maharishi University of Management in Iowa. "This occurs without any manipulation or control, and corresponds with subjective reports of experience without spatial and temporal boundaries." Also intriguing are findings of unusually high levels of brain wave synchrony across different areas of the cortex. "These waves of coherent brain activity suggest that the transcending process brings about a major shift in neural functioning," says Arenander.

Transcendental consciousness is, by definition, a transient state. It comes and goes with varying frequency during spiritual practices and, to a lesser extent, spontaneously. It is, however, the ground on which higher and more permanent states of consciousness are developed.

COSMIC CONSCIOUSNESS

When the mind is without care or joy, this is the height of Virtue.
When it is unified and unchanging, this is the height of stillness.
When it grates against nothing, this is the height of emptiness."

CHUANG-TZU

In cosmic consciousness (CC), the bliss, peace and Self-illumination of the fourth state never depart. The transcendent Self coexists with all the activities of the mind, body, senses and emotions. It is as if one could enjoy the flickering images of a movie and, at the same time, remain aware of the fully illumined screen on which they are projected—an analogy that makes sense only if you imagine that awareness of the screen confers upon the viewer perfect inner contentment and enhanced delight in the on-screen story. So it is with cosmic consciousness: the inner perfection creates a foundation on which the fluctuations of experience do not disturb the peace.

Cosmic consciousness represents the end of the ego's state of war with God. Now one's individuality has merged with universal intelligence and energy. All the yearning, all the doubt and despair, all the guilt, pain, shame and blame, melt into divine bliss, and the bliss is not just a mood or an attitude, it is an undying condition of Being. One is anchored in the unchanging Self, and that is the ultimate peace of God. There is nothing to fear, nothing to worry about, nothing to feel threatened by, for you own the soul's equivalent of an impregnable home and an inexhaustible source of nourishment. The inevitable losses and upsets of life are simultaneously experienced and observed from the silent, nonparticipating platform of pure consciousness. Like lines drawn on water, they are noted but fail to penetrate and leave a lasting impression.

Remembering Who You Are

The coexistence of unshakable inner silence with outward change and action has been called witnessing, a common, albeit fleeting, experience among spiritual aspirants. Here is Ram Dass on the experience of witnessing his thoughts: "When awareness goes behind thought, we are able to be free of time and see thoughts appearing and disappearing, just watching thought forms come into existence, exist, and pass away in a millisecond. And when the intensity of concentration allows us to see the space between two thoughts, we see eternity." Like those thoughts passing by on parade, *all* of human activity in cosmic consciousness is witnessed by the silent observer. "[I] am sensible of a certain doubleness by which I can stand as remote from myself as from another," wrote Henry David Thoreau. "However intense my experience, I am conscious of the presence . . . of a part of me, which, as it were, is not a part of me, but spectator, sharing no experience, but taking note of it; and that is no more I than it is you."

Individuals have been known to arrive at cosmic consciousness in a flash of illumination. Some have remained in its grace for a while, only to see it diminish and return, diminish and return, often many times over the course of years. In general, however, the growth from TC to CC is a gradual development fostered by regular spiritual discipline. The inner silence achieved through meditative practices carries over into worldly activity, only to fade again and again. Gradually, however, it clings, and eventually it becomes the very glue of existence. "With practice," writes Maharishi Mahesh Yogi, "the nervous system becomes habituated to not lose that state of awareness, that style of functioning, and then that state of awareness is maintained even during waking, dreaming, and sleeping. All the jerks and jolts of activity [are] not able to overthrow the reality of the fourth state of consciousness." That permanence is what defines the *fifth* state.

It should be emphasized that while cosmic consciousness is certainly out of the ordinary, there is nothing supernormal about it. It is not an "altered state." It is, on the contrary, our most natural state. Those who have tasted it for sustained periods of time have been surprised by its utter simplicity. It is like awakening to what has always been there, only veiled by the forces of habit, ignorance and a nervous system not yet capable of sustaining that level of awareness. This is illustrated in India by the allegory of a child prince who is kidnapped by robbers. Raised in the bandit's ways, he forgets completely his early life and his true origins. One day, the king's emissary comes across the long lost prince, now a grown man. He recognizes him, embraces him and calls him "Your Highness." The bandit shoves him away. But the man persists. He speaks of the prince's childhood, evoking scenes of palace life. Gradually, the prince remembers. "I am not a bandit," he finally declares. "I just forgot who I was." He returns to his kingdom, where he is welcomed with great fanfare and given his rightful inheritance. That's how it is to awaken and remember that one is a child of the infinite God.

God Consciousness

Peace is the first messenger to herald God's approach.
Then peace bursts into more dazzling lights of endless joy.

PARAMAHANSA YOGANANDA

Inwardly, cosmic consciousness represents the highest attainment. One knows one's Self to be infinite; one is unattached to the cravings that inevitably lead to pain and loss; one sustains unblemished peace and bliss at all times. This represents what has been called liberation, enlightenment or freedom from the bondage of ignorance. But this fifth state of consciousness is not the ultimate in human fulfillment, but rather the necessary foundation for subsequent development. For even in this exalted state, one still experiences the outer world as separate and apart, and one remains separate and apart from God. Growth toward higher states entails the closing of that gap, and the means by which that occurs is the refinement of perception and feeling.

From the fullness of inner freedom, it is said, one is naturally inclined to greet outer experience with open-armed appreciation. As one lives in this state of consciousness and grows toward the sixth state, the world becomes increasingly a thing of beauty and a joy forever. The senses become more acute, capable of perceiving deeper, more subtle qualities of sight, taste, touch, smell and sound. The heart's capacity for the finer qualities of feeling—love, devotion, tenderness, gratitude, compassion, reverence—expands. The direction of this growth is something any of us can relate to simply by noting how we respond to the world on a good day—when we feel happy, peaceful and energetic—and comparing that to a day when we're tired, needy, frustrated or sad. Think of the times you've fallen in love, accomplished something for which you worked hard, slept like a rock and spent the morning on a secluded beach or heard your child speak her first words—at such times you might have seen something radiant and sublime in a view you've seen a thousand times, or heard as if for the first time birdsongs or wind choruses that were always present, or tasted something fresh and luscious in a dish you'd eaten countless times before, or swelled in gratitude for no particular reason. Same people, same objects, same circumstances—different consciousness. It is as if you'd been running software on old, faulty hardware and transferred it to a spanking-new, flawless system. Growth toward God consciousness is like upgrading your hardware.

"The world is charged with the grandeur of God," wrote the poet Gerard Manley Hopkins. "There lives the dearest freshness deep down things." That freshness and grandeur is normally hidden from our feeble senses. We take in 90 percent of our information through our eyes, for example, and our eyes have the magnificent capacity to respond to a single photon of light. Yet what our eyes see is only a narrow band of the electromagnetic spectrum. Beyond that lies an enormous range of infrared and ultraviolet waves, gamma rays and cosmic rays and light detectable only by radar, x-rays and other technological aids. But we are capable of becoming detectors of a different, peculiarly human kind. When properly attuned, our nervous systems have the capacity to perceive the finest, most radiant qualities of matter, deep down at the level where changing substance and unchanging spirit merge like the sea and the sky at the horizon.

Celestial Perception

This sublime perception has been called celestial. It has been called numinous. It has been called divine light. It has been personified and given names, such as Shekhinah in Judaism and, depending on the interpreter, the Christian's Holy Ghost and the Hindu's Ishwara. "The world outside will now stand transformed as the very expression or manifestation of God," wrote Swami Ramdas of this perception. "Everywhere the Light of God will dazzle your eyes; even in the apparent diversity and activity of nature you will strangely be conscious of an all-pervading stillness and peace of the Eternal—a consciousness which is unshakably permanent . . . followed by the crowning experience of an abiding state of ineffable ecstasy."

Such awakened feelings can, of course, occur at any time. It is the soil in which sacred music and poetry takes root. As a temporary experience, this magnificent mode of awareness can be life transforming. The memory of the ecstatic moment can keep faith and persistence alive on the long spiritual quest. But there is a potential downside as well. Visions and ecstatic sensory experiences can be so intoxicating that they can, in a seeming paradox, distract you from the pursuit of complete enlightenment and the peace of God. The craving for a repeat performance can become as feverish as the pursuit of any material objective, and the frustration of not attaining it can trigger a spiritual crisis or an excruciating dark night of the soul.

"From a young age I had a flaming desire to serve God," says Amy Gallagher, the editor of *Passionate Living* magazine, "to hurl myself head first into the welcoming arms of the Divine. I embarked on a spiritual path of intense meditation, purification, prayer, and various techniques in the hope of achieving Divine Union. I had wondrous and ecstatic experiences, yet my heart was still not at rest." Then she met a teacher who taught her that "returning Home was as easy as opening and softening within [to] pure and simple Being." What she found, says Amy, is that merging with God "is not quite the rapture and ecstasy that I had previously imagined, nor does it measure up to the lofty spiritual ideas that once towered in my mind. Yet this tenderness and softness is unequivocally what I love most." She is not the first person to have ecstatic encounters with the Divine and *not* have inner peace or Self-realization. She was fortunate to learn the wisdom of integrating ecstasy and serenity.

For divine perception to rise to permanent God consciousness, the inner stability and Self-awareness of cosmic consciousness must be established first. It is in that sense that these seven states can be considered sequential, for glimpses of higher awareness—whether brief or sustained—can occur at any time. "If a man wants to be a true devotee of God," writes Maharishi Mahesh Yogi, "he has to become his pure Self; he has to free himself from those attributes which don't belong to him, and then only can he have one-pointed devotion . . . For his devotion to reach God it is necessary that he should first become purely himself, covered by nothing."

It is through the escalating interaction of refined perception and exalted feeling that God consciousness grows and becomes stabilized. The more you appreciate the world, the more you love it; the more you love the world, the more you appreciate it. This loving appreciation is no mere emotion. It is an immense, dynamic, coherent state of consciousness in which everything is embraced as part of one adorable whole.

To a certain extent, the process occurs naturally once the freedom of Self-realization is attained. But it can be aided—at *any* state of consciousness—by devotional practices. The qualities of feeling we associate with devotion—love, reverence, gratitude, worship—can, of course, be directed in any number of ways: toward one's spouse, children and other loved ones; toward the abstraction of one's heritage or tradition; toward a guru or a revered spiritual figure; toward a personification of the Divine such as Jesus or Buddha; toward the image of a deity. But those are just intermediaries for anyone seeking God. Eventually, devotion must culminate at the highest level, where ultimate credit is due. Just as appreciating a work of art naturally leads to esteem for the artist responsible for it, the feeling of ecstatic wonder before the magnificence of creation opens the heart to adoration of the Creator.

When God consciousness is attained, every perception is saturated with celestial glory, every thought is a ceaseless prayer and every action is a sacred offering. It is here that human love and divine love come together, and one achieves the goal that mystical Judaism calls *d'vekut:* to glue oneself to God. "To adore [God] means to lose oneself in the unfathomable," writes Pierre Teilhard de Chardin, "to plunge into the inexhaustible, to find peace in the incorruptible, to be absorbed in defined immensity, to offer oneself to the fire and the transparency, to annihilate oneself in proportion as one becomes more deliberately conscious of oneself, and to give of one's deepest to that whose depth has no end."

It must be emphasized that the fullness of God consciousness is not a matter of being conscious *of* God. It is not thinking about God, remembering God or having loving feelings for God. It is an intense state of being, beyond thought and beyond mere emotion, where you dwell in the awareness that there is no place you can go where God can be left behind.

UNITY CONSCIOUSNESS

The eye with which I see God is the eye with which God sees me.

MEISTER ECKHART

As magnificent as God consciousness is, it is not yet the ultimate. The next and final step is to actualize what are perhaps the ten most profound words ever strung together, the Upanishads' declaration, "I am That, thou art That, all this is That."

Even in the unending presence of the Divine, there is still separation—between subject and object, Self and non-Self, knower and known, lover and Beloved. What remains to be found is the ultimate grace: the union of I and Thou. Pure love can't stand separation; it craves the intimacy of perfect union. That is the living reality of the seventh state of consciousness.

Whereas in the previous state God is there all the time, in unity there is *only* God. Put another way, there is no longer a separate self that adores the Creator, only a singularity in which worshipper and worshipped come together in perfect oneness. The pure consciousness that was glimpsed in transcendence and stabilized in cosmic consciousness is now apprehended as the innermost essence of all that is. One has awakened to the truth that everything is Self, always was Self, always will be Self, and the journey from one state to another was a laughable illusion, because there was never really anywhere to go. The whole notion of separation was a colossal mistake. To cite the traditional analogy, it is as if one had been frightened by the appearance of a snake in the dark, only to realize when the light came on that it was a stick all along.

Apparently, the realization comes of its own accord to the person grounded in God consciousness, through the natural inclination of the lover to unite with the Beloved. The leap is propelled by refined feeling and perception, but the intellect is also said to play a role, because enlightenment is, to a large extent, a matter of *knowing* the ultimate truth. In well-prepared soil, what is called in Sanskrit a *mahavakya*, or great utterance—a penetrating statement by a teacher, a reading from a sacred scripture, even a profound truth heard or read countless times before—can suddenly lift the final veil to the supreme Aha! experience. Who knows? For you the source of the mahavakya might be J. D. Salinger. In his short story, "Teddy," a child describes watching his sister drink a glass of milk: "All of a sudden I saw that *she* was God and the *milk* was God. I mean, all she was doing was pouring God into God, if you know what I mean."

Duality Dissolves into Oneness

The momentum that began with cosmic consciousness, of projecting the awareness of the infinite Self outward, is now complete. All of creation is in me and I am in all of creation. "We always begin as dualists," said Swami Vivekananda. "God is a separate Being, and I am a separate being. Love comes between, and man begins to approach God, and God, as it were, begins to approach man. . . . and at last the point is reached when he becomes one with the object of worship. 'I am you, and you are I; and worshipping you, I worship myself; and in worshipping myself, I worship you.'"

Duality has disappeared into the formless, boundless nondual One. St. Teresa of Avila called this Spiritual Marriage, "a secret union" of the soul and God. Like all the blessed ones who have experienced this marriage, she was forced to describe it with metaphors: "[It] is like rain falling from the heavens into a river or spring; there is nothing but water there and it is impossible to divide or separate the water belonging to the river from that which fell from the heavens. Or it is as if a tiny streamlet enters the sea, from which it will find no way of separating itself, or as if in a room there were two large windows through which the light streamed in: it enters in different places but it all becomes one."

Unity consciousness is the ultimate in wholeness, harmony and intimacy. Everything is not only part of you, but *is* you. This does not mean, of course, that the wondrous diversity of the universe dissolves into some colorless broth; one could not function in the world without the ability to distinguish one form from another. Indeed, in this liberated state one is now equipped to extract more delight than ever from what has been called *lila*, the play of the Divine.

But with a difference: the ever-changing focus of perception no longer over-shadows the eternal silence of Oneness. Instead, unity is the dominant feature of awareness. Metaphorically, it is like gazing at the vast, eternal ocean while at the same time enjoying the dance of individual waves, which you know to be nothing but ocean.

First, the realization that I am That. Then, thou art That. Finally, all this is That. And that is that.

Ah, but not entirely. It is said that the enlightened ones retain, happily, a remnant of ignorance. The illusion of separation that sticks to the awareness, like the grease left on the hand when it lets go of a butterball, not only makes it possible to function in the world but to keep on feeling the ineffable rapture that comes with the love of God. Dnyanadev, a thirteenth-century poet-saint, described this cosmic trick, with apologies to the goddess to whom he was de-voted: "I see no way of truthfully praising you, for except silence you do not put on any other ornament. Your true praise consists in perfect silence, your worship is no outer act, and union with you is being nothing myself. But, if, like one whose mind is crazed and wildly babbles, I sing your praise, bear with it, Oh dear Mother."

The Quintessential Path to the Pathless

If you seek God,
You shall never find God.
But if you do not seek God,
God shall never reveal himself to you.

SUFI POEM

It has been said that the notion of a path to God-realization is absurd. God is everywhere present; there is no place to go. There is nothing to find, noth-ing to seek. We are already perfect, already divine, already one with all that is;

we do not have to do anything to become what we already are. The logic of those statements is flawless, and their truth at the highest level of awareness is self-evident and incandescent. But it is not the reality most of us live on a day-to-day basis. To put it simply, it is not enough to do as some have suggested: just wake up and realize you're already enlightened; stop striving and accept that you already have the peace of God. Just Be! Too often the attempt to do that amounts to confusing an intellectual concept with a genuine state of being, or using the power of suggestion to affect a mood that imitates what you *think* realization or enlightenment must be like.

We don't live the truth of what we are for the same reason we don't know the sun is out when the shades are stuck and we can't lift them because of ignorance or limited skills. We are blocked from apprehending the light of Reality because of the veils, and sometimes walls, of individual consciousness. The spiritual technologies developed over eons by every wisdom tradition were designed to remove those obstacles and snap us out of the illusions of the ego. It is not a matter of becoming anything different from what we are, but of ceasing to be what we are not. And, as paradoxical as it may sound, that requires intention and discipline.

The story is told of a devotee who goes to a guru and says that he wants to know God. The master takes him to a river, where he shoves the student's head under the water and holds it there. He lets the young man struggle before finally allowing him to surface. "What did you want most when you were under the water?" he asks.

"Air," the disciple replies. "I would have done anything for a breath of air."

"When you feel that way about God," says the master, "then you will find him."

Evolving toward the peace of God in higher states of consciousness is as natural as a plant growing toward the light. But, to bear fruit, plants need sun and water and rich soil—and the occasional bonus of fertilizer, nutrients and tender loving care to boost their chances. Similarly, spiritual progress is best not left to the vagaries of chance or grace. The section that follows suggests an integrative approach to establishing and stabilizing the peace of God, bringing into play all five aspects of the Quintessential Self.

At its core, the Quintessential Self is radiant light, the essence of essence, the holiest of holies, the part of you that touches God. Each aspect of the Quintessential Self radiates out from that core of eternal Being. However, while we are evolving toward the full enlightenment of Self-realization, the rays emanating from the core are, as it were, hazy, just as individual rooms might grow cold and dark when they are blocked from the fire in a central furnace. Because they do not glow with their full potential, the five aspects of the Quintessential Self overshadow our true nature as beings of light. Our core essence is obscured by the suppressed, repressed and depressed feelings of the emotional self; by the habitual roles that the relational self learns to play for survival, turning us into "rolebots"; by the doubts, misbeliefs and over-intellectualizing of the mental self; by the constraints of dogma and religious delusion on the spiritual self; and perhaps most of all by bodily needs, pain and the habit of identifying with the physical self, which is in reality nothing more than eternal light concentrated in solidified form (as Einstein revealed in his famous equation, $E=mc^2$, mass is merely concentrated energy).

By taking steps to remove those obstructions, we can reveal more and more of our essential light. Bear in mind that the effects of most practices are not confined to any one area of the Quintessential Self. A physical practice such as hatha yoga, for example, will affect not only the body but also the mental, emotional, relational and spiritual dimensions. Like the legs of a table, if one of the five is moved, all the others move as well.

The Spiritual Dimension of Reuniting with God

As in the illustration on page 23, the spiritual self sits atop the star of the Quintessential Self, receiving energy from the other four and at the same time watching over them and unifying them. By awakening our dormant spiritual power, we can bring peace to all aspects of our lives. While *everything* we do to secure the peace of God can be considered spiritual, we limit the discussion here to a few specific practices.

THE TRANSCENDENT PEACE OF MEDITATION

Be still and know that I am God.

PSALMS 46:10

The centerpiece of any path to higher consciousness, meditation is recommended as the most direct route to the Divine by virtually every spiritual tradition. There are, of course, a multitude of meditation forms. Some are more properly called contemplation, in that they involve pondering the meaning of a scriptural passage or a profound spiritual concept. Some entail highly rigorous mental workouts designed to discipline the mind and train it to concentrate. Others are more like sedatives, meant to elicit a soothing sense of relaxation. Some forms of meditation involve visualizing imaginary scenes or the image of a deity. Some utilize the sound of traditional mantras, and within that category are methods that range from rhythmic inner chanting to effortless repetition. The purpose of some is to cultivate certain qualities such as love, compassion or surrender. And some aim directly at awakening the limitless Self.

Every viable form of meditation should produce at least a measure of inner peace, but those that produce transcendental consciousness open the door to the *source* of peace, where individual presence meets the divine Presence. James Finley calls that quality of meditation a process that "lays bare our nature, and in so doing lays bare God's nature, which is given to us as our own nature." Just as removing the heat under a pot of boiling water reduces the excitation of the molecules so the bubbles cease their feverish activity and dissolve into their source, deep meditation reduces the excitation of the mind so it settles into the eternal stillness at the core of the soul. It becomes non-active but awake in itself, knowing "I am That."

It is fashionable to say that all meditation practices are the same. Perhaps it is more accurate to say that their goals are often the same and that they share certain features. But they are no more the same than cars, trains and planes are the same, even though they all are built to move passengers from one place to another. If it is to serve your yearning for the peace of God, your choice of a meditation practice should be undertaken with care and discernment, particularly if you intend to practice it by yourself without the ongoing guidance of an expert teacher. Generally speaking, a good form of meditation in our context would have the following features:

- relatively effortless and easy to do on your own
- taught by a properly trained teacher
- rooted in an established tradition with a long history of reliable success
- regularly elicits a state of restful alertness

That last item is the hallmark of any meditation that will promote the peace of God—inner stillness combined with an awakened awareness that transcends thoughts and concepts.

You may wish to find a meditation practice close to home, in the friendly confines of your religious tradition. That might not be easy to do, unless you stem from Hindu or Buddhist roots; few modern houses of worship feature inward practices other than the recitation of standard prayers. However, the more esoteric branches of every religion have witnessed a revival in recent years, and long-neglected meditative practices have become easier to learn. Jews in search of meditation have turned to the Kaballah and the Jewish Renewal movement; Christians to centering prayer and mystical practices derived from contemplative Christianity; Muslims to Sufi techniques such as *dhikr*. And, in the pragmatic American spirit of using whatever works, seekers in our pluralistic world are reaching beyond their own heritage with growing frequency—to Buddhist meditation forms such as zazen and vipassana, to various practices derived from the yoga tradition or to any number of meditation teachers offering self-designed techniques.

If you are looking for a meditation practice that does not conflict with your form of worship and does not require adopting a new belief system or becoming involved with a religious organization, you might want to consider transcendental meditation (TM). While its popular image is that of a simple relaxation technique, it is grounded in the Vedantic tradition and can be seen as a pure spiritual practice. Without disparaging the many forms of nonsectarian meditation available in the marketplace, we feel comfortable recommending TM because it meets the four criteria listed above, and because we have been practicing it ourselves for a combined total of over sixty years; it is taught by well-trained people in the same systematic manner everywhere in the world; and it is backed by hundreds of scientific studies on a wide range of measures—blood pressure, oxygen consumption, stress-related medical conditions, brain changes and many more—the aggregate of which point unequivocally to deep inner peace and the regular experience of transcendental consciousness.

Whatever technique you choose, it is important to learn from a qualified source and to make it a regular feature of daily life. It is in constancy that "the peace which passeth understanding" becomes stabilized.

THE PEACE OF PRAYER

Prayer is the energy feedback God gets from us, His creation.
Prayer completes the circuit of God's energy
and helps to keep it flowing.

RABBI ZALMAN SCHACTER-SHALOMI

Whereas meditation has been called a way of listening to God, prayer is considered a way of speaking to God. That distinction is useful as far as it goes, but with this important caveat: at their deepest and most profound level, prayer and meditation meet in a place beyond all speaking and listening, in the stillness of eternal union. That ineffable silence can be as resounding as a chorus of trumpets heralding the arrival of the Lord.

"Many people follow the formalities of the great religions and pray explicitly for specific events to occur," writes Larry Dossey, M.D., a leading researcher on prayer and healing. "Some people pray to a personal God or Goddess, the Almighty, or Supreme Being, others pray to an impersonal Universe or the Absolute. Others do not pray in a conventional sense, but live with a deeply interior sense of the sacred. Theirs could be called a spirit of prayerfulness, a sense of simply being attuned or aligned with 'something higher.'" As Dossey suggests, this most personal means of connecting to God comes in many forms. The content of prayer ranges far and wide, as do the intentions that people bring to prayer and the depth with which they experience it.

Take the two types of prayer described by comedian Emo Philips: "When I was a kid I used to pray every night for a new bicycle. Then I realized that the Lord doesn't work that way, so I stole one and asked Him to forgive me." A joke, yes, but an accurate accounting of a large portion of the prayers sent heavenward every day: petitions for gifts, not much different from a letter to Santa Claus, and contrite pleas to be forgiven for sins.

Compare that to the description of prayer by the thirteenth-century Christian mystic Mechthild of Magdeburg: "It draws down the great God into the little heart, it drives the hungry soul up into the fullness of God, it brings together two lovers, God and the soul in a wondrous place where they speak much of love." Here, the one who prays is asking for nothing, expecting nothing, only intimacy with the Divine and the opportunity to adore.

Prayer can range from extreme self-interest to complete self-surrender. Here is a list of different types of communication in prayer, along with the mental and emotional conditions that usually give rise to them:

- petitionary—desire, need, dependency
- for a miracle—desperation, helplessness
- bargaining—resignation
- confession—remorse
- for redemption—guilt, fear
- for guidance—surrender
- for the welfare of others—caring, compassion
- offering to serve—generosity
- thanksgiving—gratitude, fullness, contentment

- praise—awe, wonder, appreciation
- adoration—love, devotion
- silence—inner peace, communion

Evidence, such as the 1,200 studies on the effects of prayer on health, suggests that praying for specific results can often be effective. But what you pray for and how you go about it might make a difference. Rabbi Harold Schulweis distinguishes between passive and active prayer. In the latter, he says, "the petitioner views himself as an active correspondent of God" in a "two-sided relationship of co-creators and co-sanctifiers." Without that attitude of partnership, prayers often carry unrealistic expectations and a dependency on magic—a sure setup for disappointment. It is important, therefore, to ask yourself, Is my request reasonable? Is it deserving? Is it attainable?

The effectiveness of prayer also depends in large part on the sincerity with which it is expressed and the depth of quietude *from* which it is expressed. That is why meditation is often recommended as a prelude to prayer: to establish a sanctified meeting place for God by getting the ego out of the way. Said the Zen-like German priest Angelus Silesius in the seventeenth century, "God, whose love and joy are present everywhere, can't come to visit you unless you are not there."

A prayer's success also depends upon your openness to God's alternatives. You can't always get what you want, as the Rolling Stones made plain. But you might get something you need more, such as wisdom or guidance. Contrary to the notion that prayer is only for speaking *to* God, it is wise to include some listening time as well. In entering the silent parts of yourself, your small, individual mind can tap into cosmic intelligence, where everything is known. You may think of the messages that come as God's own counsel or as the subtle voice of intuition. Whatever you call it, a prayerfully receptive attitude prepares the ground for answers, even if you haven't asked any specific questions, and even if you weren't conscious of having questions in the first place.

At the highest level, prayers are *always* answered. When the true intent of prayer is not to get something but to commune intimately with the Divine, this statement by Rabbi David Cooper applies: "The urge to call out to God is *always* answered simultaneously as it is spoken, for ultimately there is no difference between the caller and that to which it calls." On that level, the matter of answered prayers becomes irrelevant. For here you have gone beyond petition, beyond supplication, beyond even thanksgiving. "For longer than I have been willing to admit, even to myself," writes John Shelby Spong, the retired bishop of the Episcopal Diocese of Newark, New Jersey, "prayers addressed to an external, supernatural God—a theistic deity—have had little or no meaning for me." He thought this was a personal deficiency, and he worked hard to overcome it. Eventually, he came to see himself as "a believer in exile," who needed to revise his understanding of prayer. Rather than "words addressed heavenward," prayer to Spong came to mean, "being present, sharing love, opening life to transcendence."

For prayer to rise to its highest spiritual potential, it should be more than a routine obligation, but rather a special time, a sacred time, one that you look forward to as you would a visit from a dear friend. It should also be deeply personal, not just rote repetition. Standardized prayers can be a magnificent and inspiring resource, but why not also choose prayers that have profound personal meaning? Remember Jesus's warning not to imitate those who pray only in public so they will be seen as devout, or those who think that the more they say the more likely it is that they'll be heard. "Go into a room by yourself," he advised, "shut the door, and pray to your Father who is there in the secret place."

You may find that as you pray you're inclined to verbalize less and less. Many resist this urge, thinking that prayer must be articulated clearly and loudly. But, as the Native American teacher Black Elk pointed out, "The Great Spirit is everywhere: He hears whatever is in our minds and hearts, and it is not necessary to speak to Him in a loud voice." You may find that you want to whisper, not speak. You may want to stop your lips and speak only in thought. You may want to stop forming sentences entirely, and speak the language of pure feeling. The original intention of your prayer might disappear entirely, as you sink into silence. Rather than fight this tendency on the assumption that prayer equates with speech, allow it to unfold. It could mean that you are moving to deeper levels of prayer, closer to God.

In his delineation of the stages of prayer, Thomas Merton describes what he calls "pure prayer." Here, he says, the soul "speaks to Him without knowing what it is saying because God Himself has distracted the mind from its words and thoughts. It reaches Him without thoughts because, before it can think of Him, He is already present in the depths of the spirit, moving it to love Him in a way it cannot explain or understand." This is the subterranean level at which prayer and meditation come together like underground streams. There occurs what Abraham Joshua Heschel describes as a "shift in the center of living from self-consciousness to self-surrender to God," where we "see the world in the mirror of the holy."

PEACE PILGRIMAGES

Since time immemorial, religious seekers have made pilgrimages to sacred sites and holy places—to Jerusalem, Bethlehem and Mecca; to Varanasi and Bodhgaya; to the Great Pyramids, Lourdes, Stonehenge, Delphi and Machu Picchu. They go to worship, to pray, to be healed, to drink the nectar of the Divine and draw closer to the peace of God. In these transformational settings, where the most sublime emotions have been deposited for centuries, the very atmosphere draws the receptive soul toward reverence and awe, like a riptide carries a bottle out to sea.

Consider making a pilgrimage to a holy place with personal meaning to you. To illustrate the kind of magic that can occur on such a journey, here is an account of a trip to the sacred sites of Egypt by a California physician:

"I was at a crossroads in my life. Not only was I unhappy with my work and considering a whole new professional direction, but it was a time of tremendous pain, physically and emotionally. An auto accident had left me with excruciating migraines, which I was treating with medical magnets attached to my forehead with bandaids, and my marriage of 18 years was suddenly falling apart, leaving me feeling abandoned and betrayed. I was shaken to my core, feeling like an invalidated invalid. When a group of business associates invited me to join them on a tour of Egypt, I saw it as a chance to get away and perhaps gain a higher vantage point on my broken life. I had no way of predicting what an amazing breakthrough would take place in Luxor, in an ancient temple within the Karnak temple complex.

"Our tour was led by Kevin Ryerson, the channeling expert who was featured in Shirley MacLaine's book *Out on a Limb*. At one point, in total darkness, Kevin said, 'Open your eyes and look into the face of the goddess. Welcome to the house of God.' I saw before me, in a beam of golden sunlight, the eerie, zoomorphic form of Sekhmet, who is, in a seeming paradox, the goddess of both war and healing. The icon had a human female form with the head of a female lion, and her eyes projected enormous compassion. As I gazed at her form, powerful emotions started to well up within me. I wasn't the only one. In the glow, I could see tears flowing freely from some of the other pilgrims. Then Kevin spoke in a voice that seemed eerily indigenous to the ancestral space we were in. He said that the temple was a model of the subconscious, that the light shining on Sekhmet was a link to the soul and the archetypal images carved on the walls could stimulate healing. He explained how Sekhmet would heal people's inner conflicts before they could turn into acts of aggression. It all made sense because I felt that my inner conflicts—about my wife, my work, my headaches and so forth—were somehow dissolving.

"Then we arranged ourselves according to our astrological signs and placed before the goddess the objects we had brought with us for personal inspiration. Then Kevin did a ritual with a large crystal. At first thousands of prisms hurtled around the room. Then he reflected a single beam of light into each person's eyes. I found myself drawn to an image of Hathor, the goddess of joy. It was then that I felt a tremendous release inside followed by a flood of blissful peace.

"Outside, Kevin pointed out that the stone core of the temple was surrounded by mud as far as the eye can see. The stone stands for the eternal, and the mud for all that is transient. It became clear that I had to let go of my marriage. It was also clear that the monetary rewards that had driven my work could no longer motivate me. It was time to focus on my long-postponed dream to serve humanity in a more lasting, spiritual way. When I told Kevin about my experience, he said, 'Well, you won't need these anymore,' and he removed the medical magnets from my forehead. The pain that had been my constant companion was gone, and it hasn't returned. The trip I thought would be a nice getaway turned out to be a pilgrimage that transformed my life in a major way."

Whether you trek over mountain passes or glide to your sacred site in an air-conditioned bus, bear the following points in mind:

- *Set your highest intention.* A pilgrimage is not just a sightseeing trip; it is a spiritual quest. Try to be clear on what your purpose is, what you hope to get out of the journey and what you are bringing to it.
- *Travel light.* By that we mean your mental and emotional baggage, not your suitcase. Try to leave all heavy items—worries, concerns, anxieties—at home, along with your preconceptions. But bring along your favorite prayers, objects with sacred meaning and anything else you feel might deepen your experience. Above all, bring with you wide-open senses and an alert mind so you can remain fully conscious at every moment.
- *Choose the right companions.* If you're traveling with a group, make sure they represent as closely as possible your true spiritual family. Incompatible personalities can make a mockery of a pilgrimage. Also, if you are joining a tour, make sure that any rituals and rites that will be performed are in tune with your spiritual beliefs.
- *Be open to everything.* Sometimes, the most enlightening moments on a pilgrimage come when least expected, perhaps on the way to or from a holy site. Try to welcome the surprises, pleasant or unpleasant, as part of the overall learning experience.
- *Keep a journal.* Take notes about your experiences. Don't just record the outer circumstances; describe the far more important events that take place in your heart and mind.

The Mental Dimension of Reuniting with God

The Vedas are useful only until the awakening.
To the awakened sage the Vedas are as useful as a
reservoir when there is a flood everywhere."

BHAGAVAD GITA II, 46

The intellect is often disparaged on the spiritual path because its tools of calculation, analysis and logic are not as useful in that arena as they are in the realm of material objects and quantifiable data. They can, in fact, get in the way. But it is for good reason that every wisdom tradition values study and discernment. The rational mind can be a valuable spiritual asset, and to neglect it would be as much a mistake as relying on it too much.

For one thing, a sharp, well-informed intellect is indispensable for making decisions about your spiritual life. It is there to remind you of God and your highest good when your mind strays to the frivolous, the trivial and the distracting. It is there to help you sort through the abundance of misunderstandings, misconceptions and mischief that abound in the marketplace of ideas. It is imperative for seekers of truth to evaluate information meticulously, and, when faced with choices, to listen to the counsel of the head as well as the heart.

Another, often less appreciated contribution of an informed mind is to properly interpret inner experiences. Without an adequate framework of understanding, profound spiritual openings can be disconcerting, or even terrifying. Many have been treated by ill-informed mental-health experts with the best of intentions as break*downs* instead of breakthroughs. Sustained glimpses of cosmic consciousness, for instance, have been erroneously diagnosed as depersonalization disorder and treated with inappropriate therapies and medications. Ecstatic encounters with God-consciousness have been glibly dismissed as hallucinations. And many an intense spiritual crisis has been handled as an ordinary episode of depression or anxiety. In most cases, the fear and confusion could have been avoided if the individuals and those around them had had a clear understanding of the nature of spiritual experience.

There is, as well, a subtler and more profound way for the intellect to serve the spirit: to lead the mind to deeper levels and ultimately to transcend itself. Branches of every tradition use methods of diligent inquiry to train the seeker to distinguish the real from the unreal, the eternal from the perishable. Sacred texts, commentaries and the discourses of revered teachers are subject to intense scrutiny. Stories are dissected, metaphors deconstructed and treatises analyzed like legal briefs. Masters are cross-examined. Passages of scripture are taken apart and reassembled like clocks. In the highest teachings, discernment does not remain on the conceptual level, but rather escorts the mind through the door to the living experience of God.

In the Buddhist and Hindu traditions, various contemplative methods are used to convince the mind of the impermanent nature of experience in ordinary waking consciousness. The mind comes to understand that everything we see, touch, taste, smell and hear is unreal. The pleasures we crave, the goals we seek to achieve, the desires we wish to fulfill, the bodies with which we identify—all are subject to change, dissolution and death. These truths are made indisputably plain to the intellect through repeated observation and analysis. So too is the complementary truth of the eternal Oneness that underlies and permeates all impermanent phenomena. Often the method used to drive that point home is one of intellectual negation, what in India is called *neti neti*: not this, not that. This is not the Real; that is not the Real; nor that, nor that, nor that. Nothing that changes can be the Real and nothing discernible to the senses can be the Real. In place of "the Real," any particular teaching might substitute "God," or "Brahman," or another name for the Ultimate Reality.

In certain schools of Vedanta, seekers are taught to inquire, "Who am I?" repeatedly. They are guided to the realization that they are not their bodies, not their personalities, not the roles they play in society, not anything with limits and boundaries, for all of that changes and yet the "I" remains. What is that "I"? Not my thoughts, for they change too. And who is doing the thinking?

Who is asking these questions? Who answered *that* question? All of this is meant to carry the mind to the witnessing awareness, where the true Self is revealed as the unchanging screen on which all mind-forms are projected. "The thought 'Who am I?' will destroy all other thoughts," said Ramana Maharshi, the early twentieth-century master of self-inquiry, "and, like the stick used for stirring the burning pyre, it will itself in the end get destroyed. Then there will arise Self-realization."

By itself, the path of intellectual inquiry can easily get stuck in the mud of the mind, endlessly spinning its wheels—particularly in the absence of ongoing contact with a skilled mentor. It is one thing to understand conceptually that God is ever present as the eternal Self, and it is quite another to live it, breathe it and truly *know* it. Another risk is that the constant contemplation of abstract ideas can interfere with the demands of everyday life. For these reasons, such paths have traditionally been confined to the contemplative life of a monastery. With that caveat in mind, however, every seeker of peace with God is encouraged to dissect sacred writings, question spiritual authorities and otherwise engage his or her mind in the service of truth.

Just as a river is different each time you set foot in it, everything you read is different each time you read it. As your consciousness and discernment grow, you invariably find nuances of meaning you could not have absorbed at an earlier stage in your evolution, and each new insight has the potential to elevate your relationship with God. Therefore, spiritual texts can be read repeatedly and never exhaust their value. But why remain within the boundaries of a single tradition? Never have so many rich sources of wisdom been available to the average person. "Reading other scriptures often throws light on your own," says Vandana Mataji, a Catholic nun who runs an ashram in India where the Upanishads sit beside the Bible. "They illumine texts with which one has long been familiar, yet which one has not yet really begun to fathom."

Try not to read spiritual texts as you would a history treatise or a science book, looking for facts. Think of every chapter as an onion of wisdom that reveals deeper meaning as each layer is peeled away. Ponder what might have been lost in translation. Consider what the original intent might have been in the context of the time and place in which it was written. Examine a variety of interpretations. And try to approach sacred stories metaphorically, not just literally. What do the elements of the tales symbolize? To what do they allude? Where spiritual growth is concerned, it matters less whether Moses actually parted the Red Sea or Jesus actually ascended bodily to heaven than what lies beneath the surface of those eternal tales. One good exercise is to think of the characters and events as archetypes for what takes place within the individual psyche on the spiritual path. What, for instance, is your inner Judas? What is the cross you bear? What demons must you overcome in your personal Gethsemane? What must be crucified in you before you can be resurrected? Alternatively, what is your inner pharaoh? What keeps you enslaved in your personal Egypt? What miracles must you perform to win your liberation? What psychospiritual wilderness must you cross before you can reach the Promised Land?

THE "LECTIO DIVINA" PROCESS

Here is an exercise for extracting deep personal meaning from sacred writings. Created by Benedictine monks centuries ago, *lectio divina* (divine reading) is best done in a small group setting. If you have no friends or family with whom to share it, however, by all means adapt the instructions for use on your own.

Have someone in the group select a brief passage (no more than a page or two) from a traditional scripture or from a book or article on spirituality. Then follow these steps:

1. A member of the group slowly reads the passage aloud. Others read along silently or listen receptively, with an open mind and heart.
2. Repeat Step 1. This time, notice which word or phrase leaps out at you.
3. Repeat the word or phrase to yourself several times.

4. Each person speaks aloud the word or phrase they chose, without explanation.

5. Repeat Step 1 again. As the passage is read, focus on the word or phrase you selected. After the reading, take a few minutes to contemplate the meaning that the word or phrase holds for you. It might be a philosophical interpretation, a fresh insight into a spiritual concept or something strictly personal.

6. Everyone briefly explains what their word or phrase says to them and why they responded to it. The personal meaning does not have to conform to the content of the selection or the source from which it comes.

7. Take an extended period of silence (ten to thirty minutes). During that time, open yourself to what God is saying to you through the passage. Visualize yourself entering the passage and in some way engaging with the words, the characters (if it is a story) or the ideas. Just go where the spirit leads you, and when you're ready, write down your thoughts and feelings.

8. Everyone who wishes to share their thoughts and feelings is given time to do so (agree in advance on a maximum time). It should be agreed that everything shared will be held in confidence. Comments should be limited to questions that might help the person derive deeper meaning. Do not give unsolicited advice, and do not or use someone else's time to bring up ideas or problems of your own.

9. Close the session with a few moments of silence, a prayer or an invocation.

The Emotional Dimension of Reuniting with God

Thou shalt love the Lord thy God with all thine heart,
and with all thy soul, and with all thy might.

DEUTERONOMY 6:5

Every emotion, pleasant or unpleasant, is part of the vibrant rainbow of feelings with which we have been uniquely blessed. We deprive ourselves of the drama of being human if we don't allow ourselves to experience their complete range. Nevertheless, some emotions are clearly associated with godliness, and others with sin, in the sense of being off the mark. As we enter more deeply into the peace of God, we naturally grow in love, compassion, kindness, joy and other feelings we associate with a spiritual heart. And, in reverse, the more we cultivate those qualities, the closer we draw to the peace of God. "Everyone sees the Unseen in proportion to the clarity of his heart," said Rumi, "and that depends upon how much he has polished it. Whoever has polished it more sees more."

Many people who are devoted to spirituality shy away from the "ungodly" emotions that remind us that we're not yet perfect, that highlight our attachments and shout, "You're selfish! You're weak! You're needy!" When those bugaboo emotions spring up repeatedly, many of us engage in "spiritual bypassing," which psychologist John Welwood describes as "the use of spiritual ideas and practices to shore up a shaky sense of self, or to belittle basic needs, feelings, and developmental tasks in the name of enlightenment." Instead of dealing with our messy emotional patterns, we assume that all we need is more prayer, more meditation, more yoga, more worship, more of whatever will bring us the awakening or amazing grace that will presumably put an end to problematic feelings. To a certain extent the heightened awareness and deep peace brought on by spiritual practices *can* erase old emotional patterns. But not entirely. Emotional tendencies can be stubborn, and as long as they cling to us, we can't fully receive God's love or express love for God.

EMOTIONAL LITERACY

To awaken the best of human feelings and diminish the worst, we have to become emotionally literate. In and of themselves, emotions are neither good nor bad. They are, to a large extent, automatic reflexes over which we have little or no control. But we do have power over what happens once they surface.

An important step in emotional literacy is to learn the vocabulary of feeling. This list will help you identify negative emotions when they arise:

Afraid	Angry	Anxious
Apprehensive	Ashamed	Betrayed
Bitter	Crushed	Cynical
Depressed	Despairing	Distraught
Embarrassed	Empty	Enraged
Envious	Foolish	Frustrated
Greedy	Grief-stricken	Guilty
Hateful	Helpless	Hostile
Impatient	Inadequate	Insignificant
Jealous	Lonely	Oppressed
Overwhelmed	Pessimistic	Resentful
Sad	Selfish	Spiteful
Tense	Threatened	Unlovable
Unworthy	Victimized	Worried

As soon as you feel it, name it. While it is unhealthy to stuff feelings into some closet of your soul where they will eventually turn toxic, it is a mark of spiritual maturity to witness their eruption, interpret the information they convey and, when possible, convert their energy to a more positive alternative. Try to recognize emotions when they are mere sprouts, before they burst into full bloom and overwhelm the mind. If possible, take the time to close your eyes and feel them completely. This will reduce their physical charge and forestall any impulsive action you might later regret. If the feelings persist, writing in a journal will help you release the energy that drives them and give you insight into their origin and meaning. Then, to the extent you can, choose a more spiritually appropriate way to deal with whatever triggered the feeling. If you can do that without being a phony, you can use negative emotions as a source of transformation.

ENLIGHTENING YOUR EMOTIONS

Here is a list of emotional qualities generally regarded as markers of spiritual maturity and peace with God. Identify those you wish were more prominent in your life but have been blocked for one reason or another. You will want to favor them when you are conscious of having a choice.

Appreciation	Awe	Balance
Blissful	Calmness	Communion
Compassion	Contentment	Creativity
Devotion	Ecstasy	Empathy
Enthusiasm	Faith	Forgiveness
Friendliness	Generosity	Goodwill
Gratitude	Happiness	Humility
Joy	Kindness	Lighthearted
Love	Optimism	Patience
Peaceful	Playful	Powerful
Reverence	Serenity	Surrender
Trusting	Unattached	Vibrant
Wholeness	Wonder	Worshipful

Choose a quality you wish to develop. Take a few minutes daily to settle into a relaxed, comfortable state of mind (perhaps following your usual period of meditation or prayer) and visualize yourself already having that trait in abundance. What would it feel like? How would it manifest in everyday situations, at home, at work, at play, with other people, and so on? How would you speak if you owned that quality to its fullest? How would you act in a crisis? How would you treat people in need or those who were upset with you? By fixing positive images in your mind, you are telling your subconscious to substitute these qualities for the less desirable patterns that may have hindered you in the past. Work with one at a time, moving to the next in order of priority as soon as you feel ready.

As you visualize yourself exhibiting desired qualities, you will become conscious of a gap between where you want to be and where you are in the present. Acknowledge these differences honestly. Being aware of the tension between the ideal and the actual will help you gravitate naturally in the right direction. It takes time, however. Negative habits do not change overnight, so it is important to be patient. And if intractable emotional tendencies continue to cause problems in your life, by all means bring them to a qualified therapist who can help you use them as a catalyst for spiritual growth.

FROM GRIEVANCE TO GRATITUDE

If the only prayer you ever say in your entire life
is Thank You, it will be enough.

MEISTER ECKHART

In a sense, gratitude is the mother of all virtues. When you can greet life every day, every instant, regardless of outer circumstances, with an unambiguous "Yes!" then all other desirable emotional qualities tend to fall into line like chicks following a hen.

Two different people experience the same trying circumstances: one bitches and moans, while the other responds with dignity and grace. Two different people find love, success or good fortune: one takes it for granted and finds something to complain about, while the other bows her head in thanksgiving. Indeed, *you* might experience the same exact circumstances in radically different ways depending on your mood, your health and other factors affecting your overall state of consciousness. Whether you deprecate or appreciate, praise God or curse God, is a matter of awareness and attitude, and, to a large extent, choice. "I have set before you life and death, blessing and cursing: therefore choose life" (Deut. 30:19). The wise ones have always advised us to pay homage to the bright shafts of light that break through the cracks in the darkness, no matter how dark it gets. The reward is a shift in feeling, from sour grapes to sweet wine.

Sometimes, finding a reason to say "Thank you" requires nothing more than a shift of attention. At other times it takes a leap of faith to trust that this moment of your life is just as it should be and that somewhere in the muck and mire lay diamonds waiting to be uncovered. Sifting them out is worth the effort. Every true gift carries with it something more than the gift itself: the love of the giver. When you can see every moment as a gift from God, you open your heart to the *love* of God as well.

One way to cultivate gratitude is to take a few minutes each night to review the day and write down five things for which you are grateful. Try to do it with full attention, not just as an obligatory ritual, and look beyond the obvious blessings to the smaller gems that often go unnoticed.

You might want to start by expressing your gratitude for all the influences that have brought you to this moment in your quest for peace with God. The Talmud says, "Every blade of grass has its angel that bends over it and whispers, 'Grow, grow.'" Acknowledge the angels whose whispers have fueled your spiritual growth. Write a list of all the people—family, friends, mentors, clerics, etc.—who were your main catalysts. Add the authors, public speakers and shining role models who inspired and instructed you along the path. Write each of those angels a brief thank-you note, whether or not you intend to mail it, describing how they influenced you and why you are grateful to them. Then go out and be an angel to someone else.

THE OCEAN OF DEVOTION

I am He whom I love and He whom I love is I.

AL-HALLAJ

As described earlier, the blossoming of inner peace into the full effulgence of God consciousness takes place largely through the act of devotion, the most refined feeling of which humans are capable. In the Bhagavad Gita, Krishna, representing the embodiment of God, tells Arjuna, after revealing his divine form, "Neither by the Vedas, nor by penances, nor by alms-giving, nor yet by sacrifice, am I to be seen in the form in which you have now beheld Me. But by devotion to Me alone may I be known in this form . . . realized truly, and entered into."

Needless to say, many of the rituals of every religion were designed to give the worshipper prescribed ways to express the most tender of feelings toward God. We can only encourage you to make the best use of those opportunities. Try to bring to those sacred moments a fully open heart and a calm, alert mind, and leave your ego at the door. It doesn't matter whether the congregants around you are restless or bored. It doesn't matter if the priest, rabbi, minister or imam is going through the motions like he can't wait to get home for the football game. This is between you and God. It is your chance to praise, to celebrate, to express your love and to say, "Thanks for everything."

Of course, you needn't restrict your devotional activity to formal occasions. You can shout "Thanks" at the top of your lungs or feel it silently in your heart at any time. One easy practice is to learn some devotional music and sing your thanks when you feel so moved. Whether they are standard hymns, gospel songs, pop tunes with a spiritual theme or devotional chants from another culture in a language you don't understand, you can also sing them when your mind is distracted by trivial, repetitive or negative thoughts, when you're out walking or jogging, when you're driving, and any other time you want to honor the Divine. In one of India's scriptures, God says to a devotee, "I do not live in heaven, nor do I live in the heart of the Yogi, but where my devotees sing my praise, there am I."

How to Create Your Sacred Altar

Another powerful way to build devotional activity into your life is to create a sacred altar in your home. Set it up on a flat surface in a special place. If you are lucky enough to have a room set aside for meditation, that would be the perfect location. If not, try to put the altar in an area without a phone, TV, computer, fax machine or any other intrusive technology. (A CD player, however, would be a nice addition, if you restrict its use to spiritually appropriate selections.) The focal point of the altar might be a photo, sculpture or other representation of a holy person, a divine embodiment or a sacred place that represents God for you. If you like, add other spiritual figures (why not have a pantheon?), symbols of religious traditions you revere, a holy book, meaningful quotes, prayers, an amulet, a crystal, a chalice, sword or shield, a plant, photos of your loved ones—anything you hold sacred and can evoke in you the highest thoughts and the most tender feelings.

An altar can alter your perceptions, your feelings, and your thoughts, lifting them above the mundane by reminding you of the sacred. Keep it clean. Place cut flowers on it regularly. Add and subtract items from time to time, or rearrange their placement. Anything to keep the altar fresh and alive. And perform the activity of maintaining your altar in the spirit of a devotional ritual, mindfully, as if you were preparing a guest room for a saint.

Don't just let your altar become part of the furniture. Spend time there (you might want to keep a pillow or chair handy so you can be comfortable). Use it. Perform rituals and ceremonies on it. Make offerings. Sing or chant. Pray and meditate. Or simply stand before it in contemplation. Its very sight can be transformational. Touch the various objects to make palpable the abstract ideas and feelings they embody. When a specific spiritual or emotional need arises, focus on an object that corresponds to that need or seems to call out to you. Hold it. Touch it to your heart or lips. Contemplate what it represents and gain strength and wisdom from it. When performed from the heart, such activities can be remarkably transformative. You might feel a shift in your blood flow or your musculature. You might feel movement in the heart area, or a sense of divine presence. At times you might even feel moved to sob, to moan, to cry out in anger or to otherwise release pent-up emotions. Your altar should be a place where you feel safe to give voice to what you feel at the moment, knowing you are in a sanctuary of unconditional love.

Here is how one person describes the use of her altar: "Sometimes I go to it knowing that I need something specific. Other times, I just gravitate to it and realize later that I needed something. I stand before it, taking a few minutes to empty myself. Then I slowly let my gaze fall on every object. After a while, the altar seems to become transparent, and my spirit is transported through a gateway to God. I find that I'm sitting with my 'God team'—the figures in the photos become real, but in another dimension. Sometimes I get guidance from them. I may get concrete advice or inspiration. I might get a vision of what to do in the next chapter of my life. Insurmountable problems become manageable. At those times I feel as though I have awakened from a deep sleep, like I've moved from the consensus reality to a higher wisdom. Above all, I feel an intense communion with God."

CONSECRATING YOUR LIFE

Potentially, everything you do can be a devotional act. Every moment presents an opportunity to remember God and offer praise and thanks. Many of us are accustomed to saying grace before meals. Why not consecrate other routine features of life as well? Jews, for instance, are called upon to place mezuzahs on their doorposts to remind them of God when entering and leaving their homes. Christians intone phrases like "God bless" and "Thank the Lord." Muslims bless endeavors with *Bismallah ir rahman ir raheen* ("In the name of God, boundlessly compassionate, boundlessly merciful"). All of life's events can be made sacred, whether it's visiting friends, cooking a meal, bathing your child or paying your bills.

Whenever devotional feelings arise in your heart, whether you're at your private altar, or in a church, a disco, a ballpark, a freeway or some holy niche in temple Earth, express them with full-hearted reverence, without the desire for personal gain—even though you know, deep down, that what you stand to gain is priceless. Devotion is an offering. Not just an offering of words, or flowers or melodies or praise, but an offering of the self. And in giving up the small self comes the ultimate gain. In the culmination of devotion, you don't just love, you *become* love. Lover, Beloved and the process of loving all unite in the singular oneness of God.

The Physical Dimension of Reuniting with God

If the doors of perception were cleansed, everything
would appear to man as it is, infinite.

WILLIAM BLAKE

Beseeching God to reveal his or her glory is like asking someone to unlock a door when it's you who holds the keys. God's grandeur is already present, not just in the depths of matter where even supercolliders can't go, but right on the surface—for those you have the eyes to see. "We kick a diamond like it's any old stone because we don't have the ability to perceive and evaluate it," says Maharishi Mahesh Yogi. "We not only ignore it, but we may complain that we have hurt our toe. But a trained jeweler has the ability to perceive the diamond for what it is." So it is with those whose perception is attuned to the Divine. In God consciousness, as we saw earlier, one is able to appreciate the objects of creation at their most glorious, where the sublime artistry of the Creator is revealed.

The ability to see not only with what metaphysicians have called the "material eye," or with the "conceptual eye" of abstract ideas, but also with the "eye of the spirit," is not entirely a matter of spontaneous grace. It can be nurtured through physiological refinement. Just as we use technological devices such as microscopes and telescopes to extend the range of sense perception, we can open our senses directly to previously unseen, unheard and unfelt glories. Some of the psychospiritual technologies already mentioned — meditation, prayer, devotional rituals, etc. — work on that level as well their more obvious functions. And there is much more we can do to further awaken our dormant perceptual abilities.

Love All God's Creation

"Love every leaf, every ray of God's light," wrote Feodor Dostoyevsky. "Love the animals, love the plants, love everything. If you love everything, you will perceive the divine mystery in things. Once you perceive it, you will begin to comprehend it better every day, and you will come, at last, to love the whole world with an embracing love." That is the task of those who wish to bask in the peace of God, and to a large extent, it is a matter of practice and intention — practice in the sense of learning to attune your perception, just as you might practice the use of a musical instrument or a high-tech device; intention in the sense of being alert and attentive instead of dull or distracted.

When asked where God dwells, a Hasidic rabbi replied, "God resides wherever we let God in." Nevertheless, just as oxygen is present everywhere, but it's decidedly easier to breathe in some places than in others, God is everywhere, but the Presence is easier to locate in the sacred places, the pure places, the places that seem to have "Entering Holy Ground" emblazoned on their entrances in invisible letters. Spectacular natural settings, where the palate is vibrant, the air is fragrant and the sounds are sonatas to the ear — that's where most of us come closest to perceiving the miraculous. Getting out into nature, therefore, can be as much of an imperative for the modern seeker of God as spending time in a meditation hall or a house of worship. That is where we are likeliest to see, in Blake's words, "a world in a grain of sand, and a heaven in a wild flower."

Another arena for energizing latent perceptual faculties is art. Museums and concert halls are cathedrals to the eternal creative spirit as it flows through human beings. The greatest art springs from the deepest reaches of consciousness, where silence finds a voice and emptiness takes on form. When you commune with a masterpiece, regardless of the medium, you connect to some degree with the artist's awareness at the time of conception, and in that communion your own awareness can be drawn toward the same pure place. Some art, of course, is sacred in intent. Whether it's a statue of a deity, a painting of a saint or an oratorio on a biblical theme, its content is spiritual and one of its purposes is to evoke in the viewer or listener a religious experience. But art does not have to be explicitly spiritual to serve the purpose of refining one's ability to perceive the Divine. Content may be less important than aesthetic quality and the depth of soul from which the work was conceived. It does not have to be soothing or uplifting by design, it just has to move your spirit and awaken your senses.

Wherever you find sensory delight, whether Yosemite or the Louvre, the refinement of perception is not automatic. We get from nature and art only what we bring to it. If we're dull with fatigue, consumed by problems, ruminating about the past or pondering the future, we cannot receive the full glory of what is being offered to us. For the sensory moment to be a doorway from the immanent to the transcendent, we need to approach it with mindful, awakened, reverent attention. "When we are mindful," says Thich Nhat Hanh, "deeply in touch with the present moment, our understanding of what is going on deepens, and we begin to be filled with acceptance, joy, peace and love."

Try to get into the habit of placing your full attention on the present sensory experience. When you look, just look—and really see. When you listen, really hear. When you sniff, really smell. When you touch, really feel. When you taste, really savor. Too often, we're distracted by the babble of the mind and fail to appreciate the sacramental fullness of the moment. At times, all it takes to come back to the present is to redirect your attention. However, because touch is the most immediately grounding of the senses, a good technique for shifting your energy away from a mental maelstrom is to grab hold of an object and put your full attention on the feeling. If you're walking, notice the sensations in your feet as your weight shifts from one side to the other.

From touch, it is an easy transition to the sight or sound on which you wish to focus. Another way to quiet the mind is to focus on your breath. Simply attend to the natural pattern, noticing the sensations in your nostrils, chest and belly as you inhale and exhale.

SACRED STROLLS

The sensory refinement and perceptual skills you uncover when communing with nature or art can be carried home to your mundane world, like buckets of fresh water hauled from a river to a village where the well is stagnant. Every place is hallowed ground. There is nowhere that God is not, and if God does not seem to be present, it is merely an illusion based on our inability to perceive, "For now we see through a glass, darkly." It takes practice to locate the sacred in the profane, but the memory of transcendent wonder that you have glimpsed in cathedrals, whether of hand-shaped stone or God-shaped greenery, can help you evoke it wherever you are. In part it is a matter of remembering that the desk lamp is as holy as the stars, the fence as holy as the snowcapped peaks, the tap water as holy as the raging river. But it is also a matter of being mindful to the magnificence of everyday life. "The time of business does not with me differ from the time of prayer," said Brother Lawrence, "and in the noise and clatter of my kitchen, while several persons are calling for different things, I possess God in as great tranquility as if I were upon my knees at the blessed sacrament."

Why not set aside some time for a sacred stroll around familiar places close to home? To help create a reverent mood, imagine that you are walking side by side with Moses, Jesus, Buddha, Muhammad or any saint or sage of your choice. Try to see your surroundings as if for the first time, as if everything had been set in its place the night before by the hand of God. Find the invisible splendor behind your familiar, visible world. To heighten your powers of observation, try looking through a rolled up newspaper, or bring along a camera and frame scenes as if they were works of art. At some point, find a comfortable place to sit and close your eyes. Notice how many different sounds you can hear—birds, insects, voices, etc.—and how many scents you've never before sniffed. When you stop to eat, place your complete, unspoiled attention on every delectable bite. And gently remind yourself that everything you see, hear, touch, taste and smell contains the same divine spark as you do. "God himself culminates in the present moment," wrote Thoreau, "and will never be more divine in the lapse of all the ages."

In the film *American Beauty*, written by Alan Ball, a teenager tells his girlfriend that he videotaped a homeless woman who froze to death looking sad. "When you see something like that it's like God is looking right at you, just for a second," he says, "and if you're careful you can look right back."

Then he shows her the most beautiful thing he's ever filmed. In what many consider the film's most arresting scene, we see on video a plastic bag fluttering in the wind, with a city sidewalk and a red brick wall as backdrops. As he filmed the dancing bag, the boy recounts, "I realized that there was this entire life behind things, and this incredibly benevolent force that wanted me to know that there was no reason to be afraid. Ever."

Even corpses and trash are "charged with the grandeur of God." But don't expect miracles of God-perception from yourself. The habit develops over time, like taking up bird watching and gradually seeing winged creatures where you never suspected they were hiding. "The ideal of man is to see God in everything," said Swami Vivekananda. "But if you cannot see Him in everything, see Him in one thing, in that thing which you like best, and then see Him in another. So on you can go."

REFINING PERCEPTION

We have known for more than thirty years, ever since Elmer Green of the Menninger Clinic first articulated the principle, that "Every change in the physiological state is accompanied by an appropriate change in the mental-emotional state," and vice versa. As a rule, the more we can stabilize the state of awareness we called restful alertness (quiet mind/heightened wakefulness), the better equipped the nervous system is to appreciate the most sublime qualities of experience. This adds a whole new dimension to how we think about physical health. Over and above the usual recommendations for avoiding illness, we can consider what will best help the nervous system sustain the peace of God. For example, vitamin and mineral deficiencies, minor hormonal imbalances and the like may be discounted as serious health risks, but they might throw off the body's chemistry and prevent the nervous system from sustaining restful alertness. Poor eating habits, exposure to toxins, substance abuse, excessive fatigue, lack of exercise—all these can dull the senses, agitate the nervous system and destroy our ability to discern anything deeper than the most commonplace perceptions. Lifestyle habits that enliven and calm, on the other hand, will heighten that ability.

The premier system for training the physiology to support spiritual experience is hatha yoga. Yoga, which derives from the same root as the English word yoke, means union, its ultimate goal being the union of the individual with the Divine. The time-tested collection of practices that comprise hatha yoga features hundreds of movements and postures (asanas) of varying degrees of ease, as well as a large repertoire of breathing techniques (pranayamas) that ranges from gentle to strenuous. Their overall purpose is to cleanse the system of impurities and stress, and to produce deep calm and heightened awareness. While less explicitly spiritual than yoga, the ancient Chinese systems of tai chi and qigong also use movement and breath to achieve similar physiological goals.

MEDICINALS OF PEACE

The medicinal use of God's bountiful plant kingdom also has a long history of helping individuals counteract imbalances to achieve inner peace. The herb valerian, for instance, has been used for centuries as a safe, natural sedative. In India, ashwaganda has long been known as a rejuvenative and calming herb. In recent years, research on St. John's wort and kava kava suggest that they might have value, respectively, in treating mild to moderate depression and anxiety. Studies also indicate that acupuncture and Chinese herbs have potential value in these areas. Most promising in restoring deep peace to the system is the ancient medical system of India, *ayurveda*. Its integrative approach to health holds as a primary purpose the cultivation of higher states of consciousness.

As modern science continues to uncover the seamless interplay of mind, body and spirit, it becomes increasingly clear that religions have always been right to regard the body as the temple of the soul. There is, of course, a great deal of conflicting health advice out there. In the present context, the rule of thumb is this: do things that promote restful alertness and refined perception; avoid that which causes either dullness or agitation, and thereby clouds perception. One good gauge is to notice how peaceful and alert you are during your regular prayer or meditation sessions; restlessness and fogginess may be signs that you need to balance your physiology.

The Relational Dimension of Reuniting with God

I want to find God, and because I want to find God, I have to find God along with other people. I don't believe I can find God alone.

MAHATMA GANDHI

What we know as the Golden Rule has been stated and restated through the ages by every religion and every ethical philosophy. In ancient Jerusalem, Rabbi Hillel told a young seeker, "What is hateful to you, do not do to others. That is the whole of the Torah. The rest is commentary."

In China, Confucius echoed Hillel: "What you do not want done to yourself, do not do to others." Islam puts it this way: "No one of you is a believer until he desires for his brother that which he desires for himself." In Leviticus it reads as a commandment, "Thou shalt love thy neighbor as thyself," words repeated by Jesus when the Pharisees challenged him, and later reframed in the Sermon on the Mount as, "Always treat others as you would like them to treat you." Perhaps Jesus had heard that Aristotle had said, three hundred years earlier, "We should behave to our friends as we would wish our friends to behave to us."

The rule is called golden because it is simple, precise and flawless. But it's not always easy to follow. The perfection of "Love thy neighbor as thyself" comes in the fullness of unity consciousness, when one literally sees the Self in one's neighbor, in every other being and in all that is. When the Other is the Self and the Self is the Other, it is only natural to act with love, compassion and kindness to all. Prior to that awakening, however, it is a challenge to say the least. Our egos get in the way. Pride and self-interest block our noblest intentions. The fire of anger consumes the seeds of goodness. Fear of pain or loss keeps us in a defensive posture. We are all selfish, and it would be naive to expect us to be otherwise. But what the great teachers have tried to drum into our thick skulls is that *it is in our best interest to be kind and compassionate.* Kindness not only comes back to us, often in rewards too subtle to notice, but it brings us closer to God by making us feel worthy of grace and protecting us from toxic relationships that throw tension and distress in the way of peace. The Dalai Lama, who once said that his religion was kindness, distinguishes between foolish selfishness and wise selfishness. "Foolish selfish people are always thinking of themselves, and the result is negative," he said. "Wise selfish people think of others, help others as much as they can, and the result is that they too receive benefit."

Why not look upon every relationship as a testing ground and a classroom? With openness, sincerity and right intention, conflict and tension can be used as catalysts for spiritual development. Each time you exercise compassion by seeing the world through the lens of someone in pain, you are loosening the grip of your ego as it clings to the illusion of separation. "A human being is part of the whole, called by us 'universe,' a part limited in time and space," wrote Albert Einstein. "He experiences himself, his thoughts and feelings, as something separate from the rest—a kind of optical delusion of consciousness. This delusion is a kind of prison for us, restricting us to our personal desires and to affection for a few persons nearest to us. Our task must be to free ourselves from this prison by widening our circle of compassion to embrace all living creatures and the whole of nature in its beauty."

That task, like the proverbial journey of a thousand miles, begins with a single step. How about practicing by seeing the spark of the Divine in the next person you encounter, as in the traditional Hindu greeting, "*Namaste*"? From there it can spread, one step at a time.

PRACTICE LOVING-KINDNESS

Buddhists have a meditative technique for cultivating universal kindness and compassion. Called *metta* practice (metta means loving-kindness), it is taught in a number of variations, but always in the same basic form and with the same precious intent: to open the heart's capacity for tenderness toward others in widening waves, from the most intimate to the most distant.

The practice begins by focusing on the person for whom it is often hardest to find compassion: ourselves. Seated comfortably in a quiet place where you won't be disturbed, take a few minutes to slip into deep relaxation. When your mind and body are settled, silently recite the following sentences to yourself, in a prayer-like manner:

May I be free from suffering.
May I be happy.
May I be healthy and strong.
May I be peaceful and at ease.

Repeat the phrases gently and slowly. When the mind is distracted, simply return to the feeling and intention of the words, without straining. Some Buddhist teachers advocate continuing with each stage until it feels complete. Others recommend keeping to a predetermined time, say five or ten minutes per stage, or simply repeating each group of phrases a set number of times.

Now, the practice moves on to other people. Think of someone you're very close to—someone you love and whose well-being matters deeply to you, and intone the phrases on his or her behalf: "May [name of person] be free from suffering," etc.

Feeling sincerity and goodwill toward a loved one usually comes easily, but don't be surprised if conflicting feelings arise; all relationships have some degree of ambivalence.

In stage three, you direct your compassion to a friend—someone with whom you're not quite as intimate as the previous person, but whose relationship you value.

In stage four, shift to someone toward whom you feel neutral. This can be an acquaintance such as a neighbor, coworker or a relative stranger.

Next, move on to someone for whom you have bitter feelings. It could be someone with whom you share enmity, or someone who wishes you harm or has hurt you in the past. Or, it could simply be someone who irritates you and for whom you never have kind thoughts. Needless to say, all sorts of resistance might arise. Continuing through that resistance is precisely what makes the practice effective.

Finally, aim your deepest feelings of love and kindness to all corners of the world, to all the unknown strangers who deserve your compassion. Use the same phrases, but begin each one with, "May all beings . . ."

Metta practice can be done for as short or long as you wish and as often as you wish. Doing it regularly is good for the heart.

"WHO SPEAKS FOR YOU, GOD?"

Religions pass, but God remains.

VICTOR HUGO

It is hard to secure the peace of God if you cannot resolve your relationship with God's representatives on earth. That goes for religious institutions—the one you grew up with and those you've adopted or explored—and for all-too-human spiritual leaders, both anointed and self-appointed, from abusive nuns in Catholic school to self-righteous rabbis to hypocritical pastors to scandalized gurus.

We tend to be deeply ambivalent about religious authority. The struggle probably goes back to the first shaman or tribal priest, but it takes on added dimensions in a culture where everyone has unlimited access to religious diversity, and where individuality and freedom of choice are venerated above all else. Americans value loyalty and tradition, but we are also fiercely independent, reluctant to obey and highly suspicious of authority. We want the community and continuity of religious affiliations, but we reserve the right to reject practices and precepts that don't make sense to us. All of which can create conflict in our hearts that has to be resolved.

In the movie *Oh, God,* John Denver's character tells God (in the unlikely form of George Burns), "I don't belong to any church." "Neither do I," God replies. Before there were religious institutions, there was God. When religious institutions decline and fall, there is still God. In between . . . well, that's where the conflicts arise. What begins with the magnificent revelation of a God-realized soul and gets codified with the holiest of intentions inevitably becomes tainted by human foibles. Like all organizations, religions magnify the best and worst of the human beings in them. But, in the end, as Gandhi said, "God has no religion."

For many of us, the subject of spiritual authority evokes volatile feelings. Some people regret the years they spent blindly following religious do's and don'ts or marking time in the superficial comfort of a community that met their social needs but not their soul needs. Others are angry with their families because religion was shoved down their throats or because they were abused (physically, emotionally or sexually) by a member of the clergy. Still others resent having been made to feel shameful or unworthy. And many walked away when they reached adulthood simply out of boredom.

Where do you stand with the religion of your ancestors? Do you embrace it wholeheartedly? With reservations? Are you bitter toward it? Indifferent? Are you deeply involved? Show up once in a while? Attend only on special occasions? Are you totally disconnected? Is it your exclusive spiritual involvement or do you explore more widely?

The Purpose of Religion: Translation and Transformation

In seeking to come to terms with your heritage, it is important to recognize the two main purposes that religions are meant to serve. Ken Wilber calls them translation and transformation. The first function, by far the most common, is to comfort, guide and fortify individuals and communities. This is accomplished through belief systems, shared stories and rules by which to live. In other words, religion translates the complexities of life into a common language, providing coherence and social glue. The transformational function, says Wilber, offers "not comfort but revolution." It is meant to shake us out of our complacency. It challenges us to grow, to enter the cocoon of radical metamorphosis, die to the creeping figure we have been and emerge flapping our divine wings. The translation function upholds the individual self; the transformation function exposes the small self as an illusion and urges us to let it go. Translation speaks to our need for security and guidance; transformation speaks to our yearning to merge with God. It is no secret that, with rare exceptions, religious institutions today excel at translation but have fallen down on the job when it comes to genuine transformation. That shortcoming has forced an exodus away from belief-oriented religions and toward experience-based spirituality.

The struggle to find the proper role for one's ancestral religion has been met in an astonishing variety of ways. A great number of God-seekers abandon the religion of their youth entirely, finding other ways to satisfy their need for spiritual transformation. Within that group, some retain rancor for their heritage, while others bear no ill will. Some find transformation elsewhere, but cannot replace the moral foundation, the shared history and the sense of community that established religions offer. Many come home to their roots later in life, especially if they have children who stand to benefit from religious participation. Some return to their origins with newfound respect and acceptance, but on their own terms. Bringing with them concepts and practices they've learned from other sources, they may reshape the religion to fit their needs, embracing what works while either ignoring the rest or finding some way to live with it. This has been denounced as pick-and-choose religion. But, when done in a responsible manner, it is no more and no less than what clear-thinking individuals have always done to accommodate flawed institutions. It allows them to stay rooted in a tradition without getting stuck in it.

One solution a growing number of people have found is to take advantage of the cornucopia of spiritual teachings to which we have unprecedented access. At no other time in history have so many seekers been able to draw from every major religion, plus an enormous number of less-known traditions and fresh, new spiritual offerings. This can only be regarded as a blessing, but one with notorious pitfalls. On the one hand, it enables everyone to create an individualized curriculum, filling in gaps in their development that their own religion or chosen path does not address. Like travel, spiritual exploration can expand your horizons and open your mind to greater possibilities.

On the other hand, the spiritual supermarket contains dangers such as charlatans, false promises, misconceptions and more imperfect institutions. It is not uncommon for people to abandon one spiritual affiliation for a shiny alternative, only to find, like men and women who leave their spouses for a sexy new partner, that the same problems crop up in the new romance as well. But perhaps the biggest pitfall of eclecticism is spiritual promiscuity. It is easy to convince yourself that you're growing spiritually when all you're doing is sampling one teaching after another and never sticking around long enough to go deep. "The problem with cafeteria-style spirituality," says religious scholar Huston Smith, "is that Saint Ego is often the one making the choices at the salad bar. What tastes good is not always the same as what you need, and an undeveloped ego can make unwise choices." Smith advocates having one main meal and supplementing it with other teachings, just as we take vitamins to supplement our regular diets.

Walt Whitman may have been overstating the case when he said, "There will soon be no more priests. Their work is done." But he was certainly right when he added, "Every man shall be his own priest." In the end, all men and women have to take responsibility for their own souls, and we each have to make peace with our religious roots in our own way. As with nutrition, finding the right diet and selecting appropriate supplements requires discernment, knowledge and a sharp intuitive sense of your personal needs. Here are some questions to ask yourself:

- Does your tradition offer means of transformation as well as the benefits of community and moral guidance?
- To what extent can you live with what you consider wrong, useless or even harmful about your heritage?
- Can you find ways to honor the spirit of your tradition even if you disagree with the letter of the law?
- Can you turn obligatory rituals into opportunities for spiritual growth rather than just occasions for catering?
- Can you forgive the institution for its imperfections?
- Can you forgive the men and women who represent your religion for their human shortcomings?
- Can you be involved with your religious community and still be true to yourself?
- When you participate, do you feel like a hypocrite or a phony?
- If you were to cut yourself off from your heritage, what would you lose?
- Are you resisting your heritage because of negative associations from the past—a bad experience with a pastor, for example?
- On the other hand, are you reluctant to explore other paths because you're afraid of ostracism, disapproval or divine retribution?
- Are you drawn to something new just because it's new, mistaking novelty for substance?

The primary reason to participate in any spiritual institution is to get closer to the direct experience of God. That is the ultimate measuring rod, just as the ultimate measuring rod of a hospital is getting well—and you may be able to do that even if you don't like every doctor or disagree with all of the administration's policies. In the final analysis, God transcends religion, and transcendence is the meeting point of all religions.

Spiritual Discipline

The world is your friend if it reminds you of God,
and your enemy if it makes you forget God.

SHEIKH TOSUN BAYRAK

The term spiritual discipline appears to be an oxymoron. It juxtaposes that which is unbounded with a word that implies control and restraint. Yet all the great teachers of spiritual transformation spoke of the necessity for discipline. Hair shirts and flagellation belong to religion's age of martyrdom, but aside from the blessed few who fall into a permanent state of grace, making peace with God calls for some degree of self-mastery. No matter how busy you are, it is vital to build into your life time to render unto God as well as Caesar.

Perhaps the most important form of discipline we need to develop is not something else to do, but rather to *not* do. We are addicted to doing. We feel uncomfortable when we're not in high gear, trying to accomplish something. But the peace of God comes not so much from doing as from *being*. "Some of us need to discover that we will not begin to live more fully until we have the courage to do and see and taste and experience much less than usual," wrote Thomas Merton. He called for "a wise alternation of activity and rest." Adding to your daily routine periods of meditation, prayer, contemplation and other practices for making peace with God should not detract from your responsibilities; it may, in fact, allow you to fulfill them with greater energy, awareness and integrity.

In addition to daily practices, consider devoting extended periods of time to making peace with God. The fourth commandment, "Remember the sabbath day, and keep it holy," is not a demand for self-deprivation but a call for spiritual renewal. Perhaps it is impractical for you to take an entire twenty-four hours once a week to shut out the hustle and bustle of life and commune with your spirit. But is half a day too much? A couple of hours? How about once a month? Can you take an annual retreat to spiritually advance? Can you spend a week in quiet seclusion instead of the usual vacation spot? However you can manage it, adding an extra dose of spirit to your life is like bumping up your regular bank deposits with an occasional large investment. It compounds the peace of God.

But as important as spiritual discipline is, it must be balanced with something equally vital. When Jesus cautioned that we can't enter the kingdom of heaven unless we become as little children, he was telling us, essentially, to adopt a childlike state of consciousness. We are born in bliss and awaken to a world of magic. Developmental psychologists tell us that young children experience every day the feeling of being passionately and wildly alive in their bodies. Their emotions flow freely, their minds are open and free of prejudice and conditioning. They respond open-heartedly to whatever arises in the moment. Then they start to mimic adults, and their innocent spontaneity is shrouded by the fears and worries of the judging, analyzing, problem-solving mind that needs to be in control. They become closed to pure, raw experience, shut off from the freedom of being alive to the moment. To "become as little children," therefore, would entail the following:

- Innocence; being open fully and naturally to God in the moment
- Relinquishing strain; being, not just doing
- Transparency
- Simplicity
- Taking things as they come; refusing to be harried or hurried
- Humor; bursting into laughter several times a day
- Delight in being a child of God
- Unconditional love for the Divine
- Feeling that you and your playmates are loved by God
- Feeling safe and secure in a friendly universe

Making peace with God is not a grim business; it's a return to innocence, and even if sometimes the road seems marked by blisters more than bliss, it is wise to remember to lighten up. Let the melodrama become the background, and the divine play the foreground.

7.

HOW MAY I SERVE YOU, GOD?

Rising Above the Lonely Ego

*Service which has not the slightest touch of self
in it is the highest religion.*

MAHATMA GANDHI

When Henry David Thoreau lay on his deathbed, he was asked if he had made his peace with God. "I am not aware that we had ever quarreled," he replied.

What would it take for you to feel that quality of peace at the end of your life? Everything we've explored in the previous chapters will help ensure that you will. In addition, there are three things you can start to do right now—if you haven't already.

1. *Accept the reality of your death*. Shunryo Suzuki once said that life is like setting sail on a boat that you know will one day sink. Wise people throughout the ages have advised us to face squarely the immutability of death. They were not advocating morose resignation or romanticizing a heaven to come. Instead, they urged a stark, honest acknowledgment that the forms we have inhabited all these years will one day die and disintegrate, ashes to ashes, dust to dust. Because it can be disturbing to contemplate death, it is tempting to simply not do it. But denial can be perilous. One reason some people are *not* at peace with God at the end of their days is that they are simply not prepared for

the immensity of that moment. And if you're not prepared, someday—when you get ill, or have a narrow escape or awaken to the signs of physical decline—death's ferocious inevitability will stun you like an icy wind in May and the great gaping void will open before you like a hungry lion's jaws.

About three years after the death of his wife, and again after the death of his son, Ralph Waldo Emerson, Thoreau's fellow transcendentalist, had his loved ones' bodies unearthed. Gazing upon the rotted corpses was his way of forcing himself to confront the naked truth of their death. That is, perhaps, a bit extreme for most of us, but many cultures have used rituals to reinforce the awareness that with every step we take we walk deeper into the shadow of death. Meditative practices in various mystical sects are designed specifically to remind practitioners of the impermanence of the bodies they inhabit.

But the value of accepting death is not just to prepare you to greet that moment in the spirit of the Native American affirmation, "Today is a good day to die." It can also profoundly enrich your existence, right now and every day until there are no more days. Deeply acknowledging that you have limited time in your present form can nudge you to clarify your values and priorities, and awaken in you a determination to make the most of your remaining years. "One can experience an unconditional affirmation of life," observed Joseph Campbell, "only when one has accepted death, not as contrary to life, but as part of life." This unconditional acceptance of your own mortality is essential to being at peace with God.

2. *Transcend the fear of death.* For many people, of course, the fear of dying is ameliorated by a deeply held belief that something more, and presumably better, is to come in the hereafter. Whether that conviction is attained by accepting the precepts of one's religion, reading accounts of near-death experiences or from a deep intuition of eternity, it pacifies our natural anxiety about dying. But belief alone is seldom enough to remove all mystery from the great unknown. "If you see death as the moment when you engage the deepest mystery of the universe," said Ram Dass, "then you prepare for that moment . . . so that you'll be open, curious, equanimous, not clinging to the past. You'll just be present, moment by moment."

Ultimately, however, the surest path to fearlessness is to experience clearly and profoundly what Emerson called "the presence of the Eternal in each perishing man." One of the stated values of practices that open one's awareness to the undying, transcendent Self is to reveal the illusion of death and make the eventual dropping of one's body a peaceful, even blissful, transition. When you realize through direct experience that your spirit is using your body the way light uses a bulb, you can presumably watch without fear or tension as the bulb grows faulty with age and starts to flicker out. This may well be what Plato had in mind when, as he was dying, someone asked him to summarize his life's work: he propped himself up on one elbow and said, "Practice dying."

3. *Be of service.* "Make me always ready to come to you with clean hands and straight eyes," goes a Native American prayer, "so when life fades, like the dwindling daylight, my spirit may come to you without shame." A major reason people are not at peace when they die is that they are tortured by regret over how they have lived. Of course, that torment is most often based on a fear of divine judgment and a permanent assignment to hell. But a surprising number of people who do not accept that model of the afterlife—who don't see doing good as a ticket to paradise—nevertheless suffer an agony of conscience when they remember the wrongs they have done to their fellow human beings. Even more surprising, perhaps, is how many good, decent people are not at peace at the time of death because of what they view as sins of omission: they feel they have not done enough for others, have not contributed enough, have no worthy legacy to leave behind. In short, they feel they have not lived as they believe God expected them to live.

It is that aspect of making peace with God that we focus on in this last chapter. Not just for the sake of dying in peace, but for deepening your peace in the present and living a full, complete and satisfying life. For anyone who succeeds even a little at achieving the peace of God will feel it imperative to ask, "How can I serve? What is expected of me? How may I help?" And anyone who asks those questions moves closer to the peace of God.

Service That Satisfies the Soul

The tools of illumination are the will to know,
the will to love and the will to serve

Wu Li

In his small Texas town, Bill grew up loving his Baptist church. He loved Sunday school, loved the preacher and the ladies who served cookies, loved the youth activities and the sense of community. His affection was sustained until his senior year of high school. Unable to ignore the urges that had stirred in him since puberty, Bill realized that he was gay. Now, on Sundays, he heard fiery denunciations of who he was ringing from the pulpit. Now the institution where four generations of his family had worshipped made him feel like an abomination. Now, instead of affection, he felt anger, which mixed with self-loathing to form a lethal combination. He had to change or leave, and after a year or two of trying to change, he understood that he could not. With a heavy heart, Bill told his father he was leaving the family's construction firm and was moving to Los Angeles.

In the cosmopolitan environment of L.A. he found acceptance, joined a gay and lesbian church and forged a successful career in television as a set designer. On one Christmas visit to Texas, he revealed his sexual orientation to his family. They renounced him. For the next six years, his only contact with his parents was an occasional phone call to see how they were. His mother would always say the same thing: she loved him and hoped that he would repent his sinful ways before he ended up in hell. His father wouldn't speak to him. The calls became less and less frequent. Then he received word that his father was dying of cancer. He flew to Texas. For a week, as the pain-riddled old man slipped in and out of consciousness, Bill tended to his needs. "Despite all my resentment, some primal feeling of love took over," he says. "I didn't think, I didn't choose, I just did what had to be done for this poor, sick man who had loved me and cared for me until I bumped up against his superstitions. It was truly an amazing grace. I was washing his body and emptying his bed pan, and I felt closer to God than I ever had in church." Before he died, his father took Bill's hand and said, "I love you" for the first time ever. As he and his mother wept in each other's arms, Bill was filled with a sense of forgiveness, resolution and rebirth.

Bill had come to Texas with a heart filled with hate and left with a heart filled with God. "Something opened up in me," he says. "I felt like I'd been embraced by the Lord and given a very clear message." Back in Los Angeles, his usual pursuit of money, merchandise and men came to feel insufficient. "My life was fulfilling in its own way," he says, "but it could not completely express the love I felt for God." He began to volunteer at a hospice. Now, depending on his work schedule, he might spend as many as twenty hours a week caring for the dying. "My design work satisfies my creative needs," he says, "but hospice work satisfies my soul."

Contrast Bill's story with Martina's. Martina fell in love with Jesus as a child and kept up an intimate conversation with him through Catholic school, confirmation and college. As an adolescent, she prayed daily, attended mass regularly and went to confession to unburden herself of sins, most of which were so trivial as to amuse her priest. Through marriage to a kind-hearted radiologist she met at church, the birth of three children and the busy life of a soccer mom, she kept up her pious routine. By every standard, it would seem, Martina's prayers had been answered. Now, with all three kids in school and a live-in maid, she was blessed with a good and easy life. So why, she started to wonder, did she feel abandoned by Jesus? What had she done to cause him to pull away from her? And why, why, why, did she feel so empty inside, so dreary, so bereft of God's grace?

The answer came one day in the familiar voice she had come to associate with Christ. "Who do you serve?" it asked. Startled into seeing herself as complacent and self-involved, she immediately began to volunteer time at a homeless shelter. What began as a way to absolve her guilt and win the approval of Jesus soon grew into something nobler: a new calling. Elated by the peace and joy she experienced when serving the less fortunate, she dusted off her college degree, earned a teaching certificate and requested a position at an inner city school that most teachers were begging to leave. "God is back in my life," she reports. "Not because I'm a 'good girl,' but because I feel his presence when I forget myself and give to others."

Bill and Martina represent the two sides of service. For the former, the impulse to give more of himself flowed spontaneously from a heart touched by divine love. For the latter, the seeds of service blossomed in a spiritual desert, from an empty heart that ached to be filled. For Bill, service work was an overflow of peace with God; for Martina it was the path to it.

In the movie *Agnes of God*, the psychiatrist assigned to assess Agnes's state of mind when she's accused of killing her newborn infant gets her to free associate. When she asks Agnes to say the first thing that comes to her mind, the aspiring nun says, "God." Not knowing quite what to do with that response, the shrink says, "What's the second thing that comes to mind?" Agnes replies, "Love." First God, then love—a holy one-two punch by which service flows naturally from nearness to the Divine. God can be seen as infinite generosity, ever and always giving him- or herself away like the sun gives away light—or, to use biblical imagery, like a burning bush that is not consumed by its flame. As manifestations of the sacred, created so to speak in the image and likeness of God, our very nature is generosity. The more access we have to the inexhaustible source of love and goodness at the center of our being, the easier and more natural it is to give some of it away, just as it's easy to be philanthropic when you're rich.

Seen another way, as you draw closer to the peace of God, the substance of your needs and desires changes; self-centered goals that once seemed indispensable, and objectives you thought you would kill to achieve, lose their urgency because you feel content in the present moment. And because you are grateful for that gift, actions that might appear to others as a sacrifice are, for you, just a way of saying, "Thank you." It is as though learning to receive the unconditional love of the Divine expands into the capacity to *give* unconditional love. And when giving and receiving become essentially the same thing, you are free to ask, without fear of deprivation or disadvantage, "How can I help?" You ask, not because you think you should, but because you can't help it; your cup runneth over. The voice that had been belting out "My Way" now proclaims, "Thy will be done." To the extent that you have made peace with the Supreme God, therefore, you automatically serve the Supreme Good.

This explains why the great religious role models of history elected to heal, teach and awaken others rather than bask in the bliss of their enlightenment. They had nothing to gain personally. They could have stayed on the mountaintop or under the tree. Instead, they ministered to hungry hearts with magnificent compassion and, in some cases, fought to correct social injustice, because that is what they were guided to do by the infinitely generous love that flowed through them. And we, in our own puny ways, would be wise to emulate them—and all the heroes of sacred stories who return from their holy quests to serve humanity—because we *do* have something to gain. That is the other side of the service equation: true giving benefits the giver first and foremost, by bringing him or her closer to God.

What Must I Do, Lord?

Man discovers his own wealth when God
comes to ask gifts of him.

RABINDRANATH TAGORE

Before our cup runs over, it is often necessary to prod ourselves to perform what the East calls *seva* and the West calls charity or service. The habitual self-interest of the ego is hard to shake, even after we begin to experience the peace of God—and experiencing the peace of God can make us want to withdraw from the troubles of the world and soak up even more of the bliss. To nudge us toward the higher good, every religious tradition has made service a virtue, if not a requirement. Here is a sampling of scriptural inducements to serve*:

Christianity: It is more blessed to give than to receive.
Taoism: Extend your help without seeking reward. Give to others and do not regret or begrudge your liberality. Those who are thus are good.

---

*From *Oneness: Great Principles Shared by All Religions*, by Jeffrey Moses.

Sikhism: In the minds of the generous contentment is produced.

Islam: The poor, the orphan, the captive—feed them for the love of God alone, desiring no reward, nor even thanks.

Hinduism: Bounteous is he who gives to the beggar who comes to him in want of food, and feeble.

Judaism: Blessed is he that considereth the poor: the Lord will deliver him in time of trouble.

Buddhism: The real treasure is that laid up by a man or woman through charity and piety, temperance and self-control. The treasure thus hid is secure, and does not pass away.

Of course, mainstream religions often use the threat of damnation and the promise of heaven to motivate us toward charity. But for those who are more concerned with life after birth than life after death, it might be best to link arms with the eighth-century Sufi Rabia Basri. She is said to have wandered the desert with water in one hand and a flame in the other. Symbolically, she was quenching the fires of hell and setting heaven ablaze, to convince people to love God for the sake of loving God, not out of concern for the afterlife. The same could be said for doing good while you're on the planet.

Perhaps a better motivating force in this day and age would be these two simple facts: One, it's obviously good for society when individuals give generously and care for one another and for the needy. Two, giving is good for the giver.

An impressive body of research suggests that those who regularly engage in acts of service are healthier, happier and may even live longer than their counterparts who do not take on such activities. A thirty-year study at Cornell University, for example, found that those who did volunteer work were more satisfied and had a greater sense of purpose in life. Another study found that a selfless attitude made it 2.4 times more likely that a person would be happy, while a selfish attitude made *unhappiness* 9.5 times more likely. By all indications, helping others improves one's mood and promotes greater optimism. Those who volunteer are also physically healthier than those who do not, as measured by factors such as lowered stress levels, heightened immune response and sounder sleep. A University of California at San Francisco experiment found that self-centered people may run a greater risk of developing coronary artery disease. And a thirteen-year study of men and women between the ages of sixty and ninety-four found that remaining useful and performing meaningful activity as one ages can significantly improve longevity. On average, seniors who volunteer outlive their compatriots who do not.

Why should reaching beyond your own needs and desires be good for you? Shouldn't you be better off when you're looking out for number one? Perhaps it's because thinking only about yourself is the surest route to discontent. Self-centeredness invariably focuses the mind on what is missing, on which unmet desire to satisfy next, which personal problems have to be solved, which wound must be soothed and which grievance has to be addressed—in short, on the half-empty glass of your life. Thinking about the welfare of others shifts the attention and more often than not leads to the half-full glass.

When singer-songwriter Beth Nielson Chapman was undergoing chemotherapy for breast cancer, she was not only in ghastly physical pain but she was overwhelmed by contradictory feelings toward God. She was angry at God because her teenaged son faced the possible loss of his mother only a few short years after his father's death. At the same time, she was reaching out for the healing power of God's love and compassion. As she alternated between feeling abandoned by God and comforted by God, what helped her most, she says, is prayer. She didn't pray for a cure. She didn't pray for relief from pain. She didn't even pray for her son. She prayed for a child she had never met, who suffered from an incurable disease. Someone had told Beth that Mother Teresa used to have terminally ill patients in different parts of the world pray for each other rather than for themselves. Something about this made sense to Beth. So she prayed for the child of the woman who told her the story.

"Whenever I felt depressed, or in pain from the side effects of the chemo," she says, "I would offer up my suffering for that boy, like it was some kind of currency." The shift of attention from herself to the afflicted child removed the overlay of fear and loathing, she explains, and that made her physical pain

more manageable. "After praying, I could accept the pain. I would stop struggling against it, and an enormous grace would come from that." Just as you
can't feel gratitude and resentment at the same time, you can't feel empathy
and self-pity at the same time, and you can't feel generosity and anger at the
same time. For Beth, the act of compassionate prayer was an offering that
came back to her with dividends.

But service to others, whether in prayer or action, brings an even higher
level of benefit. It brings you closer to the peace of God. "The more we come
out and do good to others," said Vivekananda, "the more our hearts will be pu-
rified, and God will be in them." In that sense, service is not just a moral imperative; it is a vehicle for spiritual advancement. We are never so much our
Selves as when we are not thinking about ourselves. Since God's infinitely
generous nature is expressed, in part, *as us*, when we allow that generosity to
flow through us unimpeded, we touch that which is most noble in our nature.
When we give ourselves away, we are doing what the Talmud calls mimicking
God, and what Muslims call being worthy of the world that Allah created. Just
as in meditation or prayer, we get closer to our divine nature when we get our
egos out of the way. Hushing our endless preoccupation with personal gain reduces our identification with the small self, enriching our sense of connection
to the Whole.

A TV documentary called "The Heart of Healing" showcased the Starcross community, a Christmas tree farm in Northern California. The three
clerics who run the place, Brother Toby, Sister Marti and Sister Julie, adopt
children with AIDS who have no homes and are considered beyond the powers of medicine to help. Normally, the kids would be in hospitals or state institutions. Starcross cares for them until they die. Brother Toby explains what
he and the sisters get from dealing daily with tragedy, pain and loss: "It's a lot
easier for us to find what we're spiritually looking for in the children than it is
sitting under a tree meditating. We always have this question, 'Where is God
and what is God?' You don't have that question when you're dealing with children. I mean, you look into a child's eyes and you see God. It's very simple.
You hold a child who's dying, you know that you're in the presence of what-

ever mystery there is in life that we label God." The dying children remind them of what's important, adds one of the sisters. It forces them to concentrate on making the present good, since there is not much of a future to think about.

If God can be said to have wishes for us, by all indications he or she would like us to laugh, live and love with exuberance. But also to serve. These are not contradictory aims. We can serve others and ourselves at the same time. When you think about it, to do otherwise would be to deny part of what makes us human. "The more I think of helping others," says the Dalai Lama, "and the stronger my feeling for taking care of others becomes, the more benefit I reap for myself. This is quite extraordinary . . . Since overcoming negative tendencies and enhancing positive potential are the very essence of the spiritual path, the practice of developing altruism is really the greatest, most effective, and most compelling practice of all."

To Whom Much Is Given, Much Is Expected

Speak Lord, your servant is listening.

1 SAMUEL 3

As peace with God strengthens and deepens, generosity of spirit naturally arises, and the urge comes forth to let it flow into action. Questions may then arise: What should I do? How should I do it? When? Where? With whom? How much time should I devote to it? The first thing that must be said is that there are no universal answers to questions like those. We each must do what we can, finding our own appropriate ways to serve and setting our own sensible limits. Certain points, however, can be made:

1. *Look around you.* There are countless ways to give. Worthy organizations designed to meet every conceivable human need are begging for volunteers.

Many are in your own backyard. Also in your own backyard are numberless needs that cannot be met by charitable organizations or public institutions—sick people, illiterate people, homeless people, disabled people, dying people, lonely people, unloved people whose days would be made by one stranger's smile.

What about your immediate circle? Sometimes it's most appropriate—and in some ways more challenging—to tend selflessly to the needs of family, friends and acquaintances. Service does not have to be limited to strangers or to those whose needs are dire or to actions that are normally thought of as charitable. It does not have to be grand. It does not have to be all-consuming. Not everyone is Mother Teresa. "Every good act is charity," said Muhammad. "Your smiling in your brother's face is charity; an exhortation of your fellow-man to virtuous deeds is equal to alms-giving; your putting a wanderer in the right road is charity; your removing stones and thorns and other obstructions from the road is charity." It is not hard to find an opportunity to do some good. Just look around and see what needs to be done. Think godly, act locally.

2. *Use your gifts.* A few years before her own cancer was diagnosed, as she mourned the loss of her husband to lymphoma and cared for her adolescent son, Beth Nielson Chapman poured her pain and all she had learned from it into the ten songs of an album called "Sand and Water." A moving chronicle of grief and healing, the album was integral to the spiritual growth that emerged from Beth's sorrow. "Every aspect of my life has deepened in meaning," she wrote in the liner notes. "That has been a gift in the midst of this loss." Upon its release, the music also became a gift to thousands who were touched by it. That prompted Beth to conduct workshops on grief. She uses music to help people in mourning tap into their feelings and teaches them to use self-expression to accelerate their healing.

Beth is an example of using your talents and natural inclinations to serve a higher good. We have a tendency to think that unless an activity is difficult, unless it involves great sacrifice or doing something you don't like doing, it's not worthy of being called service. But what heals you can heal others. What teaches you can teach others. What nourishes you can nourish others. One way to serve, therefore, is to take what you do well—what you might consider your calling or the thing you were placed on earth to do—and channel it for a greater good. It could be the way you earn your living. It could be your most passionate hobby. It could just be something you do well and enjoy doing. That it enriches *you* does not mean it can't be a gift to others. In fact, that might make it a more powerful and meaningful gift.

3. *Do it with intention and attention.* As the old song goes, it ain't what you do, it's the way that you do it. One person cuts hair in a salon; the other is an aide in a nursing home. The hair stylist does her work with gracious good cheer and tends to each customer as if she were washing the feet of a saint; the nurse's aide is surly and indifferent. Who is performing the greater service? Who is doing more good in the world? Who is doing God's work? "It is not how much we do," said Mother Teresa, "but how much love we put into the doing."

Can you perform your service in the spirit of innocent giving? Can you get your ego out of the way? Can you give it away as an offering? It is in that spirit, for instance, that B. J. Gallagher goes to work as an organizational consultant. "My work is my ministry," says Gallagher, the coauthor of *What Would Buddha Do at Work?* "I preach the Gospel of humanistic management. I give managers and executives the skills to create a kinder, gentler workplace, so they work as a community and not beat each other up in the process." Part of her mission statement reads, "I try to embody God's love in action in the world as best I can."

4. *Serve with humility.* Beware of that insidious form of spiritual materialism, performing service to inflate your ego, to impress others or to score points with God or guru. Mother Tessa Bielecki points out that there is a difference between being "spirit-propelled" and "self-propelled." "People want to feel good," she says, "and can in a very tricky way be serving themselves rather than serving others." It is very easy to let your goodness go to your head, or to puff up with pride and grandiosity over your supposed holiness. So keep an eye on your motives. Find out how much of your eagerness to serve is driven by a desire for personal reward, however subtle it might be, and how much is driven by generosity of spirit. One good test is to see if you can do service that no one else knows about, where you receive not an ounce of recognition and simply give for the sake of giving.

5. *Serve with joy.* A gas station chain used to advertise "Service with a Smile." If the smile is genuine, it's a service in and of itself, and it serves the smiler as much as the recipient. Service does not have to be a somber duty. In truth, there are few sadder spectacles than people who try so hard to be virtuous that they become humorless, passionless and prudish. In the name of healing the suffering of others they become insufferably grave. Said a priest who, for obvious reasons, chose to remain anonymous, "Being around some of the volunteers at the church makes me long for the company of thieves and reprobates. At least they know how to have fun." Perhaps that is why the workers at Mother Teresa's Home for the Destitute Dying are required to play for an hour every day.

> I slept and dreamt that life was joy
> I woke and saw that life was service
> I acted and behold! service was joy.
>
> RABINDRANATH TAGORE

6. *Serve yourself.* We gain the most from service when we lose ourselves in the process. However, we can take the spirit of self-surrender to an extreme and turn ourselves into martyrs. Compassion burnout is a very real problem, particularly in religious communities that exhort the faithful to greater and greater sacrifice, as if each hour spent doing good earns you a coupon to be redeemed in heaven. Genuine service is not motivated by guilt, and it needn't be measured by the standards of sainthood. You are called upon to be authentic, not sacrificial, and you are called first and foremost to take care of the one person you *know* God wants you to serve: you. That means setting appropriate limits on the time and energy you devote to others. Doing good should feed your soul, not drain it.

"People see being Christian as being a do-gooder," says Reverend William Grimbol, author of *The Complete Idiot's Guide to the Life of Christ.* "They do good works, but they do it through gritted teeth and get exhausted." He says he constantly has to remind certain congregants to take care of themselves and enjoy their lives. "You have to learn to *receive* so you can give more genuinely," he says. That same point was made in the *Chicago Hope* episode we mentioned earlier. A character asks the spirit of his departed friend to tell him what the Divine Plan is. His friend writes down a quick answer. The man is incredulous: "This is *it?*"

"That's harder to understand than you think," says the spirit. "Those two are of equal importance—that's what's hard."

Later we see what he wrote: "Giving and Receiving."

Archetypal Service

Do God's will as if it were your will, so that God
may do your will as if it were God's will.

JEWISH PROVERB

To guide you in your path to greater service, here is how each of the nine archetypes tends to relate to the issue:

Reformers are naturally drawn to worthy causes. They love to help people change their lives for the better, and they are at their best when they can help individuals or institutions correct shortcomings and function more effectively. Tendencies to guard against: self-righteousness; forcing their dogma or ideology on those they serve (like missionaries who feed hungry people in order to convert them); and needing everything to be perfect.

Lovers are wonderful at working one-on-one with those in need, as health-care providers, counselors or in circumstances where empathy is valued. Natural caregivers, their compassion would make them assets in hospices, crisis shelters and children's services. Tendencies to guard against: using service as a way to earn love; not loving themselves enough to protect their own health and well-being; and turning themselves into martyrs.

Achievers are ambitious leaders and efficient planners who would be at home at the head of large-scale projects with far-reaching humanitarian goals.

They would also be drawn to programs designed to enhance the prosperity of a community or an institution, especially if its purpose is to better people's lives. Tendencies to guard against: competing with colleagues and allies; self-aggrandizement; and the need for control.

Creators might be drawn to projects that beautify and inspire, especially through the arts. Their familiarity with intense emotions might also draw them to helping people who are going through major upheavals; they might, for example, help disaster victims, counsel the grieving or run a suicide hot line. Tendencies to guard against: letting narcissism draw them away from service; getting too depressed to be of use to others; and the need to create drama and pathos.

Thinkers bring to any worthwhile project a discerning intellect and an ability to uncover pertinent facts; this makes them terrific assets in the fact-gathering and planning stages, and indispensable when a situation calls for a fresh way of looking at things. Their ability to think clearly under pressure also makes them useful when the chips are down. Tendencies to guard against: being stingy with their time and energy; staying emotionally detached from those they serve; and letting their minds dominate their hearts.

Security-Seekers excel at causes that provide security and comfort for the unfortunate: shelter for the homeless, food for the hungry, adoptive parents for children, etc. Because they take duty and responsibility very seriously, and because they are attracted to longshots, they can be relentless workers for an underdog cause. Tendencies to guard against: letting distrust of authority get in the way of service; and letting their own need for safety and security detract from their efforts to serve.

Adventurers are great at lifting others out of the doldrums and leading the way to fun and pleasure. They would do well organizing activities for shut-ins or taking inner-city kids skiing or white-water rafting. If they are allowed to think out of the box and given free reign to turn doing good into a high adventure, they can be of great help to any cause. Tendencies to guard against: impulsively moving on to a new project before the present one is complete; slipping into laziness as soon as things become routine; and expecting others to do the tedious stuff.

Bosses can be the George Washingtons of the world—strong, take-charge types you want at the head of an important mission, especially one that's up against formidable enemies or major obstacles. They might be drawn to political action, protest groups or ad hoc organizations that fight against threats to the common good as they define it. Bosses at their best lead so effectively and unobtrusively that no one knows they're being led. Tendencies to guard against: despotism; belligerence; the need to dominate and control; and fighting to be top dog at the expense of the task at hand.

Peacemakers make excellent mediators and conciliators. They might be attracted to service that involves conflict resolution, perhaps as a diplomat, a judge in family court or as a marriage counselor. They can be found in the Peace Corps or the United Nations, volunteering in groups advocating disarmament or advancing peace efforts in strife-torn parts of the world. Where a formula for a win-win solution is needed, they're quick to answer the call. Tendencies to guard against: passivity; sensitivity to criticism; and compassion burnout.

As in our other discussions of the archetypes, please remember that we all have at least a trace of each personality type within us.

"Thy Will Be Done"

Use me, God. Show me how to take who I am, who I want
to be, and use it for a purpose greater than myself.

OPRAH WINFREY

Every spiritual seeker who wishes to serve wants to report for duty as an instrument of God and be given a personal assignment. For enlightened souls who are permanently vested in higher consciousness, knowing what the Divine intends for them and acting accordingly is not an issue. God's will runs through them like air through the nostrils, and they express it through every gesture with the natural ease of inhaling and exhaling. They are the ones the

Persian mystic Abu Yazid al-Bistami probably had in mind when he said that the only true prince is "the man who cannot choose," because for him, "God's choice is the only possible choice."

For the rest of us, "Thy will be done" is a fine idea, and "Let go, let God" is a wonderful aphorism. But just what do those fine sentiments mean, and exactly how are we supposed to live up to them? Even if we're willing to do God's will, our resistant egos hold on for dear life, as our personal needs and desires cry out for immediate attention. At times, surrender seems as enticing as a dip in cool water on a blistering day; at other times, it seems as frightening as a plunge through thin ice. "What if God tells me to do something really hard?" "Will I lose my individuality and my freedom of choice?" "What's in it for me anyway?" We're afraid that if we relax the ego's grip on our narcissistic self-interest, we'll somehow become spiritually enslaved. These fears may be projections onto God of tyrannical, authoritarian parents, oppressive religious authorities and self-righteous fanatics of every stripe who call themselves servants of the Lord. Surrendering to the will of God is not like capitulating to a repressive regime or having a set of moral handcuffs chained to your wrists. It does not mean giving up your liberty like a prisoner handing over his weapons. It does not mean having to be something you're not. It simply means acting in accord with your Higher Self and marching in step with the natural laws that regulate everything from microscopic cells to galaxies. Until we accept that "Thy will be done" represents freedom, not sacrifice, the ego will kick, scream and resist.

How do we discern the will of God? How do we know what is expected of us? After all, it's not like asking mommy or daddy what we should do. God works in much more mysterious ways, and few of us are asked to take dictation from a burning bush. Some would say, turn to scripture and simply do what is held to be virtuous and refrain from that which is considered sinful. But, as Moses Maimonides said, "The literal meaning of the biblical words may lead us to conceive corrupt ideas and to form false opinions about God." Clergy and religious scholars continue to disagree on how to interpret scriptural injunctions, just as they have for thousands of years and probably always will.

Ultimately, aligning with God's intent is not a matter of will or intellect.

The ability emerges naturally as you evolve to higher consciousness and become secure in the peace of God. Your heart beats on its own. Your lungs take
in oxygen and expel carbon dioxide without your willful assistance. Nature
puts you to sleep and wakes you up. Why shouldn't life-supporting choices
flow just as freely from a mind that's attuned to the evolutionary currents of the
cosmos? "We lie in the lap of an immense intelligence," wrote Emerson,
"which makes us receivers of its truth and organs of its activity. When we discern justice, when we discern truth, we do nothing of ourselves but allow a
passage to its beams." God's will is nothing more than the mind of God working through your mind *as* your mind.

The eternal formula seems to be: move the ego out of the way and tune
in to the highest channel on the cosmic dial. *"Yogastah kuru karmani,"* says
Krishna to Arjuna in the Bhagavad Gita. "Established in divine union, perform action." Or, as Jesus put it, "Seek ye first the kingdom of God." From that
sacred space where individual awareness is a pure expression of Supreme Intelligence, right action will surely arise, whether you call it serving the will of
God, acting in accord with natural law, or doing your duty. God's will may not
come to you in verbal or visual messages, or as anything you can articulate. It
might just come as a deeply felt sense of where to go, what to do and how to
act in the world from moment to moment. Clues might arrive in dreams,
reveries or flashes of intuition, or in synchronistic meetings and moments, like
a seemingly chance encounter with another person or a passage in a book you
open in a random instance.

Chana Silverman was living on the coast of Oregon, working as a waitress
in a Native American casino. She liked the job and her coworkers, and, as a
recent widow, she needed the money and the medical benefits. But she
missed the sense of community she enjoyed in her previous location, and
she lived far from her autistic daughter, who was in a facility in Portland. She
prayed for guidance. Then she opened the Bible to a random page and placed
her finger on a passage that read, "Maiden of Israel, return to your cities."

Chana took it as a sign. But which city? She had lived in many, and her
grown children were living in several different ones. Then she had a dream.
She was in the living room of her former home with some other women. A

snake lay curled in a corner. "You're the snake woman," the others said. "Do something." Fearfully, Chana grabbed the snake and threw it out of the house. As she did, it bit her in the chest. Somehow, in the next scene, before a roaring fire, the snake was curled around her head, and Chana was not afraid. When she woke up she heard the word, "California" as a clear directive to move there.

Moving to California made no sense at the time and it was a financially risky proposition. But she could not ignore the experience. Her Native American friends told her the snake was her spirit animal. She then learned that, in dreams, fire represents cleansing by the Holy Spirit; a snake curled around the head stands for spiritual awakening; and a snake bite on the chest symbolizes opening up to love. Putting together all the signs, Chana moved to Los Angeles. It did not take long for everything to fall into place. She found a job; she formally converted to Judaism and found a new spiritual home at a local synagogue; she began to cleanse her psyche of a dysfunctional past; and most surprising of all, she found a form of service that changed her life. The love that opened her heart was not for a new mate, as she'd hoped, but for her autistic daughter, who came to live with her. In the past, Chana had seen the child as a burden, and she turned her care over to others; now the child became her greatest blessing and her most profound teacher. Of the dream and all it led to, says Chana, "God can use anything to reach you."

It's a good idea to take note of the magical moments and surprise gifts that turn up in your life, especially those that send chills up your spine. It is equally important to note that dreams, signs and inner voices are easily distorted by a deluded ego angling for advantage. We have to also be open to the promptings that come in subtle, undramatic ways, in signs that blend with the scenery of life and whispers that can barely be deciphered amidst the clamor—as well as the power of reason through which the Divine also speaks. Aligning with the sacred will is primarily a matter of being receptive. "God does not force itself upon us," says Reverend Michael Beckwith. "It is not God who limits its givingness, but we who limit our willingness to receive. . . . It is a shift from trying to make something happen to allowing that good which is happening everywhere in the universe to happen through us. Willfulness is transformed into willingness."

The surest way to display that willingness is to turn toward the quiet spaces of awareness where the divine will is most easily located. "To the mind that is still," said the Taoist sage Lao Tzu, "the whole universe surrenders." You might do this regularly during prayer or meditation, but you can also do it anytime the need arises. Susan Quinn, an organizational development consultant in Los Angeles, conducts workshops on conflict resolution. Before beginning a session, and *during* a session if she finds herself struggling, she finds a quiet place where she can sit, take some deep breaths and "invite God's presence." She does not petition for anything. She does not ask specific questions. "I open up a space for receptivity," says Quinn, author of *The Deepest Spiritual Life*. "It's a shift in consciousness, a way of connecting, and it changes the whole dynamic. God comes in the silence."

Peace on Earth (As It Is in Heaven)

The time of the lone wolf is over. Gather yourselves.
We are the ones we have been waiting for.

TOMAS BANEYA, HOPI ELDER

In *Oh, God*, George Burns, as God, tells John Denver's character, "I gave you a world and everything in it. The rest is up to you to make it work."

"But we need help," says Denver.

"That's why I gave you each other."

On one level, peace with God reveals the awesome truth that the universe is perfect as it is. Some take that to mean that we don't have to "save" the world or try to fix things that we perceive to be problems because, from God's perspective, they may not be problems at all. In this view, nonjudgmental detachment from the sorrows and anxieties of "real life" is prized above social engagement. The only duty of a spiritual aspirant is to achieve Self-realization.

That endeavor, by itself, is held to be a way of healing the world, for the peace of the awakened individual spreads, not only through acts of goodness but by pulsating outward like radio waves through prayer, meditation and the pure emanations of the soul.

Others feel that the spiritually evolved have a special moral responsibility, a call to higher citizenship. Deeply rooted in the Judeo-Christian tradition, for example, is the Hebrew concept of *tikkun olam:* to repair the world. It is said that God left a piece of the world unfinished so that humans could complete the job, like a parent who assembles only part of a puzzle so her child may learn from the challenge of making it whole. Throughout time, that challenge has been taken up by spiritually driven activists from every tradition, who feel a sacred responsibility to make the planet a more hospitable place and contribute to humanity's great dream of peace on earth.

Clearly, very few of us are called to renunciation. The rest of us are left to contemplate the undeniable fact that, no matter what state of consciousness we're in, or how close we've come to making peace with God, we must, as the Zen Buddhists say, chop wood and carry water. As we chop and carry, we have to make choices. And those choices send ripples throughout the universe, altering the world for better or for worse. Since we're already changing the world with every action we take, why not do it with the highest intention? Why not make choices that heal, that promote goodness and well-being, that minimize suffering, that make it easier for others to love, to laugh, to enjoy material abundance and spiritual treasures, to realize their full potential and make peace with God?

It seems certain that the old ways of addressing our collective problems—political action, social engineering and technological fixes—are not sufficient for dealing with the well-known issues facing the planet today. They won't forestall the looming crises, like terrorism, global warming and worldwide pollution, and they won't end the old ones, like poverty, hunger and incessant warfare. It is simply unreasonable to expect too much from attempted solutions that arise from the same limited consciousness that got us into the mess in the first place. As long as we continue to use a small fraction of our brain's potential; as long as we skimp on compassion, generosity and fairness; as long as we see ourselves as apart from—rather than as part of—one another, our natural environment and God, we will continue to create more problems than we solve. We can't depend on experts and institutions; they are only mouthpieces for the collective brain in which every human being is a neuron. "Homes are made by individuals," says Maharishi Mahesh Yogi. "Shops, ships, farms, and factories are manned by individuals. The external harmony and peace of the entire human race is founded on the internal harmony and peace of every individual." That is why those who awaken to the peace of God bear great responsibility.

BE THE CHANGE YOU WISH TO SEE

By their fruits you shall know them.
MATTHEW 7:20

Undoing the damage we have inflicted upon one another through the centuries begins with each of us choosing the good, the kind and the compassionate at every turn—as Mahatma Gandhi famously put it, to *be* the change we wish to see. Each time we meet hate with love, fear with courage, selfishness with generosity, despair with hope, cruelty with benevolence, we strike a blow against the forces of darkness. But there are also collective concerns that must be addressed directly if we wish to evolve from an era of domination and submission to one of dominion and cooperation. If the divine intent is for all God's creatures to live in peace and harmony on this small blue-green marble in the vast black universe, we must each do what we can to show the way, by word, by example and by deed.

The fruits of our actions are born in the seeds of awareness. Each of us has a circle of concern in which we hold the people and places we regard as extensions of ourselves—the "we." Unfortunately, we have tended to define the "we" in extremely narrow terms. We include those who look like us, or believe what we believe or live in the circumscribed area we call home. To those within our circle, we do no harm; we offer sharing, cooperation and help; we treat the "we" as we would treat ourselves. Those outside the circle we ignore, compete with, defend against and sometimes attack. But as long as we act like little boats afloat on an ocean of indifference, life on the planet will remain precarious. It is imperative, therefore, that we awaken collectively to the truth that naturally arises when an individual turns inward and connects to the Divine: we are all roommates, cohabitating in a universe of unbroken wholeness. Only then will we embrace all beings and all things as "we."

It is an old vision, an eternal vision, but one that has remained for the most part an easily ignored concept, not a living truth. Now, at this turning point in human evolution, when we teeter on the brink of either a golden age or the extinction of our species, we have more than the perennial insights of the visionaries to remind us of our Oneness. We also have scientific corroboration. Science has been progressively peeling back the onion of creation, exploring the depths of matter to see what underlies the forms and textures of outer existence. At each step a greater unity has been revealed. There is nowhere left to go but to the ultimate Union that scientists of the spirit have always perceived. One day, perhaps, we will have a mathematical equation for it. But we know enough now to state unequivocally that everything is connected, that we are all part of one another and everything each of us does affects the rest of the planet. We are also blessed with communication and transportation technologies that shrink the globe and bring together minds and bodies in ways that illuminate the unity of our diverse species. Most of all, we have the *spiritual* technologies to make Oneness a conscious reality not just an abstract idea, and to make kindness and compassion a felt experience not just a noble aspiration. The more "I am That, thou art That, all this is That" becomes a living truth, the more our circle of kinship expands. Instead of a You-*or*-Me world, it becomes a You-and-Me world.

ALL GOD'S CHILDREN

The world was not left to us by our parents.
It was lent to us by our children.

AFRICAN PROVERB

Roberta Forem, a Montessori teacher in Ventura, California, witnessed the following scene in her classroom one Good Friday morning. Three four-year-olds were huddled in a corner, playing quietly with blocks. "Are you going to church today?" asked the Christian boy. "This is the day they killed God."

"He wasn't God," protested the Jewish boy. "He just said he was, and you're not supposed to say that."

"He was the son of God," the first boy insisted.

The Jewish boy raised his voice. "You're not supposed to say that!"

The third boy, the son of immigrants from India, had been listening in, looking rather confused. "But God is in our hearts," he said. "We're *all* God's children."

The other two thought that over for a few seconds, then all three resumed playing as if the subject of religion had never come up.

Wouldn't it be nice if it were that easy for adults?

The moral of that story is not about the children's respective religions. It is about two different ways of understanding our relationship to God. One way focuses on the differences among belief systems, arguing over their respective merits and defending the one it favors. The other way focuses on our commonality and the essence of spiritual experience. One divides, the other unites. If you think of religions as spokes of a wheel radiating outward from the numinous hub of the Holy Source, then the belief-centered view looks at the periphery, where the distance between the spokes is wide. The experience-centered view dwells closer to the hub, where the spokes converge and their differences fade.

In a world that cries out for a unifying vision, religions should be in the vanguard, bringing us all together as children of God. Sadly, all too often they have done the opposite. Three hundred years ago, Jonathan Swift said, "We have just enough religion to make us hate, but not enough to make us love one another." It remains ever thus. Religions strayed further and further from the hub, and further and further from one another on the outer rim of the wheel of spirit. They let themselves be used to justify all manner of prejudice and oppression, setting brother against brother and sister against sister, as exemplified by the tortured history of Jerusalem—literally, City of Peace—where the children of Abraham have bludgeoned one another for centuries. It is as though no Jew ever prayed, "In that which we share, let us see the common prayer of humanity. In that in which we differ, let us wonder at the freedom of humankind," and no Muslim ever prayed, "O God! Make good that which is between us, unite our hearts and guide us to paths of peace."

The history of enmity and violence between religions is perhaps the saddest feature of the human saga. It is one thing for humans to fight over land or water or access to food, or to hate one another because of acts of cruelty and greed. But to fight over God, whose nature is love? To take a stance of superiority in the name of that which should evoke humility? To pit one form of worship against the other when we should all be down on our knees together? Nothing could be more contrary to the spirit of the holy ones whose revelations birthed and nurtured the world's religions than the sight of arrogant men bickering over which god or scripture or precept is better than the rest. It is more than a dishonor; it is a disgrace.

If we are to make peace with God collectively, we must make peace with the God of *all*, not just the God we imagine is watching over our exclusive club. The challenge to religious leaders in this time of global crisis is to grow out of their chauvinistic boundaries—to not just tolerate other religions, but respect them, and even more, to celebrate them, cherish them and humbly listen to their wisdom. Religions have more to learn from one another than to fear from one another. It is time for the clergy of all faiths to direct their energy not just to the preservation of their institutions and their power, not to converting and persuading and proclaiming "the one true way," but to calling attention to our oneness and our interdependence, and lighting the spark of divinity in every human soul. "We require a spirituality that promotes the unity of the human family," says Brother Wayne Teasdale, "not one that further divides us or maintains old antagonisms."

There are welcome signs of progress in relations among the religions, in the interfaith movement, in the attempts by various leaders to heal ancient animosities, in the rediscovery of the mystical roots of every tradition, as well as in other efforts large and small. But the main impetus for change will come from the millions of individuals like you, who are experiencing directly the peace of God and thereby know—not just believe, not just understand, but *know*—that the spokes of all religions merge at the hub of divine union. Those who embrace that truth can lead the way to a collective spiritual awakening by emulating the boy in the Montessori class and proclaiming—in shouts and whispers, in large deeds and everyday actions—"But God is in our hearts. We're *all* God's children."

Let There Be Peace on Earth, and Let It Begin with Me

Where there is no vision, the people perish.

PROVERBS 29:18

What is your vision for the world? How can you help to realize it in your sphere of influence?

There are many who say we are entering a new age in which the way we look at the world and relate to one another will give way to a more advanced paradigm. We will cooperate rather than compete, unite rather than separate, empower rather than dominate. The forces of ignorance and illusion will be replaced by wisdom and peace. Spiritual and humanistic values will take precedence over the materialistic, hedonistic drives that have exploited, assaulted and pillaged for centuries, polluting the land, air and sea, turning fertile soil into deserts, decimating coral reefs and rain forests and causing immeasurable human suffering. The hungry will be fed, the poor will be upraised, the oppressed will achieve equality and, in the immortal words of Isaiah, "We shall beat our swords into plowshares and our spears into pruning hooks, and nation shall not lift up sword against nation or learn war anymore."

Some speak as though this global evolution is as inevitable as spring. There are certainly signs that a planet-wide time of transcendence and transformation is upon us. We stand at the brink of the greatest leap in collective consciousness the world has ever seen, global in its reach and cosmic in its implications. It would be comforting to believe that this is preordained. It would be more realistic, however, to believe that it is *possible*, and that the transformation will come to fruition only if we take effective action to bring it about. Certainly, the tools are in place. The knowledge is in place. But do we have the will? Do we have the awareness? Do we have the strength of spirit?

God-Conscious Evolution

The day will come when, after harnessing the wind, the waves,
and the tides, we shall harness for God the power of love.
And on that day, for the second time in the history
of the world, man will have discovered fire.

PIERRE TEILHARD DE CHARDIN

This book was finalized in the immediate aftermath of the terrorist attack on the World Trade Center and the Pentagon. The horror made it painfully clear how urgent it is for individuals and civilization as a whole to make peace with God—and, by extension, with one another, for we are in God and God is in us. Never before had the issues addressed in the book seemed more vital. As has always been the case in times of trauma and tragedy, doubts about God, rage toward God and feelings of isolation from God erupted, while at the same time, hearts reached out to God for comfort, guidance and sustenance. The burning questions that stand as the titles of our chapters—"Why, God, why?" "Where are you, God?" "How may I serve you, God?" etc.—roared forth from a shocked and grieving humanity. The gaping wound in our collective body, caused by an old, festering wound in our collective soul, made painfully obvious how urgent it is to achieve the spiritual awakening that alone can bring about true universal peace.

We are evolving because we must. But we must evolve consciously. We can't settle for a peace defined merely as the absence of war. Not when the earth clamors for the peace of God. Not when it cries out with the cumulative ardor of humanity's anguish. Exactly *how* a spiritual awakening would play out in the public sphere is impossible to predict. But it is safe to say that it will be what we make it, as each of us offers his or her unique contribution to the pieces of the puzzle God left for us to complete. Spiritual people have to make some decisions. What is closer to God's will: to dig more holes in the earth and burn more of nature's resources so we can drive bigger SUVs, or to use our God-given ingenuity to keep the planet's air, water and land unspoiled for the future? Would God rather we rape the earth or protect it? (To answer that question, simply envision for a moment that the planet is a living cell in God's body.) To what extent would God want us, with our limited awareness and our short-range vision, tampering with the Rosetta stone of God's genetic code? Would God want us to look out for number one or to care for the least of us? Would God want us to raise children to be consumers or to be contributors?

Is it in the spirit of making peace with God to fight holy wars in God's name? To claim that one nation's missiles and troops have God on their side? Or is it more holy to ask, "What do we have to do to be on God's side?" What would be closer to God's intent: for individuals, groups and nations to impose their will on others through coercion, or to cooperate, negotiate and accommodate? What would God prefer, that we demean, hate and condemn to hell those who worship differently from us, or to rejoice in the variety of names and forms that humans have attributed to the Divine? To state what we hope is obvious, *we are all the children of one God*—not a Christian God, a Jewish God, a Muslim God or a Hindu God. There are no heathens. There are no infidels. There is only God, formless, nameless and Absolute, a singular holy Essence to which humans have attached a variety of images, and from which humans have to end the illusion of separation.

The inner work of Self-awakening and the outer work of serving a higher purpose are not incompatible. Indeed, because you have begun to make peace with yourself and God, you are automatically enlisted in the service of waging peace. You are turning on the light, whereas in the past, most well-meaning souls have battled valiantly with the darkness. And, as Swami Beyondananda cleverly puts it, "A little peace here, a little peace there, pretty soon all the peaces will fit together to make one big peace everywhere." What else can you do? Making peace with God brings its own assignments. As the uncompromising light of the Divine brings the sordid consequences of ignorance into high relief, solutions to seemingly unsolvable problems will make themselves known.

You make a difference. And if whatever you choose to do, no matter how seemingly small, is presented to the world as a peace offering on the altar of God, it will be an enormous contribution. "Serve the Lord with gladness," as it says in Psalms. Let your service flow joyfully from your heart, with both the invincible power of God's might and the healing force of Goddess's love. "When you are inspired by some great purpose, some extra-ordinary project, all of your thoughts break their bonds," taught Patanjali, the great sage of yoga, 2400 years ago. "Your mind transcends limitations, your consciousness expands in every direction, and you find yourself in a new, great, and wonderful world. Dormant forces, faculties, and talents become alive, and you discover yourself to be a greater person by far than you ever dreamed yourself to be."

Now is the "some day" of our myths, a time to realize humanity's ancient dream of Heaven's peace on Earth. One by one we awaken ourselves; all in one we awaken the planet. We human beings, fashioned out of stardust millions of light-years ago, are capable of remembering and re-experiencing our original home in the peace of God. With that awareness, we can cocreate with God a world that is fully worthy of our stature as spiritual beings in human form—a civilization that delivers divine peace to every soul, turning Homo sapiens into Homo universalis, the human race into human Grace.

Acknowledgments

While writing a book is a profoundly solitary adventure, it is also collaborative. We wish to express our deepest gratitude to the many individuals whose assistance and support were indispensable at every stage of this book. First, while it might seem odd, we would like to thank each other for a joyous collaboration of the highest order. This was a true partnership in which two sets of skills, experiences and knowledge merged to create an authorship greater than the sum of its parts. Special thanks go to our respective agents, Joelle Delbourgo and Lynn Franklin, for their long and continuing support and guidance; to Jeremy Tarcher, Mitch Horowitz, Joel Fotinos, and Ken Siman for their commitment to the highest vision for this book and their wise assistance in helping us to realize it.

A heartfelt thanks to the many people who were kind enough to tell us their stories, share their expertise or simply talk with us, formally and informally, about issues pertinent to the book. We list them here alphabetically: Brad Adams, Robert Alderman, Alarik Aranander, Swami Atmaswarupananda, Michael Beckwith, Brent BecVar, Rustin Berlow, Ed Bernstein, Dana

Brecke, Russ Brue, Mary Bullock, Bob Burchman, Michael Peter Cain, Ray Chambers, Beth Nielson Chapman, Bobby Colomby, Rabbi Laurie Coskey, Tom Cunningham, the Dalai Lama, Keila DeMorais, Jimmy Dezen, Larry Dossey, Wayne Dossick, Dean Draznin, Ken Druck, Carol Duncan, Carol Edlic, James Finley, Judy Firestone, Rev. Donna Fletcher, Jack Forem, Roberta Forem, Robert Forman, Franklin Fullerman, B. J. Gallagher, Maria Gallo, Swami Gopalanand Saraswati, Chris Greene, Rev. William Grimbol, Robert Grimes, Christel Hammad, Rachel Harris, Steven Hart, Helen Hays, Betsy Hoffman, Roger Housden, Suzie Hurley, Liza Ingrasci, Raz Ingrasci, Daniel Jackson, Jerry Jarvis, Susan Jorgensen, Hillary Kapan, David Kaplan, Earl Kaplan, Gurutej Kaur, Ellen Kenwood, Diana Kruschke, Doug Kruschke, Rev. Larry Lea, Norman Lear, Stanley Lewis, Kay Lindahl, Kate Lutz, Franz Metcalf, Catherine Miller, Tandie Mitchell-Firemoon, Sonny Murray, Valerie Norris, Craig Pearson, Nancy Peddle, Paul Perrotta, Jach Pursel, Susan Quinn, Kikanza Nuri Robins, Kevin Ryerson, Ayman Sawaf, Carol Schaefer, Ann Scheppach, Neil Schuitevoerder, John Selby, Shanti-Mayi, Nancy Shaw, Chana Silverman, Kathy Solomon, Jim Strohecker, Laura Van Waardenburg, Wendy Ward, Bill Woodring, Majken Youngquist and Connie Zweig.

It is with reverent gratitude that we thank all the spiritual teachers through the ages whose wisdom has not only informed this book but shaped our lives and inspired us to aim for our highest spiritual destiny. The enlightened ones are too numerous to mention. We offer our profound gratitude, however, to Maharishi Mahesh Yogi, who showed each of us how to regularly experience the peace that transcends understanding.

On a personal note, Harold would like to convey his deep, heartfelt appreciation to Maria Tonello for her radiant love and intelligent, precise and creative feedback on the book from its inception through various stages of development. Special thanks to all of my clients, with whom it has been my privilege to learn with and grow in Del Mar, California. Heartfelt appreciation to my daughter Shazara and godsons Damien and Michael who have taught me so much. All love and gratitude to my mother Fridl, departed father Max, sister Nora and brother-in-law Gus.

Phil wishes to express his profound and everlasting gratitude to Lori Deutsch. Her daily infusions of intelligence and good sense, along with her unqualified concern, support and love, were indispensable at every stage of this project. Thanks as well to my spiritual compatriots in the Forge Guild and to my Interfaith colleagues, whose dedication to the truth of all paths inspired and informed me throughout. And special appreciation to my departed parents, Archie and Ann, for their basic goodness, and for their staunch agnosticism, which fueled, unknowingly, my drive to know the unknowable.

Finally, our profound thanks to you, our readers, for the privilege of serving your psychospiritual growth.

Recommended Reading

Bloomfield, Harold, M.D. *Healing Anxiety Naturally* (New York: HarperPerennial, 1998).

———, Candice Carter, Susanna Palomares, Linda Williams, and Bradley Winch. *Chicken Soup for the Peace Lover's Soul* (Deerfield Beach, FL: Health Communications, Inc., 2002).

———, Melba Colgrove and Peter McWilliams. *How to Survive the Loss of a Love* (Allen Park, Michigan: Mary Books, 2001).

——— and Peter McWilliams. *How to Heal Depression* (Allen Park, Michigan: Mary Books, 2001).

——— with Leonard Feldes, *Making Peace with Your Parents* (New York: Ballantine, 1983).

——— with Philip Goldberg. *Making Peace with Your Past* (New York: Harper-Collins, 2000).

Chögyam Trungpa. *Cutting Through Spiritual Materialism* (Boston: Shambhala, 1973).

Chopra, Deepak. *How to Know God* (New York: Crown, 2000).

Concept Synergy. *Making Peace with Your Shadow* (audiotapes and workbook) (Orlando, FL: Author, 1997). To order: 800-678-2356.

———. *Ending Shame* (audiotapes I-IV) (Orlando, FL: Author, 1997).

Cooper, David A. *God Is a Verb* (New York: Riverhead Books, 1997).

Dalai Lama. *Ethics for the New Millennium* (New York: Riverhead Books, 1999).

Dosick, Wayne. *When Life Hurts* (San Francisco: HarperSanFrancisco, 1998).

Dossey, Larry, M.D. *Healing Words* (New York: HarperCollins, 1993).

Fellowship in Prayer. *The Gift of Prayer: A Treasury of Personal Prayer from the World's Spiritual Traditions* (New York: Continuum, 1995).

Ferucci, Piero, Ph.D. *Inevitable Grace* (New York: Tarcher/Putnam, 1990)

Finley, James. *The Contemplative Heart* (Notre Dame, Indiana: Soren Books, 2000).

Forman, Robert K. C. *Meister Eckhart: Mystic as Theologian* (Rockport, Massachusetts: Element, 1991).

Fowler, James W. *Stages of Faith* (New York: HarperCollins, 1981)

Fromm, Erich. *The Art of Loving* (New York, HarperPerennial, 1956).

Goldberg, Philip. *The Intuitive Edge* (New York: Tarcher/Putnam, 1983).

———. *Real Life on the Spiritual Path* (Emmaus, PA: Rodale Books, 2002).

Goulston, Mark, M.D., and Philip Goldberg. *Get Out of Your Own Way* (New York: Perigee/Putnam, 1996).

Harvey, Andrew. *The Direct Path* (New York: Broadway Books, 2000).

Housden, Roger. *Ten Poems to Change Your Life* (New York: Harmony, 2001).

Hubbard, Barbara Marx. *Conscious Evolution* (Novato, CA: New World Library, 1998).

Huxley, Aldous. *The Perennial Philosophy* (New York: Harper & Row, 1944).

Khan, Pir Vilayat Inayat. *Awakening: A Sufi Experience* (New York: Tarcher/Putnam, 1999).

Koenig, Harold G., Michael E. McCullough and David B. Larson. *Handbook of Religion and Health* (New York: Oxford, 2001).

Kornfield, Jack. *A Path With Heart* (New York: Bantam Books, 1993).

Maharishi Mahesh Yogi. *Bhagavad Gita* (New York: Penguin, 1967).

———. *The Science of Being and Art of Living* (New York: Penguin, 1966).

McLennan, Rev. Scotty. *Finding Your Religion* (San Francisco: HarperSanFrancisco, 1999).

Merton, Thomas. *New Seeds of Contemplation* (New York: New Direction, 1961).

Mitchell, Stephen. *The Book of Job* (Berkeley: North Point Press, 1987).

———. *The Enlightened Mind: An Anthology of Sacred Prose* (New York: HarperPerennial, 1993).

Moody, Harry R. and David Carroll. *The Five Stages of the Soul* (New York: Random House, 1997).

Newberg, Andrew, Eugene D'Aquili and Vincent Rause. *Why God Won't Go Away: Brain Science & the Biology of Belief* (New York: Ballantine, 2001).

Schuller, Robert H. *My Journey* (San Francisco: HarperSanFrancisco, 2001).

Schulweis, Harold M. *For Those Who Can't Believe: Overcoming the Obstacles to Faith* (New York: HarperCollins, 1994).

Sluyter, Dean. *The Zen Commandments* (New York: Tarcher/Putnam, 2000).

Smith, Huston. *The World's Religions* (San Francisco: HarperSanFrancisco, 1993).

Smoley, Richard and Kinney, Jay. *Hidden Wisdom: A Guide to the Western Inner Traditions* (New York: Penguin Arkana, 1999).

Sogyal Rinpoche. *The Tibetan Book of Living and Dying* (San Francisco: HarperSanFrancisco, 1993).

Taylor, Brian C. *Setting the Gospel Free: Experiential Faith and Contemplative Practice* (New York: Continuum, 1996).

Thich Nhat Hanh. *Living Buddha, Living Christ* (New York: Riverhead Books, 1995).

Tutu, Desmond M. *No Future Without Forgiveness* (New York: Doubleday, 1999).

Vardey, Lucinda ed. *God in All Worlds* (New York: Pantheon Books, 1995).

Wilber, Ken. *Sex, Ecology, Spirituality: The Spirit of Evolution* (Boston: Shambhala, 1995).

Yogananda, Paramahansa. *Autobiography of a Yogi* (Los Angeles: Self-Realization Fellowship, 1969).

Walsch, Neale Donald. *Conversations with God* (New York: Putnam, 1996).

Zweig, Connie and Steve Wolf. *Romancing the Shadow* (New York: Ballantine, 1997).

About the Authors

Over the past 30 years, Harold H. Bloomfield, M.D., has been dedicated to spiritual enlightenment and emotional literacy as a renowned teacher, healer and bestselling author. Dr. Bloomfield has written 18 books, which have sold more than 8 and a half million copies and have been translated into 34 languages. Two of his *New York Times* bestsellers, *Making Peace with Your Parents* and *Making Peace with Yourself,* introduced personal and family peacemaking to millions of people. *How to Survive the Loss of a Love* and *How to Heal Depression* have become self-help classics. *TM: Discovering Inner Energy and Overcoming Stress* helped introduce meditation to America. *Hypericum (St. John's Wort) & Depression,* his most recent *New York Times* bestseller, and *Healing Anxiety Naturally* helped catalyze the herbal medicine revolution (for information on herbs call 800–255–8332).

Dr. Bloomfield has appeared regularly on national television, including ABC's *20/20, Oprah, Good Morning America, Larry King Live* and CNN. His work has been featured in *Time, Newsweek, U.S. News & World Report, People, Forbes, Cosmopolitan, Ladies' Home Journal, Prevention, USA Today, The New York Times,* the *Los Angeles Times,* and numerous other magazines and newspapers.

Dr. Bloomfield received the 1999 Theodore Geisel "Best of the Best" Book Award, the *Medical Self-Care Magazine* Book of the Year Award, the Golden Apple Award for Outstanding Psychological Educator and the American

Holistic Health Association's Lifetime Achievement Award. A frequent speaker at conferences throughout the world, he brings a friendly, compassionate, inspiring presence to public lectures, professional meetings and seminars.

Now retired from the practice of medicine, Dr. Bloomfield is in private practice as a spiritual counselor and personal life coach. For information regarding Dr. Bloomfield's professional services, please call 858-635-1235, e-mail *harah@adnc.com*, or visit his Web site at *haroldbloomfield.com*.

Philip Goldberg, Ph.D., a spiritual counselor, meditation teacher and ordained Interfaith Minister, is the author or coauthor of 17 books, including *The Intuitive Edge*, which has been called the definitive book on intuition, *Get Out of Your Own Way, Passion Play, Pain Remedies, Making Peace with Your Past* and *The 6 Secrets of a Lasting Relationship*. His forthcoming book, *Don't Hurry, Be Happy: Road Signs for the Spiritual Path*, is about the challenges of integrating authentic spirituality with everyday life in the modern world. He has lectured widely on topics related to human development and spirituality, and has appeared on numerous television and radio talk shows, including NBC's *Today Show*. His work has been featured in magazines and newspapers, including the *Los Angeles Times, Newsweek, Prevention, Cosmopolitan* and *Ladies' Home Journal*. A novelist and screenwriter as well as a nonfiction author, his first novel, *This is Next Year*, is currently in development as a motion picture.

Dr. Goldberg is on the board of directors of the Forge Guild of Spiritual Leaders and Teachers, a professional association dedicated to fostering a renaissance of spiritual wisdom. He lives in Los Angeles, where, in addition to writing, he counsels individual clients, leads spiritual support groups and conducts seminars. For more information, visit his Web site, *www.philipgoldberg. com*, or contact him at 310-827-8266 or at *philgold@flash.net*.

Readers may visit the authors online at *www.makingpeacewithgod.com*.